MA
T

The Meteoric Rise
and Tragic Fall
of Hector Camacho

Christian Giudice

MACHO TIME

HAMILCAR
PUBLICATIONS
BOSTON

ISBN: 978-1-949590-13-5

Publisher's Cataloging-in-Publication Data
Names: Giudice, Christian, author. | Acevedo, Carlos, foreword author.
Title: Macho time: the meteoric rise and tragic fall of Hector Camacho / Christian Giudice; foreword by Carlos Acevedo.
Description: Includes bibliography. | Boston, MA: Hamilcar Publications, 2020.
Identifiers: ISBN 978-1949590135
Subjects: LCSH Camacho, Hector, 1962–2012. | Boxers (Sports)—United States—Biography. | Boxers (Sports)—Puerto Rico—Biography. | BISAC SPORTS & RECREATION / Boxing | BIOGRAPHY & AUTOBIOGRAPHY / Sports
Classification: LCC GV1131 .G52 2020 | DDC 796.83092/2–dc23

Hamilcar Publications
An imprint of Hannibal Boxing Media
Ten Post Office Square, 8th Floor South
Boston, MA 02109
www.hamilcarpubs.com

Printed in the United States of America

On the cover: Hector Camacho celebrates his victory against Jose Luis Ramirez to win the WBC world lightweight title at the Riviera Hotel & Casino in Las Vegas on August 10, 1985. The Ring/Getty Images

Frontispiece: Hector Camacho punches Roque Montoya during their fight at the Memorial Auditorium in Buffalo, New York, on April 29, 1985. The Ring/Getty Images

Contents

Foreword

H e was garish, crude, outlandish, lewd, reckless, and loud. Everybody paid attention to him—he made sure of that. Hector "Macho" Camacho was the first fighter since Cassius Clay/Muhammad Ali appeared in the early 1960s to master the art of negative appeal.

This wide-eyed wild child, whose love of joyrides earned him a bid on Rikers Island when he was still a teenager, lived out his vivid dreams of being a perpetual commotion. Wherever Camacho went—Detroit, Los Angeles, Florida, Puerto Rico, Alaska, New York, Atlantic City, Las Vegas—he brought his own peculiar fantasia with him, in the neon palette of his peak era: magenta, gold, fuchsia, mauve, lavender, metallic silver. "I always wanted to dress in leather suits," he once said. And because Camacho barely recognized limits, he went far, far beyond the leather suit.

In *Macho Time*, the first comprehensive biography of Hector Camacho, Christian Giudice uses the same methodology that made his biographies of Roberto Duran, Wilfredo Gomez, and Alexis Arguello models of reportorial legwork: complete immersion in his subject. Thoroughly researched (Giudice interviewed Camacho's son, Junior, most of his family, friends, ex-friends, writers, managers, trainers, promoters, and opponents), *Macho Time* is a revealing portrait of a gifted athlete who blurred image and reality to such an extent that he ultimately seemed unable to tell the difference between them. In the end, like some sort of postmodern conceit, Camacho succumbed to the image he had created.

In tracking down one Camacho associate after another from his early days, Giudice also captures the era and the place—Spanish Harlem—that not only formed a unique fighter, but a unique celebrity as well. Crime, drugs, arson—El Barrio was then a neighborhood that epitomized urban squalor. This was also the Golden Age of street gangs, and Camacho was part of one. "Around this time," writes Giudice, "prevalent Spanish Harlem gangs included the likes of the Spanish Kings, the Wild Aces, the Renegades of Harlem, and the Baby Satans, and people had to respect their 'blocks.' Hector was associated with the Jefferson Crusaders. Although it fashioned itself as a neighborhood-watch group in the Jefferson Projects, it used violent tactics when outsiders interfered."

While his outrageous flair would eventually overshadow his accomplishments, the fact remains that, in the 1980s, Camacho was one of the most talented fighters in the world. During the early Reagan years, nothing succeeded like excess, and Camacho personified the hedonistic philosophy of the decade with boorish aplomb. But if Camacho burned his candle at both ends, he lit the wick with a blowtorch. As a fighter, he was through by the time he was twenty-five years old, his startling combination of athleticism and precision already looking as obsolete as ColecoVision.

Still, between the first retirement of Sugar Ray Leonard and the arrival of Roy Jones Jr., Camacho was the fastest fighter in the world. His pinpoint combinations resembled futurist blurs, and his ability to throw multiple hooks and uppercuts in microseconds left average fighters overwhelmed. Timing, speed, coordination, defense, reflexes, balance, a surprising mean streak: Camacho had it all before fame sabotaged his talent.

Late nights, promotional squabbles, inactivity, and a drug habit robbed him of his physical gifts long before his cruel vocation could. Is it possible that a fighter who would someday win titles in multiple divisions and enter the International Boxing Hall of Fame could be a disappointment? In the case of Camacho, the answer is **yes**—in bold letters. As promising as Camacho was during his rise, as accomplished as he was after only a few years as a pro, nothing less than crossover stardom would have been enough for him. But the superfights that marked the 1980s—starring Sugar Ray Leonard, Marvelous Marvin Hagler, Roberto Duran, Thomas Hearns, Aaron Pryor, Alexis Arguello, and Larry Holmes—did not include "The Macho Man."

To accompany his painstakingly detailed accounts of fights and controversy, Giudice even investigates the fashion sense of a man who designed his own over-the-top outfits to stand out from the herd. The stripes and piping of the average pug (not to mention the ubiquitous terrycloth robe) were replaced by tassels, epaulets, masks, fringe, diapers, capes, ponchos, codpieces, loincloths, sequins, glitter, Cazals, and a variety of bizarre headdresses (including a pharaonic domepiece and a strange Norfin troll sprout that topped a bizarre Venetian ensemble). At various times Camacho entered the ring decked out as if to attend a Halloween party. Down the aisle he would bop: now a matador, or a fireman, or a centurion; now some sort of Darth Vader character, or even a Chinese peasant (wearing a conical hat). Once, it was a Native American outfit, complete with war bonnet, almost certainly inspired by the Village People or a TV viewing of Chief Jay Strongbow. "Occasionally, Hector would become secretive about his next ring costume," writes Giudice. "He would sketch it on a pad and then cover it up so Junior could not see. 'No one could touch or see his outfits,' said Junior. 'I remember the only time he got mad at me, he was like, 'Did you fucking touch my outfit?' His style was unique, and it didn't come from anywhere. That was just him."

While Giudice traces the life of Camacho from his turbulent days as a child raised in a dysfunctional family to his rise as a three-time Golden Gloves champion to his early pro career, when his future seemed limitless, to his last lost years in the ring and out, he also captures poignant snapshots of Camacho through the eyes of his son, Hector Jr., a former fighter himself, whose childhood was dominated by the bedlam that trailed his volatile celebrity dad. For Junior, there were other issues as well. "I never wanted to fight," he tells Giudice, "but I didn't want to be a pussy. It was hard to hold that Macho image, but I wanted to show my father that I ain't no sucker. I wanted to be Macho too."

When he died in 2012, shot to death while sitting in a parked car full of cocaine with a friend (who happened to be a pimp and drug dealer),

Camacho had come full circle from his days as a Rikers Island inmate. Between those endpoints, however, Camacho came close to achieving what he had desired ever since he was a child growing up in the Johnson Houses: "When I was young, I always said, 'I want to be a hero. I want to be one of a kind.'"

Macho Time reveals the often-moving circumstances behind the man who made at least half of his dreams come true.

Carlos Acevedo
New York City
August 2020

"It's Macho Time"

1

"I created me."
—Hector "Macho" Camacho

The late Jose Torres, writing about "Hispanic machismo," explained: "There is the notion that poverty creates bullies, that in such subcultures only the strong survive, the super macho." Hector Camacho, who made the nickname "Macho" famous, started out as a bully, challenging anyone to fight as he ruled the streets of Spanish Harlem. A "macho" man is defined as someone who is excessively "proud of his own masculinity," and so it is no surprise the other nicknames for Hector Camacho eventually fell away and "Macho" stuck.

Torres later expounded on the topic when he wrote that Mexican boxing icon Toluco Lopez "embodied every ingredient essential to the making of a macho prizefighter." At that point, it was too soon for Torres to anoint Hector the next "super macho," but it would have been appropriate. Brash, unforgiving, and full of panache, Hector did not give a shit what others thought about him.

And now he was looking across the ring at one of the best fighters in the world.

Chiseled, handsome, and wearing leopard-print trunks, Macho was fighting Mexico's Rafael "Bazooka" Limon for the WBC junior light-weight title in August of 1983. Like Limon, Macho abided only by the referee's decrees, but he continued to bend those rules to his liking. In his previous twenty-one fights, Macho had faced men he could hit at will. But none of those fights had been fought on this stage in front of so many Puerto Rican fans.

In fact, more than ten thousand fans had filed into Hiram Birthorn Stadium in San Juan, Puerto Rico, to see Camacho, a Nuyorican (a New Yorker of Puerto Rican descent), dismantle Limon, a Mexican. The Puerto Rican faithful had not completely accepted Camacho, but he was no longer fighting in front of a thousand local fans at New York's Felt Forum. Nothing that Camacho had been exposed to before could have prepared him for this moment. Fans clamored to touch him as he made his ring walk. His handlers crowded around him to shield him from the onslaught of well-wishers. Years later, Camacho's ring entrances would feel like vaudeville, all pomp and no substance, but now, as he headed to the ring, he was merely a young, charismatic fighter who possessed otherworldly skills.

Past his prime, Limon no longer had the ability to fight with the same skill that earned him a world title. Even though Limon had challenged—and beaten—some of the best fighters of his generation, he had never encountered a fighter in his prime with Camacho's speed.

In the first round, Macho shuffled quickly toward Limon, a tactic that he rarely displayed later on. He glided and attacked; Limon stood and delivered, always one step behind. As the rounds progressed, Macho started to dabble with his uppercut and other weapons. Limon, on the other hand, threw punches in long, looping arcs that a quick fighter like Camacho could expose. Limon was tailor-made for him; Macho looked good as he inched closer to becoming the new champion.

As skilled as he was, Hector was still twenty-one years old and raw. Over time, he would understand how to approach a world title with more patience, but now, as he chased after Limon, he was still an immature kid, lacking composure. Taking his time to ease into the bout was not an option. Most young fighters made errors early on in such a high-stakes match, and Camacho was no exception. He needed to settle down, but he wasn't sure how—yet.

In the end, the pundits who had predicted an easy night for Hector were not disappointed. Although there were great Puerto Rican legends who had preceded him—Wilfred Benitez impressed his people with his defensive acumen; bantamweight champion Wilfredo Gomez gained fans' respect from his blend of speed and power—Camacho was something different. Up against Limon, he awed his fans, quickly reducing Limon to a plodding fighter who settled for one harmless punch. But there was something else about Hector: He had an aura about him that forced people to look. He sparked euphoria. He was young, good-looking, and unafraid to show how "Macho" he was.

As Hector jumped into the arms of Puerto Rican cruiserweight and friend Carlos "Sugar" De Leon after the one-sided bout was stopped in the fifth round, all of Puerto Rico seemed to celebrate his ascent. In the process, Camacho had perfectly embodied what Torres revealed when he wrote, "'The Hispanic Machismo' is your capacity to anticipate punches and moves; to have perfect timing and to have the skill to see every incoming punch." Hector's ability to anticipate Limon's moves made Limon seem to fight in slow motion, and Hector took advantage of every slight opening. One thing was certain: A star was born.

A New Life Begins in Spanish Harlem

2

Hector Camacho started his life in 1962 in a little shack in Bayamon, Puerto Rico. His mother, Maria Esther Matias, had married his father, Hector Luis Camacho Matias Sr., when she was just fourteen years old and Hector Sr. was seventeen. Maria fell in love with the handsome young Hector when her family sent her to vacation in Puerto Rico one summer. She knew very little about his violent tendencies at first, but she quickly realized that he was brutal and self-destructive.

In 1961, Maria gave birth to her first child, Racquel, and then a year later, on May 24, 1962, Hector Jr. was born. Unfortunately, Hector Sr.'s violent nature wasn't the only issue the family had to contend with. They were also very poor. "When we were living in Puerto Rico, we were living on the poor side," Racquel recalled. "I will always remember that my grandmother had to cook for us on brick. We were walking with no shoes."

Maria called Hector Jr. "Tito," after her father. When Hector was four years old and Racquel was five, Maria became fearful of Hector Sr.'s escalating violence and decided to send the children to New York, where her family lived, so that they could be safe. First, family members came to get Hector; soon after, they arrived to take Racquel. Maria knew that if her husband found out that she had sent the children to New York permanently for their safety, he would have killed her on the spot.

When Maria eventually escaped Puerto Rico and Hector Sr.'s clutches herself, the emotional strain of separating from him was overwhelming. "I was crying because he was my husband and I loved him," recalled Maria. "I [had known] him since I was fourteen years old."

Once in New York, the family stayed with Maria's father Tito and his wife. Unfortunately, when Hector Sr. found out his wife and children were not returning to Puerto Rico, he followed them to New York. The family moved several times to different locations in Manhattan and the Bronx to evade Hector Sr., but he persisted, pursuing and terrorizing Maria and the children. Racquel, only seven at the time, witnessed the abuse and threats, as did little Hector. Soon, Hector—who was very attached to his mother—began hitting his father to protect Maria. "Don't hit Mommy, don't hit Mommy," Hector pleaded, but he could not stop the abuse.

The story often told in boxing circles is that young Hector was fighting in the streets ever since he was five years old.

"Macho was always Macho," recalled Racquel. "Lovable, crazy, always crazy. It didn't surprise me that he became a boxer, because this little boy was in trouble since he was born. You knew that he was going to be something."

Trying to find a world where comfort and hope supplanted fear and terror, Maria had whisked them away from Hector Sr., whose violence knew no boundaries. Yet when the family settled in an apartment in the James Weldon Johnson Houses on 112th Street, between 2nd and 3rd Avenue, Hector Sr. showed up once again. This time he did not leave.

Persistent and controlling, Hector Sr. forced his way back into the family's life. Despite her father's objections, Maria took him back, hoping that things would change. On June 27, 1966, Felix, whom everyone knew as "Boo Boo," was born.

"My family was mad with me because I would leave [Hector Sr.] and then come back to him," recalled Maria. "[But] I had no money for my kids."

Despite her family's pleas, Maria saw something in Hector Sr. that gave her an inkling of hope for improvement. Yet the endless cycle of abuse never stopped. Maria did her best to shield her children.

"We saw what was happening with our own eyes, and we used to try to save our mother, but he used to push us [down on the ground] so we could not intervene," remembered Racquel. "At other times, my mother used to put us under the bed or in the closet so we wouldn't see things. We had to get on welfare because he didn't want to support us."

"I put Macho in a box under the bed," Maria confirmed. "I didn't want him to see anything. . . . He was scared. [He] said, 'Mommy don't go back with him, please don't go back with him. He gonna hurt you.'"

In the early 1970s, after a stint of two years of being alone with the kids, Maria met a handsome man at a party whom she would eventually marry. His name was Alejandro Oliveras, or Ruben. When Ruben entered the family's life, it got easier. Ruben and Maria would have two more children: Estrella and Esther. For Maria, Ruben allowed the family a fresh start and a chance to heal old wounds.

"I was alone and he started to help me with the kids," recalled Maria. "And Hector would look at me and say, 'Mommy I like him. He's gonna be my father. He's better than my father. I want us to live with him.'"

Before Ruben came along, the children had always had a male figure in the household. "We always had my uncle, Julio," recalled Racquel. "We always had uncles and cousins who would look out for me and my mom and Macho. [But when] Ruben came, he was like a father figure. . . . He took care of us."

Despite all the trauma and abuse, Racquel remembers her childhood fondly. "We really didn't miss much," she said. "We had a good childhood. We were poor, and my mother was suffering by herself, but we, me and Mach, had a good childhood."

Maria eventually landed a job at a Kentucky Fried Chicken in the Bronx. Little Hector ("Tito") would sit by her side and watch her during the whole shift from morning until night. Maria recalled, "They looked at me and said, 'Maria Camacho, your son can't stay here all day.'" But Hector would not budge.

"Tito, please go home," Maria would beg.

"No, Mommy, I will stay right here! I will stay and watch you because somebody can do something to you."

"Nobody can do anything to me. I'm working for you, Tito. The money I am making is for you."

"I don't care, Mommy. I be here for you."

Hector's attachment to his mother ran deep, and this connection never wavered, even when he became a professional boxer. Never leaving his mother's side, Hector, at seven or eight years old, wanted to create a protective shell around her to ensure that she would never suffer again. Everywhere Maria went, she needed only to turn around to see Hector trailing behind her, telling her, "Mommy, you're going to be the richest woman in the world. Because I am going to buy you a car, a house, and give you money. I swear, all of it for you. You don't need Ruben or anyone else, just me Mommy."

Soon Maria had to look for another job, but the promises never stopped.

"Don't worry, Mommy, I will give you everything!"

"No, Tito, you are a little boy. You can't think that you will give me everything."

Maria soon got a job working with her sister in a factory in the Bronx, far away from home. Hector could no longer sit nearby and watch her every move, which made it easier on everyone. Determined, young Hector tried to make the walk to see his mother, but it was too far. Not giving up, Hector tried to negotiate with her.

"Mommy, you have to give me money so I can take the train," said Hector. But it was too much, so Hector would stay home with Ruben.

Able to keep a sense of self in the midst of the brutality, Maria held the family together. "We were on welfare, but my mother always took care of us and made sure that food was on the table," remembered Racquel. "We were always dressed, always clean, and always there was food for us. I didn't need anything, and Mach, especially, didn't need anything."

Hector Sr., an alcoholic, was still in the children's lives, but he did not have a loving relationship with them. He rarely engaged his son; he never hugged him or told him that he loved him. Maria had to do everything in her power to make up for this void of affection. She filled that gap with unconditional love, spawning an extremely tight-knit family structure, one that fended off poverty and the difficult moments that emerged. According to Racquel, there was no lingering animosity or personal grudges toward their father, but by that time, he had been replaced.

Throughout his childhood, Hector reminded his mother that she could not go back to his father. Maria promised him that the relationship was over. For Hector, the fear lingered. "I used to cook, and he used to sit right there [pointing next to her in her apartment], and stare at me," Maria recalled. "I said, 'Go play, Macho, please go.' But then he looked at me and said, 'No, Mommy, I will stay here for you.'"

Soon Hector turned his focus to karate and Maria enrolled him in classes at the Boys' Club on East 111th Street. "He always asked me, 'Mommy, buy me the clothes, buy me the picture,'" said Maria. "So I had to put him in karate, because he had to be Bruce Lee."

Every kid knew of Bruce Lee in the 1970s and 1980s. Thousands emulated Lee's enticing mix of bravery and guile. Boys and girls lined up at the Cosmo Theatre in Spanish Harlem to spend afternoons watching his films. Young Hector saw Lee's yellow-and-black outfit and slick moves and yearned to be the iconic fighter. He needed that yellow jumpsuit with the sharp black stripe. One day it would be his.

Meanwhile, four years older than his brother Boo Boo, Hector had to look out for him. When Hector wanted his mother's attention, he also had to contend with his little brother. As much as he loved Boo Boo, it bothered him that he had to share his mother's love. "He was jealous of Boo Boo," recalled Maria. "Hector would say, 'Mommy, I'm your baby. Boo Boo's not your baby.' I said, 'Yes, he is. You are both my babies.' Then Hector told me, 'But I love you more than Boo Boo.' I would tell him he couldn't love me more than Boo Boo, because you both love me the same way."

As a fourth grader, Hector attended Commander John J. Shea, a Catholic school located in the heart of Spanish Harlem, close to their apartment. It cost Maria $30 to enroll all three children there. Making the transition to John J. Shea was not easy for Hector, who initially struggled to fit in. Dressed in hand-me-down clothing and struggling to speak English, Hector was the odd man out. Socially, the students already knew each other; culturally, these were New York City kids—tough New York City kids. The clear divisions led to the obvious questions: Where would he fit in? Would he find his niche?

"Hector comes in," recalled former classmate Austin Fenner, "and no one knows him. He became the toughest of them all in this room of tough kids. [He] was clearly the best fighter."

On the first day, Austin faced Hector one-on-one to see what the new kid was made of. In Austin's mind, "there was no better way to win a friend than fight him on that first day of school."

"I was thinking, *He's a nobody. I would take him on. I will fight him.* Seconds later at the back of the school. Whap. A jab. Whap. Move to his right. Whap. Back to his left. Whap!"

Young Austin was defenseless: "I got my hands up and he's busy jabbing me. No hooks, nothing. Just jabs. Pop, pop, pop. I was like, *What's happening?*"

Hector continued the onslaught of punches, clearly defeating his classmate. He didn't need to delve into his bag of tricks. His polished jab worked to perfection.

"He went for the weak spot," recalled Austin. "I was thinking, *This is not how it was supposed to go.* I was bigger. My clothes fit me right. I had a hard-working dad. [But] I was still standing there. Whap. Whap. Whap."

Austin's head jutted back again—and again. "It was an educated jab," Austin would pronounce years later. Austin's friend Zina and some other boys gathered around to watch, but if Austin had harbored any hope that they would step in and, at the very least, present a diversion, all hope was officially lost after five minutes of consistent jabs. Austin saw no option but to quit. He was no match for the polished fighter. Using a blend of karate and boxing, Hector had shown Austin and his supporters that picking on him was a poor choice. Round one went to the new kid on the block. In Austin's mind, it was safer to be Macho's friend.

"It was my form of surrender," said Austin. "'You win.'"

They were in the fourth grade.

After Hector established himself on that first day of school, he moved on to bigger and better opposition. As he established an identity, Hector was always clear about who he was, and where others, friends or acquaintances, stood with him.

Having started early in karate, Hector also began to develop a strict mindset that belied his age. Karate had opened up a new, more focused side of the rambunctious and jocular boy. Skilled in the movements, Hector applied what he learned and practiced his craft. When challenged to a street fight, Hector never backed down and always had an edge.

"When I was about ten I was into martial arts," Hector recalled to a boxing reporter. "I went to a lot of Bruce Lee pictures. He was my idol. I thought I was big and bad, so I stuck with fighting and went into a gym. I ran around the streets looking for fights."

Despite the discipline that karate instilled in him, Hector's restlessness and fearlessness followed him throughout his life and became a large part of who he was. One memorable encounter involved a neighborhood tough guy aptly named "Dirt." In an area called "Big Swings," Hector mentally readied himself for a difficult challenge.

"Everyone knew who Hector was, and everyone knew Dirt," said Austin. "You knew everyone and everyone knew you. No one wanted to fight Dirt."

Dirt was not concerned about Hector's growing reputation in the streets, and when Hector—who had by then started boxing—accepted Dirt's challenge, the fight, as Austin recalled, symbolized something greater than two kids mixing it up. The crowd swelled. Fights in Spanish Harlem could last for hours, so Hector went home to retrieve his boxing gloves.

"People came from the handball courts," Austin recalled. "Guys came from the corner and the other side of the Jefferson projects. Soon the whole neighborhood was watching the fight . . . kids were climbing the fences to get a bird's-eye view."

Passionately emulating his idol, Hector embodied Lee's fighting spirit and laser focus as he stood up to the toughest kids in the neighborhood.

"A guy like Bruce Lee was everything if you were a kid in Spanish Harlem," said Austin. "He represented swag . . . and he could fight his ass off. Every kid in Spanish Harlem cut broomsticks into sticks and used nails to make nunchucks, and they were all out there doing the Bruce Lee nunchuck move. The flash, the ability, the 'hiya.' No one embraced that better than Hector. No one exemplified the flash of Bruce Lee like Hector did."

Dirt persisted and kept moving ahead with abandon, whereas Hector dazzled with speed. Eventually, the fight ended, but the spectacle stayed in the minds of the people there. Hector had faced off against the toughest kid in the neighborhood and did not back down. He didn't knock out Dirt, but he stood up to him and refused to let him bully him.

His bouts with Dirt and Austin were only two of many that would get the notorious youngster kicked out of several schools. One time, Hector ripped his school jacket in a fight and dreaded going home to tell his mother what happened. Later, he would be kicked out of school for fighting with a girl.

"Every day I would get a call from the office, 'Mrs. Camacho, come right now, Hector had a fight with a girl,'" Maria recalled. "A big girl started to bother him, so he punched her in the teeth and took her teeth out."

One of Hector's first real friends when the family moved to Spanish Harlem was a boy named Eddie Pratts. Eddie and his older brother, Casey, spent a lot of time with Hector and witnessed his early fighting spirit firsthand as the three of them took turns jumping Lucha Libre–style from the Pratts's mother's bedpost. Young Hector enjoyed his time with the brothers, who lived on 110th Street and Third Avenue. All three were enamored with elaborate wrestlers' masks. In the early 1970s, *luchadores* such as Angel Blanco, Los Gemelos Diablos, and El Santo graced the covers of the famous *Lucha Libre* magazines.

Eddie and Casey, then ten and twelve, liked to go up to the roofs of the local grocery store, Key Foods, located on 110th between Lexington and Third Avenue. One afternoon, the brothers headed up there and saw Hector with his white karate *gi*, practicing his moves. Hector was too focused to even notice the brothers. With Bruce Lee's mottos, such as "I fear not the man who has practiced ten thousand kicks once, but I fear the man who has practiced one kick ten thousand times," in mind, the disciplined fighter stayed in the moment. The boys laughed uncontrollably. They could not believe what they were seeing.

"Is he for real? Is Hector crazy?" they asked each other.

Eventually the boys left the roof and went home, but the image of their friend in his karate *gi* was forever ingrained in their minds.

"We had no idea we were watching somebody who was going to become famous as a fighter," said Eddie. "We just wondered if there was something wrong with him."

Raging against a bully was one thing, but Hector also targeted his friends. Eddie and Casey had been making fun of a neighborhood kid for having big ears, and the boy went to his father, a local barber. In a scene reminiscent of *A Bronx Tale*, the father went to Hector to put a "hit" on the brothers as revenge. Needing the money, Hector went up to them and punched Casey in the face.

"We went home and told my mother, and she looked at both of us and said, 'You're going down to fight him right now!'" Eddie recalled. "We go down to the barbershop and Camacho was there collecting his money."

At this point, neither Casey nor Eddie was interested in facing Hector, who already had a reputation as a respected fighter, but their mother insisted they stand their ground. With their mother watching, Casey made a beeline for Hector.

"Casey was not able to do anything," said Eddie. "My mom is there yelling, 'Hit him! Hit him!' And my brother is like, 'I can't, Ma. He won't stay still. He's too fast.'"

"I watched the fight, and Hector is jabbing and moving like he's already developed as a fighter," Eddie remembered. "He was born to fight. There was just something inside of him. He loved to fight, and it didn't matter if you were his friend or not."

Surprisingly, all three remained friends after the organized hit. The Pratts needed a friend like Hector on their side, and that ethos reflected the neighborhood mentality: You fight, then back to friends.

Not long after his scrap with Casey in front of the barbershop, Hector beat up another friend named Ralphie Velasquez at a park. When Hector made up his mind to fight, there was no turning back. Velasquez's own indecision about whether to fight, however, proved to be a big mistake.

"Ralphie was taking his jacket off and then putting it back on, then taking it off and then putting it back on," recalled Eddie. "You know how a guy takes his jacket off when he's going to fight. Well, as Ralphie is doing this, Camacho is right there just hitting him with punches. That's how he was."

Not only did friends have to be wary of Hector's behavior, but his mother and sister had to be on the lookout as well. When Hector was around nine or ten, recalled Racquel, "he used to break all the sticks, the mops, the brooms to use as [nunchucks]. We got so tired of him beating us up that my mom put them all in the garage. That was when he started to think he was Bruce Lee."

Maria steered Hector away from karate when he started practicing moves on boys in the park. Hector soon became a mainstay in the local gyms, this time focused on boxing, not karate. When he came back from the boxing gym the first time, Hector was hooked.

"Oh, Mommy, I like that. I like that," Hector told her. "So I'm going to leave the karate and go into boxing. You like the boxing, Mommy?" he asked.

"Yes, sweetheart!" Maria replied.

"Okay, I will go into boxing.'"

Ruben gave Hector early lessons in their apartment, showcasing different punches. Despite not having been formally trained, Ruben understood boxing moves and punches. Maria always kept a close eye on them.

"Don't touch my son! You're going to hurt him," Maria would say.

"But that's how he gets tough," responded Ruben.

And, as Maria recalled, "That's the way he came. Tough."

Even back then, Hector had charisma and fashion sense. "[He] started to cut his shirts so that he could show his belly button," Racquel recalled. "He changed his style."

Although he and Racquel had joined his mother in escaping the toxic environment created by his abusive father, and although with Ruben in the picture they were safe from Hector Sr.'s abuse, they still lived with the torment of poverty.

Between the Streets and the Gym

3

I n the 1940s and 1950s, Puerto Ricans had begun to leave their homeland in waves to resettle in northeastern Manhattan, now known as Spanish Harlem or "El Barrio." Before and after World War I, Puerto Ricans were drawn to Spanish Harlem to work in the manufacturing sector. It didn't take long for these newcomers to leave their collective cultural imprint on "El Barrio," an area that stretched from 5th Avenue and 1st Avenue and from 96th Street to 125th Street. The area, however, was not always the cultural haven for Puerto Ricans that it is now. In the early nineteenth century, an influx of Italian immigrants dotted the landscape. Sicilians and Southern Italians gravitated toward the area, and more than a hundred thousand Italians lived in East Harlem, which was then known as Little Italy. German, Irish, and Jewish immigrants also called East Harlem home. After World War I, Puerto Ricans laid claim to the 110th and Lexington area, and over time their reach expanded to the rest of Spanish Harlem. From 1940 to 1960, more than half a million Puerto Ricans, mostly first generation, left the island to come to New York. By the 1950s, nearly sixty-five thousand Puerto Ricans had migrated to Spanish Harlem.

When Maria Camacho came to Spanish Harlem in the 1970s, blacks and Puerto Ricans comprised the majority of families living in public housing there. Maria felt poverty tug at her every move and looked for any job that would provide a sliver of security. Envisioning the glorious day when he could give his mother the life she wanted, Hector chose to prioritize his fists over his education. By the time he was in his teens, karate, boxing, and a penchant for getting into trouble all blended into a charming, charismatic, and sometimes toxic mix.

When Hector was young, on the streets they called him "Little Man." In the 1970s, teenagers frequented the Boys' Clubs of America as an escape from the burdens they faced. Trying to navigate the hardscrabble streets during this time proved difficult. Even as Hector got older and started to commit petty crimes, he always respected his mother, but he also sought out male figures who were not afraid to use physical measures to instill fear and demand discipline, which convinced him that they cared for him. Neighborhood guys Gilbert "Tito" Cuevas and Edwin "Eddie" Gonzalez, both living on 112th Street, were in his life from early on and rarely left his side.

With his charming smile, it was easy for Hector to think he was invincible. In and out of several schools, Hector, who had trouble learning to read, loved being around his friends and enjoyed the camaraderie that the streets afforded him. He had seen friends on the block get locked up and others killed, but he was able to navigate the streets by disarming people with a smile or a punch, whichever the situation called for.

By age fourteen, he was dating seventeen-year-old Maida Olivo, nicknamed "China," whom he had met at a party and was instantly smitten with. Maida was a member of the East Side Gang, a boxer, and a streetfighter; the first time Hector saw her, he knew he had to have her.

When Hector and Maida met, Maida was dating a local DJ named Richie, and Hector was in a relationship with a girl named Tiny. Yet because they both spent time in the same gyms, Maida and Hector's relationship started to blossom. At the time they had a number of boxing gyms to choose from. Former Golden Glove champion and Muhammad Ali sparring partner Jimmy Glenn opened up a gym and an adjacent bar called Jimmy's Corner in Times Square in the 1970s. Jimmy Gleason, formerly Peter Gagliardi, a bantamweight, had first opened Gleason's Gym in the lower Bronx on 149th Street and 3rd Avenue in 1937. In 1974, however, the gym was on the move again, and Gleason settled at West 30th Street in Manhattan.

Hector and Maida dreamed of a better life. On the way home after grueling training sessions, Hector looked in the windows of expensive department stores. "I promise you that when I make it big, I will buy you those outfits," Hector told her as he pointed to the expensive clothes. "I promise."

As enamored with him as he was with her, Maida believed every word—even the hollow promises of luxurious gifts. "I was attracted to him because he was a boxer," said Maida. "He exercised all the time, which I loved because I was a jogger myself. Also, he was good-looking and he reminded me of Rocky."

Having started out in karate and then transitioned to boxing, Hector was always defined by one or the other as he hauled his gloves wherever he went. When he went to Negro's Gym (run by Negro Gonzalez and later renamed La Sombra Sporting Club) in the projects at 108th and Park to train, Maida was often right there watching him.

"For martial arts, we both went to the Boys' Club together, which was located on 111th Street between 1st and 2nd Ave," Maida recalled. "Hector was put in an upstairs martial arts program, and I was put in the girls' cadets program downstairs. The Boys' Club was a place to keep the youth out of trouble and physically busy at all times."

The gang culture in Spanish Harlem revolved around the fight for territory. Were there fights? Yes, but, according to Maida, the prime mission of the gang was to unite and protect others who could not protect themselves. The corollary to that mission was that violence was inevitable.

"Little Man" had built a reputation that he would carry with him for decades. At times, Hector would embrace it; at other times, he would try to shake free of the pejorative labels of "street kid" or "ghetto kid." At this point, in his early teens, Hector was getting involved in both the disciplined boxing spectrum and the seedy world of drugs. One world demanded absolute concentration, the other was infested with deceit. It would have been easy for Hector, like so many of his neighborhood friends, to choose a world where deceit ruled every decision, where immorality trumped decency. For a time, Hector teetered on the edge, closer to being a product of wasted youth than a future star.

Although Gilbert "Tito" Cuevas and Edwin "Eddie" Gonzalez were Hector's closest friends, he also interacted and made friends in many different social circles. One friend from his youth who stayed loyal to him was Richie "Rich" Galvan, a local guy who lived in the Johnson Projects.

"If you needed [Hector] to protect you, he would always fight your battles," said Richie. "He would never stand down to nobody. One time he was playing basketball with us, and this big black guy fouls Hector. The guy started to pick on Hector because he was smaller. [Sensing a fight] Hector went home and got his boxing boots. The guy was a bully. Hector beat him up."

Throughout Hector's life, emotions would bubble over when he felt alone or alienated. In many ways, Hector was Macho, but in many others, he was a sensitive kid trying to sort his life out. In that regard, people in his life could give him advice, but it was rare—very rare—that he told others how he was feeling. A conversation with Hector would never start with, "This is how I feel." Instead, he was nearly impossible to pin down, jittery and energized. Whether that energy reflected a positive or negative mindset depended on the situation. With the force of his jab and straight left, Hector kept people away.

Meanwhile, Hector was in the process of becoming a hot boxing prospect, and his then-girlfriend Maida witnessed the evolution. Prone to working hard in the gym and creating a mood of lightheartedness wherever he went, Hector made sure there were few dull moments when he was around. And if somebody dared him to do something—anything—young Hector rarely turned it down.

"The same things that endeared him to fans also attracted me," said Maida. "He made me and everyone around him laugh. He was constantly joking. He was definitely a clown."

When Hector walked down the streets in Spanish Harlem, he exuded an air of self-confidence. Despite being too young to remember Puerto Rico, Hector was never far from his people. He only had to walk down Lexington Avenue to inhale the scents of La Marqueta, a market that became a staple for all Hispanics in Spanish Harlem. On the corners, Hector could take in the sounds of Puerto Rican salsa legend Hector Lavoe. "El Barrio" also provided a glorious backdrop for Roberto Roena and His Apollo Sound, which formed in 1969, and Fania All Stars, a collection of musical geniuses that formed a year earlier. It was customary to see men playing dominoes, drinking, and listening to Tito Puente, Eddie Palmieri, and Willie Colon on a corner or in an abandoned lot. Later, Hector would become enamored with Panamanian Ruben Blades, but as an adolescent he loved Elvis and Michael Jackson.

As carefree as he was out of the ring, Hector was all business inside of it. When he worked—and worked hard—his movements, speed, and focus reflected a fighter so supremely gifted that few young fighters could compete with him. Blessed with blazing hand and foot speed, Hector could throw pinpoint combinations in seconds. What he needed was a knowledgeable trainer to add polish. His stepfather, Ruben, was the first to take him to the gym, but he could only teach the young fighter so much.

"For boxing, Hector first trained in Negro's Gym on 108th Street and Park Avenue, which was located in the projects, down the ramp," said Maida. "I went to the gym for exercise and boxing, but mostly to watch Hector train. When Hector started, Negro deeply cared for him. He was a good man, and he would tell Hector, 'One day you will be somebody.'"

Around this time, prevalent Spanish Harlem gangs included the likes of the Spanish Kings, the Wild Aces, the Renegades of Harlem, and the Baby Satans, and people had to respect their "blocks." Hector was associated with the Jefferson Crusaders. Although it fashioned itself as a neighborhood watch group in the Jefferson Projects, it used violent tactics when outsiders interfered.

"When he was young, seventeen, [Hector] would get into gang fights—and whip ass," said a former member of the Crusaders. "If we had a misunderstanding or had to defend our turf . . . Hector got involved and someone got hurt. Hector was the best of everything in our neighborhood and we all looked up to him."

Hector tried to allay his family's increasing concerns about his behavior by claiming that his penchant for stealing cars and robbing people was merely child's play. Hector rationalized his behavior as part bully, part harmless rebel. In his mind, if someone was going to let him get an edge, why not take it?

At Manhattan High School on West 52nd Street, a school for troubled youth, Hector met Patrick Flannery, an English teacher who would play a significant role throughout Hector's life. It would have been easy for Flannery to brand Hector as just another product of the projects, another student caught up in petty crimes that would lead to more-substantial criminal activity, and pay him no attention. At that time, it was clear that Hector was headed down two divergent paths: one that could lead him to a bright future, and the other that could lead him to prison.

"[The first time he entered my class] he jumped on my desk, grabbed my window [opening] pole, and vaulted to the front of the room," said Flannery. "He started shadowboxing and pretending he was on television. It was like, 'Camacho throws a left. Camacho throws a right, he's down.' He acted as if he had knocked himself down, then jumped up and turned to me, smiling and waving his fists." Needing to maintain order, Flannery picked Hector up and threw him against the wall of the classroom. Some students might have retreated after such an encounter with a teacher, but Hector gravitated toward Flannery. Tough love was not a new concept to the young fighter.

"Patrick's always been a father to me," Hector told *Sports Illustrated* in 1983. "He's always taken care of me, fed me; he's the one who's always there to advise me. He loves me like a son."

One of few male figures who refused to label Hector, Flannery saw a shining light within the energetic and impulsive kid who couldn't sit still and had no discipline. At first, Hector pushed back, but when he saw that Flannery was willing to be a part of his life for the long haul, he embraced the man who would buy him his first set of boxing gloves. That buy-in from Hector marked the beginning of a beautiful friendship. Flannery witnessed the transformation of a rebellious kid into a sensitive, somewhat willing pupil who had a kind streak in him.

Despite the efforts of his teachers, including Flannery, Hector was kicked out of several high schools for fighting. When Hector started boxing on a regular basis, Maria made the decision to homeschool him. Flannery would come to the house and teach him from 8 a.m. to 3 p.m. They focused on improving Hector's reading and writing skills. A former boxer himself, Flannery understood how to motivate Hector. "If you can't read," Flannery told him, "then how will you read about yourself when you're famous?"

Eventually, Hector started making strides. And the kid many referred to as the "Rose of Spanish Harlem" saw that Flannery cared.

"He was such a nice teacher," Maria recalled. "He was very serious and strong with him. Hector would be playing around, and Flannery would tell him to be serious and stop messing around. He listened to Patrick. Hector was like a little kid, you tell him no and he wanted to do it. [But] he listened to me and Patrick."

"Like any kid," Flannery said, "he struggled. But Hector wanted it badly. And what Hector really wants, Hector gets."

Hector quickly embraced the nickname "Macho" bestowed on him by Flannery. "I been out on these streets since I was seven or eight years old," Hector told *Sunday News Magazine* in 1983. "The kids now think they're hard rocks and fly guys, but they don't know . . . they don't remember the real East Side gangs. I was called 'Macho' because I thought I was crazy, but the real crazies, they are either dead or doing life. The real macho men are in their own world, getting high, then busting out once in a while, when their feelings build up." Brash, affectionate, and genuine, Hector used sports to release the pent-up feelings that surfaced from growing up with an unstable father. To compensate, he became "Macho."

Bringing in the Wheel

4

Before Hector Camacho met Patrick Flannery, he was already focused on a future in boxing. No matter what he had done the night before, Hector woke up every morning to train. Even later in life, he rarely missed his morning run. And even though Negro Gonzalez and another trainer, Mickey Rosario, worked with Hector, he needed someone to devote more time to teach him the sport on a consistent basis. Luckily for Hector, one man showed up at the beginning of his amateur boxing career: Bobby Lee Velez, otherwise known as Robert Lee. Hector's stepfather, Ruben, had been bringing Hector to La Sombra Sporting Club (formerly Negro's Gym). That's where Lee, a former amateur star and ex-gang member who had garnered a considerable following throughout the local boxing gyms, took notice.

Lee had been a 1972 Olympic hopeful, trained by Bobby Lewis. He had grown up fighting in the streets and was well respected throughout the gyms. At the time, Lee was training his fighters out of La Sombra. The gym, owned by Gil Diaz and Negro Gonzalez, brought kids off the streets and gave them a second chance in life. Although Lee was busy working with a full stable of fighters, he did not turn Hector away. Having experienced hardship at an early age, Lee understood what the street kids who came into the gym were going through. Emptiness, depression, fear, and sorrow were emotions Lee knew well from losing his mother at an early age and searching for someone to fill that void. In the mid-1970s, Lee had a full-time job as a butcher but managed to find time to train notable fighters such as Robert "Pee Wee" Rucker, Danny Estrada, Baby Ocasio, Jose Gonzalez, Pedro Villegas, and others.

"At the time I was dating Negra . . . Maria's [Hector's mother's] half-sister, and my lady friend for twenty years," said Lee. "She wanted me to take a look at her nephew, a fighter. When he came down to the gym, I was moving to other fighters when she said, 'Here is the kid I was telling you about. That's my nephew.'"

Lee liked what he saw, partly because he recognized all of the things the then thirteen-year-old fighter lacked, specifically a strong support system. More important, Lee saw himself in the young fighter.

"I fought for him. I wanted him to have a shot," Lee said. He himself hadn't had anyone in his corner, so he figured if he turned his back on Hector, he was no better than the mentors who neglected to help him when he was a troubled teen. To give him a fair shot, Lee knew that he had to put a structure in place.

"Robert was strong and direct with Macho, but he needed someone like that, because he was strong too," said Maria.

Lee gave Hector the option of staying at La Sombra or leaving with him to go to Jimmy Glenn's Times Square Gym and Bobby Gleason's Gym on West 30th Street. Understanding that in order to grow, Hector had to have access to the best amateurs and professionals, Lee sold him on the proposal. No one had taught Hector like Lee did, and Hector enjoyed watching Lee's footwork. The young fighter was eager to begin working with the technical trainer known as "The Box Man."

Lee wanted Hector to know from the outset that he would care for him and not take advantage of him. "I saw something different in him," said Lee, "someone who really was in need of help. He needed my attention. You know, people didn't want to give him a shot. They said he wasn't worth it. That he was buck wild. But I saw affection and curiosity."

After spending his early days with Negro, Hector started to feel comfortable with Lee. But in order for the relationship to succeed, Hector had to be willing to make sacrifices. As enticing as the block was, Hector was one of the few kids on the street who could boast of a future in boxing. So many of his stablemates would fall short of gaining stardom or making a career out of the sport, so more was expected of him.

"Robert Lee used to care for him and look out for him," said Maida. "If Hector hung out on the benches, Robert Lee would say, 'Go train or go home. Don't hang out here.' And then he used to slap him. [Robert] was strong, but in a positive way."

Content to freelance from gym to gym, Lee brought Hector across the city to experience complex, pressure situations with accomplished, professional fighters. Trying to acclimate to the mental and physical challenges that Lee presented, Hector battled professionals like Terrence Alli, Howard Davis Jr., Ray Mancini, and Roberto Duran. During these brief but intense sessions, Lee implored Hector to not back down and to be willing to try new techniques. "Just try it," he urged, as Hector trained.

Ultimately, Lee wanted Hector to *feel* the difference—the texture of a sparring session—and what it meant to fight a guy who had already faced the best out there. Professionals were intent on getting to work with Hector, not hurt him. With Lee protecting him, Hector was getting educated by men who already knew what strategies to use to resolve conflict. Through sacrifice, Hector would learn too. Lee told him upfront: "The only time you stand still is when you want to set them up. Pivot and side-step, then crack." Hector complied. In his mind, Lee knew precisely how long his fighter would last in the ring.

About a year after the two started working together, Lee brought a local trainer, Billy Giles, to work with Hector, then fourteen. Giles's prized pupil was another dynamic prospect, Pee Wee Rucker. No one, however, was as highly touted as Hector.

"I put him in with [Roberto] Duran and he was too fast for him," said Lee. "Hector would not stand still. He had such fast hands and legs. But after three rounds, I took him out. [Duran's trainer] Freddie Brown was angry with me because he wanted me to leave him in there. Duran wanted to get off, but he couldn't. After the last round, I said, 'See you later, Freddie. My guy's just an amateur.' They wanted to let him open up more, but I wouldn't allow it." Later Lee told Hector, "You keep practicing, and you will bypass all of [the professional fighters] in the gym."

To many young fighters, Duran was an iconic figure, but Hector was not as enamored with the Panamanian. "I wanted to be like Bruce [Lee]," Hector said. "But I never wanted to be like Duran in style. When

I watched him, I said, 'Wow!' But I never wanted to be mean like him."
When Hector fought Howard Davis Jr., Lee warned him to stay alert
and not lose focus. Later in their careers, the two fighters would meet
up again. Before Hector's Amateur Athletic Union–sanctioned fights,
Lee supplemented his boxing education with underground bootleg fights
called "smokers" because spectators smoked in the venue as they watched
the fights. But the illegal shows would not last, and, soon enough, Hector
began to feast on amateur opponents. Former *New York Post* journalist Michael Marley witnessed the evolution: "[Hector] was the best
amateur of his generation out of New York. He had smoker fights and
then won three Golden Gloves titles back when the Gloves were very
competitive."

Gestures reveal a lot about the path of a relationship. A soft touch.
A gentle nudge. A welcoming glance. Hector was not the type to openly
express his love for someone. Instead, he let those people know in subtler
ways. Whether Lee was in the park playing handball or playing chess,
Hector was nearby picking his brain. Soaking up all he could learn from
the older fighter.

In the beginning, Hector was consumed with boxing and the mental
warfare involved in a prizefight. "I watched him and another kid duke it
out in the streets," said Lee. "I would take a rope, tie it against a chair
or a tree, and then [say], 'Now you can fight.' I knew anything goes in
the streets, so I stopped playing chess and got the gloves and set it up
for them."

By taking the initiative with Hector, Lee felt he was making up for lost
time. His mother had died when he was two years old, and he did not
know his father until he was thirty. No matter where he went, Lee ran
into problems and lived in a world where "no one took care of [me]."
Lee stressed, "Boxing was my savior."

It was Hector's too.

With another male role model in his life, Hector felt more secure. Each
man, whether it was Ruben Oliveras, Patrick Flannery, or Robert Lee,
played a different role, but all were guiding him in the same direction.

Like Flannery, Lee had to keep close tabs on Hector. Boxing may have
been a savior for him, but Hector still liked to walk on the wild side. Lee
followed him everywhere and knew all of his haunts and hideouts. When
Hector diverted from his training routine or broke curfew, it was Lee who

went to find him. "His friends would all hide him under a park bench," Lee remembered. "I would make them get up. I would tell him, 'We're going home.' He was pissed off at me. I would walk him home." Lee knew what Hector was capable of and what happened to neglected fighters whom no one invested time in. He saw the tragic street stories play out in front of him and knew that there was a fine line between potential and wasted talent.

So the boxing education began as Lee's imprint was indelibly etched on Hector over the first quarter of his career, when he began to distinguish himself from nearly every young fighter in the world. When he first met Lee, Hector liked to slug, but Lee reshaped him and made him use his legs. Everything that Lee taught Hector was based on frustrating his opponent and taking him out of his rhythm. *Jab. Spin. Fake. Spin. Hold. Use angles. Don't stop, Hector. Always try new things. Spin your opponent and hit him on the spin. Jab, turn that wrist over, push over to the side and then come back with combinations. Jab, move, and throw a quick one-two combination. Focus, Hector. Step off, throw an uppercut, and catch him in between. Check left hand, step off, and land a right hand under his chin.*

After Hector showed Lee that he could master these moves, Lee pulled him out of the ring. That was it. Lee's frugal approach did not win him many friends in the gyms. That did not bother him though. To be a great trainer, one needs to be able to read one's fighter, and, in that regard, Lee felt confident that he was doing everything in his power to prepare Hector for a brutal profession that chewed up and disposed of great talents.

Hector adhered to Lee's demands in the ring, but more important, he trusted Lee to steer him away from adversity. When Hector got arrested, Lee maneuvered to bail him out. When Hector started to get too absorbed in street affairs, Lee smacked him across the face to wake him up. By taking these liberties, Lee created friction with Maria. *Who are you to hit my son,* she wondered? Lee saw it as a by-product of his love; Maria saw it as disrespect. There was evidence, however, that Lee was doing something right, and when Hector wanted answers, he knew where to find his mentor.

"[Maria] used to get upset with me," Lee recalled. "She thought I was too hard on him. But I was hard on him in my way. It was only later that she would embrace me, and say, 'God bless you.'"

★ ★ ★

When Lee, Flannery, and Giles brought the then fifteen-year-old Hector to the New York Golden Gloves tournament in March 1978, they had to forge his birth certificate and claim he was sixteen years old because he was too young to compete at the time.

"When he made up his mind to fight in [the Golden Gloves], I did everything I could to discourage him," Flannery told *Sports Illustrated* in 1983, "but when I saw how determined he was, I gave him my boxing shoes and helped him fill out the forms."

Fighting out of the 112-pound sub-novice division, Hector was prepared to face the best competition in the state. He was starting to attract attention. A small blurb in a local newspaper read: "Hector Camacho of 1839 Lexington Ave., NYC. Senior at Manhattan High. Steered into gloves by father, former amateur boxer. Tournament record: one knockout, one decision, and one bye."

After earning a bye in the first round, Hector stopped John Byrnes from the Police Athletic League at 1:24 in the first round to reach the semifinals. He then beat Tyrone Jackson from the United Block Association Gym to reach the finals. In the final round of the Golden Gloves, on March 10, 1978, Hector, fighting out of La Sombra Boxing Club, beat Daryl Hall of Castle Hill Athletic Club for the 112-pound title, after absorbing some tough shots. More important, Hector recovered after one especially hard shot in the third round. In the ensuing coverage, a journalist described Hector as "perpetual motion." That same year future professionals Billy Costello, Davey Moore, and Alex Ramos won titles. In all, Hector won three straight bouts to get the title victory.

As a Golden Gloves winner, Hector was awarded a Gloves necklace, which felt like pure heaven in his hands. It symbolized his hard work and mental fortitude, and he showed it off to everyone. When his younger brother, Boo Boo, got his hands on the necklace, he sold it, but Hector traced it back to where Boo Boo pawned it and got it back. Still young, Boo Boo had no idea of its worth. "Oh, the trouble I had with those two boys," Maria recalled with a smile.

As Hector's career took off, Lee felt the need to monitor him more vigilantly. He knew of Hector's penchant for sneaking out at night. One night, after Hector snuck out, Lee brought him back home, gathered all of his shoes, and took them away to teach him a lesson—and to keep him from going back outside. Not to be outdone, Hector wore Racquel's shoes out.

Despite the unconventional tactics, Maria held Lee in high regard. "I liked that he did that," she said. "Hector was supposed to be in the gym. He shouldn't have been [out on the streets]. I told [Lee] to take everything, so [Hector] don't run into the streets."

Flannery and Lee both helped shape Hector but, according to Maria, her son acted with a little more defiance toward Lee, whose tendency to slap Hector may not have had the same effects as some of Flannery's tactics. Despite the presence of caring men in his life, Hector was still conflicted and caught between the lure of the streets and his success at the gym. Hector struggled.

As Hector's star rose, Maida felt stuck between the love she felt for her family and the loyalty she felt for members of the East Side Gang. Not only did Maida have to contend with the pressures of gang life, but she was also aware of the impact she was having on her younger sisters, Yolanda and Maritza. The sisters fought, made up, cried together, and relied on each other, but Yolanda and Maritza lived in a world much different from Maida's.

"At the time, it was a totally different dynamic," Maritza recalled. "[Maida] was going to the boxing gym when it wasn't popular for a girl to be going to the gym. I admired her for that. She was like a trendsetter. She would bring me to the gym and show me off to her friends. It was cool."

Back home, Maritza was trying to make sense of Maida's world. What she did know about her sister was that everyone knew her and she was extremely popular. But why? It was not until later, when she found a jacket that Maida had left lying around the house, that Maritza realized that Maida was the leader of a gang. This was a shock to young Maritza, who saw firsthand the strain that her sister's gang life had on her mother and the family. It was one thing for Maida to exist in this highly secretive world represented by her gang jacket, but a much different one to have an element of that world reach their doorstep.

"One day this girl came to the house looking for my sister. She had two black eyes," Maritza recalled. "[Maida] had beaten the crap out of her.

Imagine a five-foot-ten girl coming to my house saying my sister, who was five feet five, beat her up. She wanted to get her back."

Frightened, Yolanda also recalled the incident: "I answered the door, and this monster asks, 'Does Maida live here? Is she here?'" Shaken and stunned that her sister could administer such a beating, Yolanda covered for her. To this day she recalls those piercing, swollen eyes. "I couldn't believe my sister could hurt a woman like that."

At times, Maida's aggression seemed a comforting protective mechanism, but Yolanda started to fear the way she lived. Still mesmerized by that "monster's" two black eyes, Yolanda had difficulty reconciling the fact that it was her sister who had done such damage.

Maria pleaded with Maida to change. "As a mother, it made her worry," said Maritza. "[Maida] was rebelling. She would disappear for a night, and at one point she ran away for a day or two. It stressed my mother out."

During that difficult period, a girl in Yolanda's class had begun to bully her nonstop. Yolanda prayed that she would stop, but the taunts continued. It became impossible for Yolanda to ignore the girl's threats but, at the same time, she did not want to get Maida involved. When Maida found out about the bullying, she responded exactly how Yolanda had expected: "She's bullying you? We will wait outside your school and I want you to fight her." Everything that Maida stood for, Yolanda resisted. The mere thought of fighting another girl created a level of anxiety in Yolanda that left her yearning for any other recourse.

But she had no choice. It was too late to turn back. When Yolanda and the girl left school, Maida was there waiting. With Maida watching, the fight started and ended swiftly. "I just started hitting her," Yolanda recalled.

Meanwhile, blossoming into a young man, Hector was seeing things in his household that boys his age should never see. Amid the love and joy there was much heartache and sorrow. His occasional belligerence and unbreakable confidence masked his pain. Few were able to see beneath the welcoming smile and mischievous grin—Hector would never allow it. Trying to get beyond his "Macho" façade was nearly impossible. He closed off any discussions about his personal welfare. Instead, as Hector grew in stature, people just assumed that the cheerful young fighter was always content because he never expressed himself in any other way.

"I think he was dating someone before my sister, and I just remember hearing, 'There goes Camacho,'" said Maritza. "And he was stealing a car or something. [What I was hearing] was not real positive. He was a real troublemaker in a very dysfunctional household."

When Maida started dating Hector, Maritza viewed this "troublemaker" in a different, more welcoming light. Hector was known to dance, pretend he was Bruce Lee, and fight in the streets. Unless he was in the middle of a fight or preparing to get into one, he was always in a good mood. He made people feel good about themselves—a trait that never disappeared, even when he became famous.

"He would leave his bike in the house," Maritza recalled. "He didn't really know me at the time, but he let me use his bike. He was very giving. . . . [On one] side he was this bad boy bully, and on the other side he was a loving, charming, and charismatic guy."

Those who got on Hector's bad side were hunted down and eventually paid for their sins. But not everyone. Some were able to reason with him. Phony people enraged Hector though. He wanted people to be upfront with him and he would be the same. Living in a neighborhood populated by different ethnic groups, Hector knew that whenever he walked down Lexington or went for a run in the morning, people were watching.

"It felt like he was my height, maybe five feet three, but he walked around like he was five feet ten," said Maritza. "A big presence. Very confident. That was his energy. He made you look up to him."

Hector and Maida tried to make their relationship work despite the distractions. One major difficulty that they faced was trying to maneuver around Maria, who had a strong hold on her son and sometimes invoked strict policies. Being Hector's girlfriend had its perks, but rarely did a girlfriend get the approval she was seeking from Maria. No one was good enough for her son. Maria doted on him regularly and was adamant that he could not bring girls into his room. So when Hector did try to bring Maida home, he had to be strategic. Once, Hector hid her in the back of a closet in his room while he went to make eggs in Maria's kitchen. From her perch in the closet, Maida could not help but giggle at the absurdity of it all. *What the hell am I doing in here?* she thought to herself. But nothing at the Camacho household was ever normal. They lived by their own set of rules. She knew Maria would interrogate Hector at some point and imagined the conversation went something like this:

"Hector, what are you doing come in and out of your room?"

"I'm making eggs, Ma!"

"But you already ate eggs, didn't you?"

"Yeah, but I'm still hungry, Ma."

Hector, on the contrary, did not have to hide when he visited Maida's home. Instead, he received preferential treatment from her mother, Luz. "My mother used to buy him boxes of cornflakes," said Maida. "He loved those cornflakes. She made sure they were there when he wanted them. Then my mother would say, 'Hector, go out and get me bread.' And he put on her pajamas and went to the store. He did so many funny things. He was a happy guy. You would never see him depressed. Despite being poor and living in East Harlem, he always made sure that people had fun."

Hector was a star wherever he went, so Maida was used to being in the background. "I was the kind of girl who wanted to be away from the cameras," said Maida. "When they brought cameras to our house, I used to hide. I was never a show-off."

The couple experienced moments of joy and tension, but when Maida found out she was pregnant, it transformed the relationship. Although both families agreed to help raise the child, Hector started to hang out more at the local clubs in Spanish Harlem. One of his favorite spots was The Lion's Cave on 104th between Lexington and 3rd. A local guy, DJ Ray, had started the club with friends. Having grown up on the same street, DJ Ray was also friends with Hector's childhood friend Eddie Pratts. One evening, Hector and DJ Ray began arguing over a girl. The fight quickly escalated and suddenly DJ Ray was trying to run Hector over in his Chrysler LeBaron sky-blue convertible.

"Camacho beat him up real, real bad, and DJ Ray was considered a tough guy," Eddie Pratts recalled. "Back then there were no cell phones or cameras. There was no proof about a fight—it was your word versus his word. Nobody ever went to the cops. In order to survive, you either fought or got beat up."

Fearless, Hector was the type of guy to return to the club the next week without concern for repercussions. Many believed he had built the perfect blueprint for how to survive and thrive in a hard neighborhood.

"Everybody fought in our neighborhood," said a close friend of Hector's from that time named Tommy, who was also part of the Jefferson Crusaders. "You fight, take a break, shake it off." Occasionally people in the neighborhood instigated fights just to see Hector react. One afternoon when Tommy went with a large group to Orchard Beach, there was a controversy over a large bill at an ice cream truck. Immediately, the employee called out everyone to a fight, to which there was a collective response: "You can fight him," and they pointed to Hector. Hector took care of the driver, and the rest of the group looted ice cream from the truck.

Before the baby arrived, Maida moved in to the Camachos' ninth-floor apartment. With Hector boxing and Maida preparing for the birth of the baby, things worked out for a brief time. Maria made sure the house was clean, and there was always enough food for the family.

One day, though, Maida saw a camera across the projects filming her. She recognized the person behind the camera as a local boy. Enraged, she told Hector, who peered out the window.

"You want to look at something," Hector said to the boy and then pulled down his zipper. "Look at this."

Hector could not let it go. When the couple was crossing the Johnson Projects near the Lady Queen of Angels Catholic Church days later, they ran into a familiar face.

"Sit down," Hector said to Maida.

"Why?" she asked.

"Just sit down."

Maida looked over and saw the culprit, and she braced for what happened next as Hector approached him.

"Were you looking at my girlfriend?" Hector asked.

"So what?" the boy responded.

That was enough for Hector. He knocked the kid out and then threw him in the bushes.

"Hector didn't care. He was defending what was his. He was crazy," said Maida.

Fearless, Hector took on anyone in the neighborhood. It did not matter who it was or how big they were. His nickname preceded him.

"His friends were going to call him 'Payaso,'" Flannery said, "which means 'clown' in Spanish. I named him 'Macho.' The rhyme is something everybody won't forget. He used it in his first professional fight, against

David Brown at the Felt Forum. He was introduced as Macho Camacho and the audience went wild. It's a name that suits him perfectly."

No one from either family agrees on why Maida moved home, but it was clearly a tumultuous time for Hector and Maida as they prepared to become parents.

"There were a lot of girls," Maida recalled. "He liked a lot of girls. A womanizer. I saw him with a girl when I was pregnant. It was a big problem."

During the pregnancy, Maida also had to cope with Hector's constant crime sprees. One day, Hector stole a car, took it home, and then went to work and didn't come home. Maria and Maida were forced to go to court to get him. During the hearing, Maida started to experience labor pains and was taken away in an ambulance. The judge let Hector go home.

"He didn't realize how his actions impacted me," said Maida as she recalled the stress from that ordeal. "We were ignorant. He would just walk around the Chinese supermarket and take six or seven oranges and keep walking. He didn't care about anything."

In one of her rare admissions about the severity of Camacho's actions, Maida added, "He made me suffer a little bit."

A Bright Light Shines in the Projects

5

With the exception of quiet moments with Hector, where he showed concern for her well-being and the baby, Maida's pregnancy was a rocky one. She had to cut her ties with the East Side Gang, move back in with her mother and sisters, and then wait. Yet everything was worth it when, on September 20, 1978, Hector Camacho Matias Jr. ("Junior") was born.

Immediately, both families converged on Mt. Sinai Hospital. Weighing 6.8 pounds, Junior had already surpassed his famous father in popularity as the women in both families doted on him constantly. Ebullient and proud, Hector, just sixteen years old, let everyone know he was a father. "I am a father. I have a boy. I have my son." For a while, he would not let his son go, kissing and hugging him. Not long after, Hector passed out cigars to friends and strangers, and the party began. The scent of smoke pervaded the air.

"He was in his element and his world changed forever," Maida remembered. "He ran with excitement to tell the world he had a baby boy. He was a proud dad and the world knew it."

Raising Hector Jr.—who was also nicknamed "Machito"—was an endeavor shared by four proud women of the Olivo household: Junior's aunts, Yolanda and Maritza; his grandmother, Luz; and his mother,

Maida. As an adult, Yolanda was the more protective one, the proverbial "good girl," always home with her mother, Luz. Maritza was fashionable and extroverted. Maida was still a tough "street girl." The three young sisters recognized that the absence of a consistent male figure in the household would leave a considerable gap in Junior's life. They knew they could not make up for Hector's absences while he pursued his path to superstardom, but they did their best. Each woman pitched in differently. Not once during Junior's childhood did he feel lost or alone—a testament to the collective efforts of the four women.

Knowing Junior was growing up in dangerous projects, Luz felt the need to shelter her grandson from a young age. To describe her as strict would be an understatement, as she was suspicious about everything Junior encountered outside of the home. In addition, Junior was not just *any* grandson; he was the only son of Hector "Macho" Camacho, who was already becoming an icon and a hero to his people.

"My grandmother would not let me go outside because she was afraid I would get kidnapped because I was Hector Camacho's son," Junior remembered. "I had to just sit and look out the window. I would just sit there and wait for my dad to come around. Man, she was tough."

Eventually, Maida and Hector briefly moved in together in an apartment at 109th Street and 2nd Avenue, but that setup didn't last long. Although Hector clearly respected Maida, he had moved on from the relationship.

Being a good father took time and commitment—a boxer's lifestyle did not allow for either in abundance. Thus, Hector's discipline as a boxer did not parallel his behavior as a father. Sure, he loved his son, but his livelihood was based on devotion to and concentration on his craft. Once his professional career began to take shape, Hector would be gone for long periods of time. While the women in Junior's life could fill it with smiles, laughter, and unconditional love, life for the son of the great Hector Camacho was not always easy when he was alone and forced to fend for himself. *I don't fucking care if you're Camacho's son, let's fight!*

When forging their own identities, children without famous fathers do not have to contend with the looming shadow of a man with blazing hands, charm that went for days, and a smile so vibrant that its mere presence immediately softened any friction. The neighborhood lit up when Hector drove one of his sports cars down the street to get his son.

Anxious, Junior peeked out the window to see what the commotion was. Deep down, he already knew.

Hector's mother and sister also took turns caring for Junior—both Hector's and Maida's families shared the responsibilities and enjoyed the joint partnership. One day Maida would have Junior, the next day, Maria and Racquel.

"[My father's] family was crazy," recalled Junior. "They were wild over there. I knew that when I went to stay with my father's side, I was free. I could do whatever I wanted. I respected my grandmother. Everybody—Felix, my father—never disrespected her. I respected her because I saw everyone else respect her. It was a different kind of affection: you could laugh, joke . . . it was cool. But you never crossed the line."

Although both families loved him in different ways, Junior still felt whole. Bouncing back and forth like a ball in a Spanish Harlem hand-ball game at the park, Junior received real love from both households. In his father's house, there were no limits and few rules. Yet, when Junior came home to Maida's house, he quickly acclimated to the calm, more controlled atmosphere. In this world, Junior had limits; they were not haphazardly set, but instituted out of love.

Meanwhile, new to fatherhood, Hector wondered whether his son would grow up in his image or chart his own path, and whether he would break under the pressure of trying to find himself, burdened by his father's long shadow. It was unlikely that Hector told confidants that—as a father—he would be the antithesis of his own father. That was not his style. But he would never be like his father—absent, abusive, a drunk. His father was a nonentity, which is hard to imagine because Hector was so exuberant and protective—sometimes, too protective.

"I was in the hospital after giving birth and a guy I used to know came by to see me," Maida recalled. "Hector was there the same day. Poyo was my friend's name and he came to congratulate me. Hector looked over, 'What the hell is he doing here?' It was a big commotion. Hector wanted to fight him. He made a big thing out of nothing. He was always starting fights."

However much he tried, though, Hector was not prepared to handle balancing boxing and having a child.

Navigating the Ring and Rikers

6

Becoming a father did not entirely convince Hector that he needed to mature; at this point, he was teetering on the edge of destroying everything that he, Patrick Flannery, and Robert Lee had built. Yet Hector needed only to look at his newborn son, Junior, and rub his sparkling Golden Gloves pendant to grasp the significance of the world he was living in. If those were not strong enough deterrents to avoid a life of crime, then the filthy walls inside Rikers Island might have been a final plea for him to change his ways.

On probation for an earlier car theft, which he claimed someone else had committed, Hector was hanging out on the block with friends when someone dared him to steal a car, a Pinto. Without any hesitation, he and a friend geared up to go. In the past, the process of stealing a car and then bringing it back was a simple one, but this time, Hector's friend and accomplice got into an altercation and stabbed the driver. With the immediacy of a right hook, Hector's bright future blurred in a split second. No longer was he part of a drive-and-return-safely scheme; now he was looking at years in jail. The two men took cops on a car chase over thirty blocks that netted Hector thirty stitches. Trapped on the driver's side, Hector had to squeeze through the passenger's side to escape the car. He was then cornered by officers inside a building and arrested after getting his head split open with the butt of a gun. Still on probation from his earlier car theft, Hector expected the worst.

The judge gave him six months for grand theft. Next thing Hector knew, he was on Rikers Island. After getting into a fight there, Hector was placed in solitary confinement. Languishing in a hole, staring hopelessly at those confining, paint-chipped walls, he asked himself, *What the fuck am I doing here?* Whether it was the isolation, the harrowing nights, or the loneliness—something happened to make Hector promise to abandon his reckless lifestyle, at least for the moment. He vowed to focus on his career.

"He wrote me a letter and put a picture in it," said Maria. "In it he wrote, 'Mommy, help me! Help me. Get me out of here.'"

Sadly enough, Patrick Flannery had no idea what had happened to Hector. Knowing what Hector was capable of, Flannery went to the neighborhood to piece together the facts. Friends, fearing the repercussions, told Flannery that Hector had moved back to San Juan, Puerto Rico. Doubtful of these accounts, Flannery kept searching until he discovered the truth. Having already lost one of Hector's friends, Jerry Cruz, to a street fight, Flannery felt relieved when he finally learned that Hector was still alive. If he could get out, Hector could salvage his boxing career.

Maria says that Negro Gonzalez helped put up the money to get Hector out of jail. Several people take credit for getting Hector out, specifically Robert Lee, who said he signed the papers to get him out with the help of his friend, Big George Hankins. "I signed him out of Rikers," said Lee. "I signed papers, and they released him under my custody. No one else did it. I had promised him I would get him out. It was rough in there. I went to court and battled for him to get out. None of his family did anything." Maria, however, recalled that she, along with Lee and Ruben, were part of the team that got Hector released after he served three and a half months.

Things changed for Hector once he got out. They had to.

"I told him, 'Fools don't take advice, and wise men don't need it,'" said Flannery. "'End up doing what you feel is right, but learn from your mistakes.'"

After getting another chance, Hector had no choice but to stay clean. He stood in front of the judge and promised that he would come back with a world championship belt.

Later in 1979, Hector won the Spanish Golden Gloves title and the Intercity championship. Instead of defending his 112-pound title in the sub-novice division from the year before, he moved into the 118-pound open division. There he moved through the ranks to face a tough fighter from the Yonkers Police Athletic League named Paul DeVorce in the final. The bout between DeVorce and Hector created considerable buzz for the almost nineteen thousand spectators. Participating in the prestigious event represented a source of immense pride for all the combatants. The Gloves featured nine bouts in the sub-novice division and nine in the open division. Relying on a straightforward style, DeVorce engaged in an entertaining bout, but Hector prevailed to win the decision and his second Golden Gloves title. On March 17, 1979, after beating DeVorce, Hector was acknowledged in the *New York Times*. Two titles were not enough for Hector, and he and Lee combined to win a third Golden Gloves title a year later, in the 119-pound open division, by defeating highly touted prospect Tyrone Jackson.

During this time, Hector developed close friendships with two other fighters: Davey Moore and Alex Ramos, who had both won multiple Golden Gloves titles. Often, their gyms would square off against each other.

"He was a beautiful soul," Ramos recalled. "But you didn't want to fuck with him. He didn't take shit from anybody. You get on his bad side, he lets you know what's happening. I remember when Hector started a riot at the Apollo Gym on 125th Street. He got into an argument and went nuts. I was downstairs; he was upstairs. It was over some bullshit."

Ramos loved Hector dearly and saw him as someone who was fiercely loyal. Out of the ring, they clicked and would stay close friends for years. And during some of Moore's darkest moments as a professional, Hector did everything he could to help him cope. People who knew Hector loved him, while those on the outside often could not see past what they perceived as arrogance.

As he closed out a brilliant amateur career with a 96-4 record, Hector had earned raves for three consecutive Golden Gloves titles, four Intercity titles, two Empire State Games championships, a Spanish Gloves title, and thirteen total amateur titles. Next, he focused on an Olympic berth. Leading up to the Olympics, Hector traveled to Atlanta, Georgia,

A Path to Glory

7

When Hector joined the professional ranks, he engendered all the toughness of a typical New York fighter. He discovered a natural fit at the Felt Forum, located in Madison Square Garden. So many great fighters before him had sharpened their skills at the Felt, and Hector, who had a relationship with the Garden's matchmaker, Harold Weston, felt a level of comfort there. On September 12, 1980, eight days before Junior's second birthday, Hector, then 127 pounds, won his professional debut against David Brown at the Felt. By notching a four-round unanimous decision, Hector, fighting out of the super featherweight 130-pound division, easily moved from the amateurs to the professional ranks. Billy Giles and Robert Lee shared the training and managing duties with Jerry Villarreal Sr. (and often with Villarreal's son, Jerry Villarreal Jr., who was learning the game as a high schooler as well). Often accompanying Hector was fellow stablemate and close friend from the amateurs, Pee Wee Rucker, and another mainstay, Tony Kidd, who was brought in to do all of the office tasks. Giles later hired Don Thibodeaux from Detroit as Hector's cutman.

Later, Long Island promotor Jeff Levine would join the Macho team (through a New York guy, Bob Uchitel) as a co-promoter and manager and would play a vital role in transitioning Hector into a more prolific and lucrative future involving Don King. "My father loved Hector dearly, wild and all," said Laura Levine. By all accounts, Levine brought a fabulous business sense and leadership qualities to a team that benefited from both aspects. Before Hector became champion, Levine signed with King for six options, including a world-title fight. In the process, King promised Hector a new car as part of his bonus. Hector, a car aficionado, demanded a Lamborghini.

The Macho team was based out of New York, but Hector tried desperately to find sparring partners who challenged him, and eventually his team opted to head to Detroit to sharpen the fighter's skills. When in Detroit, Giles brought Hector and Pee Wee Rucker to work at the famed Kronk Gym. Giles had a relationship with Emanuel Steward, who ran the Kronk, and had helped get Steward introduced to key people in the sport when Steward did not know anyone. "At the time, the Kronk was the hottest gym around," said Jerry Villarreal Sr. "So Hector was getting all that work over there and kicking everyone's ass. Every Kronk guy around."

There were no comfortable hotels or luxuries for Giles, Pee Wee, and Hector; the only amenities they had were each other. But their shared laughter during that time irrevocably linked the men.

"They were all staying in one room on the East Side of Detroit," Jerry Villarreal Sr. recalled. "The room smelled so bad because Hector used to sweat so much. I had to take him out to buy him clothes and socks. But one time, Billy [Giles] locked him out of the room, and Hector was saying, 'I'm going to knock it down.' Billy told him, 'Get the fuck away from the door.' Next thing you know, down goes the door. Hector kicked the door completely off the hinges. The manager comes up, and I ended up paying him like $300 and told him everything was okay. But he kicked everyone out. Then, I took them to stay at the Residence Inn in Southgate and got them hotel rooms."

In Detroit, Hector was on a mission, and, although he heard Giles's voice loud and clear, it was Lee's technical advice instilled in him as an amateur that played in Hector's ears. When Hector needed someone to give him direction and chart a path to harness his energy and skills, Lee taught him the fundamentals—*his* fundamentals. It was Lee who orchestrated how Hector should move in the ring, not a small task for one of the most graceful young fighters to emerge in decades. Likewise, it was Lee who chased Hector down after curfew and steered him clear of the drug trade. "No one else wanted to give him a chance," said Lee, "but I wanted him to know that I believed in him." Lee saw a gem of a fighter, and a kid with a good heart. Deep down, Lee knew the world that Hector grew up in, and he felt an affinity for the young kid. Hector was tough and didn't take shit from people, but it was more than that. In order for Hector to feel good about himself, he adhered to a moral code that disallowed him from dealing with people he deemed fake. Intuitively, Hector saw through people who speciously tried to present themselves as genuine.

"He was real," Lee recalled. "If he didn't like you, he told you."

During this time, Jerry Villarreal Sr. was working with a young and popular prospect, Mickey Goodwin, who also trained at the Kronk Gym. Every morning, Mickey and Jerry Sr. drove to Belle Isle, an island in the Detroit River between Michigan and Canada, to do their road work. The fresh, early morning air on the island was perfect for fighters to run a five-mile loop. One day, when Mickey and Jerry Sr. were driving to the island, they spotted Billy Giles and Hector.

"Pull over, pull over," said Goodwin.

"Why?"

"There's Camacho and Billy."

From that point on, every morning, Hector, Giles, and Pee Wee would make the long, arduous trek to Belle Isle. Once Jerry Villarreal Sr. and Mickey joined their forces, a new boxing family took hold. They would go watch club fights at Detroit's 20 Grand ballroom, and Jerry Sr. would show them the sights. Meanwhile, Jerry Sr.'s wife would cook for Hector and Giles and became a surrogate mother for Hector whenever he came to Detroit. By this time, Hector would often sport his yellow-and-black, Bruce Lee–inspired jumpsuit, wearing it so often it eventually got holes, and he had to bring it to Mrs. Villarreal to mend.

"We really hit it off," said Jerry Sr. "But Billy never taught Hector how to pick his hand up. It was all Robert Lee, but he never got the credit for it. Billy's biggest thing was that his mother's boyfriend was Bobby McQuillan, who was the plug to Harold Weston. At that time, Weston was the matchmaker for Madison Square Garden. McQuillan introduced

Billy to Harold Weston and that's how Hector started getting on the cards at the Felt Forum."

One afternoon, Hector got into the ring with Hilmer Kenty, WBC world lightweight champion, who had no fear of this prospect who was only starting his professional career. It didn't matter. Hector easily bested Kenty, and as Jerry Sr. recalled, Hector "beat him like he stole something."

"I remember talking to my dad and him telling me, 'You have to come see this little southpaw Puerto Rican kid,'" said Jerry Jr. "'He just kicked the shit out of Hilmer Kenty.'"

Kenty was infuriated and refused to believe that Hector—or anybody for that matter—could best him so soundly. "Hilmer said, 'That's bullshit. We'll do it again tomorrow,'" Jerry Jr. recalled. "And the next day when I get to the gym, Hilmer is waiting for Hector with his gloves on and said, 'Let's go, let's go.'"

Hector tagged Kenty after some feeling-out rounds, but pulled back when he saw that Kenty was hurt.

"Are you okay?" he asked.

Immediately, Giles chided Hector for not going for the kill. It was a rare moment of compassion for Hector, who would earn a reputation for going full tilt in sparring sessions.

"Hector beat the shit out of him again," Jerry Jr. recalled. "He was seventeen years old. Kenty never sparred with him again."

While Giles wanted to simulate the adversity of a real fight, Lee often had Hector get in good work and pull back when his fighter completed the task. No matter what style Hector adhered to, he often achieved the same result—pure dominance.

Quickly intimidating fighters who knew little about him, Hector succeeded everywhere he went. Most people recognized the famous Kronk Gym name, but other gyms also drew big crowds, especially when Hector was sparring. Cutman Don Thibodeaux had his own gym, and William and Norman Dabish owned the Powerhouse Gym, another popular spot for the Macho team.

One afternoon at Thibodeaux's gym, boxer Tommy Hearns's younger brother, John, challenged Hector, and they agreed to spar. Tommy got wind of the showdown and rushed over to the gym. Tommy went straight for his brother and demanded he leave. "You have no business getting in the ring with him," said Tommy, pointing to Hector. "Go get your stuff and we can go home."

"If he doesn't want to fight," Hector joked to Tommy, "I can always take you."

One day, Hector sparred with the Kronk mainstay Bret Summers, an undefeated professional at the time.

"I want you, white boy," yelled Hector, pointing at Summers as he entered the gym. "I want you, white boy." Summers then looked to gym owner Emanuel Steward: "Who the hell is this kid running his mouth?" Summers knew Hector by name and growing reputation, but Macho had not yet reached the heights of stardom.

"You don't want to do this. Not with this kid," Steward warned the competitive Summers, who was open to a sparring session. Nothing materialized as Summers went on with his training session after the brief distraction.

About a year later, Hector returned to the gym while Summers was in the middle of another training session. "I want you, white boy."

This time around, Summers responded, "OK, bring it on," and talked Steward into letting him face the young phenom. Hector was set to spar fifteen rounds with a couple of different sparring partners, but, unfortunately for Summers, he went first. "I had to fight a fresh Hector Camacho. Boy, oh, boy, did he start roughing me up. His jab came in so fast." After a round of elbows, low blows, and other rough tactics, Summers looked to Steward for answers. "You have to keep going," Steward told him.

"Then, he breaks my nose with a headbutt," said Summers. After the headbutt and some brief sparring, Summers proceeded to pull a "wizard," an old wrestling move, slamming Hector face first into the canvas. This caused both corners to spill into the ring. After the session, Hector went over to Summers and shook his hand as if he had completed a rite of passage.

"He never called me white boy again," recalled Summers.

Although some recalled a slightly different scenario, the violent nature of the sparring session remained the same.

"Emanuel was always trying to find fighters who could beat Hector in the gym," recalled Jerry Jr. "When he brought Summers in, Hector busted him up so bad that his father had to step in when it got too bad to say, 'No, no, that's enough.' And he pulled him out."

Some fighters use sparring sessions to focus on specific areas—defense, movement, offensive game plan. But Hector didn't differentiate between the fight and the sparring session. "It was like Hector was fighting for his life every day," recalled Jerry Jr.

Coming to Detroit may have changed everything for Hector. Not only did it allow him to escape the distractions in his hometown, he also developed his own identity in the ring by facing seasoned fighters like Hilmer Kenty. And in the Villarreals he found a family who did not want anything from him and did not judge him for his checkered past. Later, their home became his retreat.

Gaining confidence with every fight, Giles knew his fighter's value. He talked a good game, and the two of them jabbed at each other incessantly. Every time Giles entered a gym with Hector and Pee Wee Rucker in tow, people noticed. *The Macho team is here!* Occasionally, Giles would announce that they had arrived. Boisterous, crude, and fun loving, Giles knew how to have a good time and when to create a scene. He lived on the go and carried his wardrobe in the back of his Cadillac Eldorado. Whenever Giles had to change, he went to the trunk to put on one of his many Adidas sweat suits.

The ongoing street banter between Giles and Hector never ceased, and the friendship away from the ring had a backstory. "Billy Giles was close to Maria. But Billy was also very close to his [own] mother," said a former girlfriend of Hector's. "Hector saw how close [Billy] was with his mother and he appreciated that. That was the one redeeming quality of Billy. In the ring, he spoke to Camacho like a trainer, and outside of it like a friend."

Always trying to outdo the other, both men fought tooth and nail to get the last word. At that time, there was an old man who used to go out on the ice near Belle Isle and skate in his underwear. Once, when Giles and Hector passed him, Giles started yelling at Hector, "You ain't no Macho Man. *He's* the real Macho Man."

Seconds later, there was Hector out skating on the ice—naked.

"Mach started screaming, 'I am the Macho Man, I am the Macho Man' and wouldn't get back in the car until they conceded that he was indeed the Macho Man," Jerry Sr. recalled.

Finally, Giles relented, "Okay, *you* are the real Macho Man, now get in the car."

Putting his clothes back on, Hector, the real Macho Man, entered the car with a huge grin. The moment encapsulated everything that made the team click. From Giles knowing what buttons to push, to Hector taking the bait, to Jerry Sr. screaming for Hector to get his "ass in the car," the scene perfectly revealed the roles that each played within the relationship.

Between September 1980 and May 1981, Hector fought seven times. During that span, he started with David Brown, then beat Benny Llanos, Herman Ingram, Robert Johnson, Jerry Strickland, Tomas Enrique Diaz, and closed out May of 1981 with a win over Kato Ali. None of Hector's opponents had a winning record, but Giles and Lee had found a winning formula. Not all fighters come into the professional ranks with a style that translates at that level. Some of the greatest amateur fighters struggled mightily when asked to make that transition, but not Hector.

"We would buy a six-pack and head to watch the fight, and only get to drink one beer because Macho was knocking people out," said childhood friend Richie "Rich" Galvan. "He gave us all motivation. Not just to box, but to achieve anything."

Hector always wanted his mother there, so Maria was also a mainstay at camps. She made sure her son stayed away from women, and, more important, that the women stayed away from him. At times, Maria aggravated her son, but her strict policies came from a good place. She only wanted what was best for him. Maria was also always the first one sprinting up to the ring apron after a fight, often giving her son a bear hug. As Maritza said, Hector didn't know how to respect women, but there was no one in his life whom he showed such love for as he did his mother.

"My grandmother was supportive," Junior recalled. "That was her baby. My dad wanted her there. She helped him read and sign contracts. He wanted her there for emotional support as well."

Maria also provided support when Hector traveled for camps later on, but Giles and Lee alternated roles as good cop, bad cop. With Weston's guidance and matchmaking skills, Hector received plaudits from the world's best fighters. Moving from super featherweight to catchweights near 135 pounds, Hector, 129 pounds, continued his string of victories with a unanimous eight-round decision over Marcial Santiago on June 25, 1981. Now 8-0, Hector returned on July 24, 1981, to the Felt Forum to face Jose Figueroa, who had replaced Jerome Artis. Hector knocked him out in one round.

"My relationship with Hector was already in place when I got him," said Weston, who worked for Gil Clancy, director of boxing at the Garden. "He only had one fight and I was negotiating with Robert Lee and Billy Giles, and both of them were involved at the time. Back then, everybody knew each other. They needed a place to put fights. And remember this wasn't Sugar Ray Leonard coming in with a corporation. Hector was not a name guy like a Sugar Ray; instead, he had to be groomed."

Over the first ten or twelve fights, Hector established himself as not just a fighter, but also as an attraction. And Weston believed Hector could become the best fighter in the world. With a knack for choosing capable opponents, Weston helped shape Hector by placing him before respected fighters who were going to force him to use a new move or approach each night out.

"Weston called me up and said, 'I got a kid for you. I need you to see him," said matchmaker, trainer, and manager Jimmy Montoya. "'He's got everything. He's fast and a bad motherfucker. I need you to help me groom him for a world title.'"

Montoya, a West Coast Renaissance man, not only made clothes for Hector and other fighters, he also had more than a hundred fighters in his stable. When promoters like Bob Arum and Don King needed a matchmaker or just an opponent, they often turned to Montoya, who deftly began lining up talent to face Hector. After only eleven bouts, Hector earned a shot to face tough Filipino fighter Blaine Dickson for the North American Boxing Federation (NABF) super featherweight title on December 11, 1981. Hector, 129.5 pounds, looked to extend his streak of victories, whereas Dickson, 130 pounds, was 15-3. Fighting effectively and weathering some difficult moments, Hector earned a twelve-round unanimous decision and the belt.

Shockingly, Hector didn't dominate the tough Dickson as he had previous opponents. In the late rounds, Dickson tagged and hurt Hector, causing him to clinch and survive. The need to clinch was something new for Hector, who rarely let opponents put themselves in a position to land such a punch. What happened in the final round left a bitter taste in the mouths of some boxing fans as Hector continued to punch after the final bell sounded, and, amid the chaos, Hector punched referee Vinnie Rainone. His behavior enraged Dickson's team and foreshadowed Hector's future mindset, in which nothing was off limits when he needed to gain an edge.

"I lost my head," Hector admitted after the fight. "I really didn't think he would come back at me."

Despite difficulties throughout the fight, Hector still managed to win decisively on all cards, with Judge Harold Lederman and referee Rainone (also a judge) scoring the fight 8-4 and Judge Tony Castellano scoring it 6-5. Some, however, were not sold on the performance. Ray "Boom Boom" Mancini was in the stands to watch the fight, and what he saw that evening stuck with him until he faced Hector in the ring years later. While some were willing to praise Hector for every cute move (he was warned twice for "clowning" against Dickson), Mancini saw a predictable fighter with a weak chin. Unimpressed, Mancini had already pigeonholed Hector as an "easy guy to figure out" if a mega-fight with him ever happened. At this point, Mancini was basking in his glory as a TV sensation and world champion in constant demand, whereas Hector was still a new kid on the block, biding his time for that inevitable world-title shot.

"When I fought [Dickson], he said, 'All Camacho does is grab, grab, grab.' What am I supposed to do if this guy's a bull?" said Hector. "He's brutal. He's coming with his head, elbow, he's hitting me below the belt. What am I supposed to do? Stand there? No, I'm gonna hit him, hold him. That's the way I fought, 'cause that was the fight I was supposed to fight."

Two months later, Hector moved to his thirteenth victory with a unanimous decision over a one-win Jorge Nina in Richmond Hill Arena, located in the southwestern section of Queens. Back in action a month later, Hector fought Rafael Lopez in front of his loyal fans at the Felt Forum, which marked his eighth appearance at the venue. Early in the third round, he used a brief respite during a break issued by referee Luis Rivera to knock Lopez out with a right hand. It took Lopez ten minutes to recover. Lopez's manager, Eddie Imondi, protested the punch, but referee Rivera supported his decision. Furious, Lopez pleaded, "Just let me get him again." Nonplussed by the controversy, Hector admired his own handiwork: "They say we can't punch; well, I guess that was a pretty good punch."

★ ★ ★

Hector was still mired in street conflicts; despite his revelatory moments in Rikers, it was difficult for him, even with the responsibility of being a professional athlete, to escape the lure of the streets. Meanwhile, laws were in place that hindered the Garden from signing fighters to long-term contracts. Thus, Weston felt that he had to earn Hector's trust to sell him on staying with the Garden, but he went about it in a most unconventional manner.

"He was a natural," said Weston. "But one time I found out that he got into a street fight and beat up a couple guys. I had him come to my office, and I shut the door. I punched him in the stomach. He looked at me like, 'What the fuck are you doing?' But I didn't tolerate that. I was trying to help these guys. He knew I cared, and I knew where he came from. He was a good kid."

Weston knew that if he did not send a forceful message to Hector, he might lose control of one of the most talented fighters he had worked with in decades. Whether he had Hector's best interests at heart is unclear, but the result was that Hector stayed focused long enough for them to continue together along the championship journey.

Weston was not the only one to act as a mediator between the street and the ring; Robert Lee also stepped in to settle a street beef that Hector got entangled in. Surely there were other scenarios where someone had to step in on Hector's behalf. Hector detailed one of his deadly run-ins: "I beat this guy up and then he came back acting like he had a gun. . . . I went upstairs and got this sawed-off shotgun. I chased him through the streets with the shotgun. I just did so much crazy stuff."

★ ★ ★

After establishing such a tightknit bond, the relationship between Hector and Robert Lee ended abruptly. Unhappy with Lee, Hector asked him to leave. What transpired prior to Lee's departure is subject to debate. One thing is clear: Giles had taken over the reins of the team and its boxing future.

"We were getting ready to fight Blaine Dickson," said Jerry Villarreal Sr. "Robert Lee had access to Hector's account and took $5,000. . . . He made the mistake of confiding in Billy [Giles] about taking the money, which he could have easily paid back after the fight. Billy went directly to Maria and said something like, 'If he takes $5,000 now, what's next?' When Robert signed the contract, Billy promised to give him his share of the 33⅓ percent, but he never did. Robert should have gone directly to Hector and he could have gotten the money, but he didn't. They let him go."

Maria recalled a different version of the events, but with the same results. Business was business, and Hector quickly became acquainted with the ugly side of a sport where relationships were fragile and tenuous.

Lee tells a different story. "Billy had started taking advantage of different things. I had the bank book with the money short, but I was going to replace the money with the TV fight. In reality, I was entitled to what I took. But I was not as focused as I should have been. [Hector] believed in me all this time, why second guess me now? I never cut his purse. They made it look so ugly. It hurt my pride."

When asked about Lee, Hector told a reporter "[Lee]'s no longer with me because of something he did to himself. I don't mind saying it because, really, it isn't hurting me. He's wrong, and he isn't right for the business. The friendship is still there, but as far as businesswise, he isn't right for it. So I just dismissed him. I said thanks for all the favors he did, and the friendship is always there. One day he might feel bad, and I don't want him to look at me and say, 'Hey I made the kid, he's making money, and now he's going around bad-mouthing me.'"

Diplomatic and clipped in his response, Hector was either holding back or repeating what Giles fed to him. Either way, the words must have stung Lee, knowing full well that *his* fighter was now under the control of a guy he viewed as a hypocrite. Now, Giles had Hector all to himself to mold as he pleased. Still contending that he was the "champ maker," Giles felt more emboldened with Lee out of the fold and often brazenly told his fighter, "You need me."

On May 21, 1982, Hector defended his NABF super featherweight crown for the first time when he returned to the Felt Forum to face Refugio Rojas, who was trained by Jimmy Montoya. Stringing fights against good opposition became a hallmark of Giles's tenure. Instead of feeding his fighter severely inferior competition, Giles challenged him. Going into the fight with Hector, Rojas had already faced stiff opposition in Rolando Navarrete, Edwin Rosario, Rocky Lockridge, and Bernard Taylor. Unable to muster a victory against those opponents, Rojas (21-9) had ample experience, which would serve Hector well. It was also the first time that Montoya got a firsthand look at the future star, and he would not be disappointed.

At the pre-fight weigh-in, Hector came in at exactly 130 pounds, while Rojas entered two pounds lighter. Not long after the pre-fight staredown, Rojas was pulling himself up off the canvas. Studious early on, Hector quickly pulled Rojas into a right hook, which sent him down. Referee Dick Young administered a standing eight count. Seeing the end was near, Hector, utilizing herky-jerky movements, sent Rojas through the bottom ropes with three consecutive uppercuts. In order to let Young step in, Hector backed off and patiently waited to celebrate. Suddenly, Rojas, using his right glove, leveraged on the bottom rope to pull himself up. Hector ambushed him, sending him down for a third time; this time, however, a punch did not trigger the final knockdown, as fatigue had set in. The New York State three-knockdown rule was in effect, and the fight was called. Hector's handlers escorted him around the ring.

The next five fights for Hector turned out to be the most significant of his career, not only because they helped him mature, but because each fight depicted him in the prime of his career. Ironically, most people would expect a great fighter to thrive *after* he wins a world title, but *this* Hector was phenomenal in so many ways. Hector fought these five bouts over a period of less than a year.

Less than two months after his drubbing of Rojas, Hector returned on July 11, 1982, to face Louie Loy. Everyone in the arena was waiting to see Hector put on his typical performance of showmanship, speed, aggression, and, always, that edge. But with a record of 15-0-1, Loy, a promising twenty-one-year-old fighter from Portland, Oregon, was not the type of challenger Hector could take lightly.

Not everyone would be willing to test himself against a fighter like Loy at such an incipient stage in his career. A mainstay at the Felt Forum, Hector (15-0, eight KOs) brandished boxing weapons so breathtaking that it was difficult to take your eyes off him. At twenty years old, Hector,

132 pounds, entered the fight as the tenth best 130-pounder in the world according to the World Boxing Council (WBC); Loy had two Golden Gloves championships on his resume.

More than eleven hundred spectators packed the Felt Forum for the nationally telecast show. Hector was headlining, marking his first television appearance. Tony Perez worked as the referee for the matchup. Only a year apart, Hector and Loy were well aware of each other's abilities.

"CBS would call me and just give me names [of opponents for Hector]," said Weston. "It didn't make a difference who it was. I didn't even ask who it was. I would just say, 'Just tell me what the price is.' That tells you how great he was. At one point I had CBS on one line and ABC or NBC on the other. I would just ask, 'How much are you paying?'"

Before the fight, CBS analyst Gil Clancy, a huge fan of Hector, gushed over the young fighter when he said, "He can out-Ali, Ali," in reference to Hector's show-stopping attributes. Clancy and the old timers admired Hector for his predilection to make deft, organic moves that it took veterans years to perfect. They admired seeing talent packaged as it was in Hector. The first time Clancy saw Hector was on one of Weston's cards in Long Island, New York, against Kato Ali. From there, he came to Weston to discuss putting Hector on CBS.

"Gil [Clancy] worked at CBS and he gave me his approval of Camacho after seeing him at the Garden," said Weston. "Gil thought he could be great, and for you to get Gil's attention—Gil doesn't just say that about anybody. When you get it from those types of guys, like the Dundees and Gil, that means you can fight."

Following Giles to the ring in a burgundy robe, Hector, focused and resolute, greeted his hometown fans. Refusing to look at Loy during the pre-fight staredown, Hector gazed at the canvas. Less than a minute later, Loy chased him down and landed a right hook. Pawing at Loy early, Hector shifted laterally and showed how flawlessly he would be able to navigate his way inside. Conversely, the awkward Loy paid for his reckless tendency to forge ahead. When Loy landed a jab in the first round, Hector shot a straight left counter; in the same round, Hector sidestepped a lunging Loy to land another straight left counter.

By the midpoint, Hector had already worked Loy over with his hold, hit, and spin tactics. Dictating the movement of the remainder of the round, Hector absorbed a jab and then swarmed Loy with a straight left counterpunch that wobbled him. As the first round closed out, Loy lunged at Hector, a risky move when attempting to leave a lasting impression on the judges. Hector sidestepped him, settled, and punctuated the waning seconds of the round with one final straight left hand. Not finished, Hector crowded Loy against the ropes and ripped off two abridged hooks to the body.

As Hector was opening up his vast arsenal of punches, Loy regressed. Within the first minute of round two, Loy hit the canvas from a left and right combination. He rose immediately. Burrowing in, Hector landed a jab and a straight left that clearly bothered Loy. In the first six minutes, Hector had opened two cuts over Loy's eyes. For good measure, Hector sent Loy down one final time with a formidable right-left-right combination on the inside. Deceivingly strong on the inside, Hector stood on the outside and used his jab or moved inside to shorten his punches and hurt Loy. At this point, Loy charged again and watched helplessly as Hector restored order in the middle of the turbulence. Something, presumably an issue with the ring, agitated Hector, who screamed toward his corner. Hector moved into attack mode for the final half of round three, which was punctuated by a big left that shook Loy.

By reverting to combinations over the first couple rounds, Hector, who promised to put on a show for his hometown fans, was beginning to get into a groove. Additionally, Hector physically manhandled the bigger Loy and used rough tactics, like holding him still with a right glove and simultaneously shooting a straight left. Most fighters get frustrated and beckon the referee; Loy looked exasperated. Highlighting the third round was the inefficiency of Hector's corner when it forgot to send him out with a mouthpiece. Appearing out of sorts, Hector adapted and finished out the round. In the fourth, Hector continued the illegal tactics by spinning Loy three times and then opened up a blistering attack at the end of the round.

After being on the receiving side of a particularly vicious four-punch combination, Loy went into the fifth round with no momentum whatsoever. Masterful, Hector landed a right hook to start the fifth and placed Loy in desperation mode in the sixth. With 1:22 remaining in the round, Hector landed one of his best punches, an uppercut, and then held on to avoid Loy's counter. Cuts worsened as the talented Hector resorted to shielding referee Perez and lashing Loy with a right hand. Not oblivious to the illegal tactics, Perez chided Hector for his actions.

Because Hector pulled off the tricks with such celerity, each one appeared to be woven in the tapestry of his style; thus, it felt more like an extension of his greatness than a cheap personal gambit. Loy had not posed a threat all night, and, consequently, had lost all six rounds on all three judges' scorecards going into the seventh and final round, when he was a victim of a vicious Camacho cheap shot. Too talented to have to resort to such illegal punches, Hector spun Loy and hurt him with a right hand. Perez jumped in to warn Hector (and the analysts called out Hector as well), but Hector's decision to walk away so nonchalantly after the punch showcased his indifference. Before the round ended, Hector had sent Loy through the ropes and then brutalized him again. Perez stepped in to end the onslaught at 1:27 of the round. Judges Al Reid and Teddy Wint and referee Perez all had it 6-0 for Hector going into the final round. A beaten Loy slowly made it across the ring; Hector acknowledged his fans and then flew into the arms of trainer Don Thibodeaux. Struggling to break free from Thibodeaux, who was taking off his wraps, Hector started to break out into dancing mode.

"I remember watching this kid with super-fast hands, who was incredible in the ring," said Sugar Ray Leonard. "And I said to myself, 'This kid is going to be a superstar.' I knew this kid was going to be special. And he turned out to be a special fighter."

The dancing exhibition was about to start, but unfortunately, the Loy bout revealed a pattern of illegal tactics employed by Hector. After the match ended, Hector told CBS analyst Tim Ryan, "[Loy] has never seen anything like my quality. I knew it was going to be this type of fight, because, first of all, I don't like to get hit." When asked about his dirty tactics, Hector responded, "It's like a habit, I have to break out of it." Less engaging, Loy countered: "He never hurt me. He's also a dirty fighter. If he did that spinning out in California, he would have never gotten away with it. He's a quick puncher, real fast. But if I hit like he hit me, he would have been gone." Loy would only fight four more times.

"Loy was good for him," said Weston. "He came forward. But Hector was too much. He was smart and had hand speed. He was very unique, very special, and, like Ali, you only have those types of guys come around once in a while."

By July 1982, Hector was a fixture in all three sanctioning bodies' rankings. The International Boxing Writers' Foundation rated Hector behind Bazooka Limon, Samuel Serrano, Cornelius Boza-Edwards, and Alexis Arguello at 130 pounds, whereas the World Boxing Council (WBC) ranked him eighth directly behind Puerto Rico's Rafael Solis. United Press International ranked him sixth. Meanwhile, the World Boxing Association (WBA) showed its true colors and left him unranked.

Keeping Hector active was vital to his career and his growth. By allowing Hector no downtime, Weston knew that he would get right back to training. Shortly after disposing of Loy, and taking advantage of the recent casino boom, Hector's team lined fights up in Atlantic City, where Hector fought his next two bouts at the Copa Room in the Sands Casino Hotel on *CBS Sports Saturday*. Hector made Atlantic City his own personal playground throughout his career, often stopping on the boardwalk to hold an impromptu dance clinic. Some joked that Hector had more of a following for his dance moves than his boxing moves as he soaked up the attention. With the intoxicating smell of funnel cakes and the soft sea air wafting off the beach, Hector felt good.

Sharing the broadcast booth before Hector's August 28, 1982, fight against Johnny Sato (18-8), announcer Gil Clancy and Sugar Ray Leonard did not have to be coaxed into heaping praise on the confident Hector. Clancy proposed that "Hector's moves are patented for a southpaw, but against Sato he will have to be a puncher." When asked about people who noticed a little Sugar in Hector, Leonard said, "It's a great comparison between the two of us. Hector's got charisma, style, and a great personality." Sato had lost two of his last three bouts leading into the August 28 showdown, one an NABF super featherweight title shot against Rolando Navarrete on May 19, 1981. Struggling to find worthwhile competition at 130 pounds, Hector, 131.5 pounds, and Sato, 134.25 pounds, faced off in an over-the-weight bout and agreed to 133 pounds. Technically, Sato did not make weight, but Hector didn't contest it. Larry Hazzard officiated the sold-out bout.

Going into the fight, Sato and Hector were ranked sixth and eighth, respectively, by the WBC. The beginning of the Sato fight severely contrasted with the Loy bout; in fact, Sato, who showed no fear, outhustled

Hector in two of three major exchanges. Hector walked into a straight left hand early on that woke him up. Hector had only needed a total of eight rounds in the previous two fights, but Sato quickly assured him that he was neither Rojas nor Loy in terms of his attacking style.

However, after moments of success in the first round, Sato revealed his limitations, including his inability to get inside on Hector. Lunging, Sato, a southpaw, could not get in range to land that same straight left again. Unveiling his uppercut on the inside early, Hector reverted to his jab to close out the round. Hector landed a litany of hooks and upper-cuts, but it was a straight left that dizzied his opponent and made Sato cover up and shift his weight and tumble backward. Hazzard sent Hector to the opposite corner and then proceeded to count Sato out at 2:15 of the fourth round. Prompted by the quick stoppage, Hector described the knockdown: "I was flicking the jab, flicking the jab, trying to stagger him. I hit him with the hook first, and the uppercut finished him off." Then, for good measure, he added, "I'm mean. I'm really mean," smiling mischie-vously. Summing up the performance, Sato stated, "I'm ready to punch him hard, but I don't block his."

In the post-fight interview, Hector admitted to "playing cautious" before unleashing the knockout punches. Michael Katz of the *New York Times* reported that Hector gave Ray Mancini's co-promoter, Jeff Levine, a six-month option to negotiate a world-title fight with Sammy Serrano (whom Hector had little respect for as a fighter) for the WBA junior lightweight crown. In addition, Hector signed with Levine to pro-mote his next three fights. There also had been speculation that Bobby Chacon and Hector would get together that fall. Either way, people were intrigued.

Some young fighters can punch. Others can box. Still others are defensive wizards. Blessed with all those skills and a little flair to boot, Hector rep-resented something new—a figure the sport desperately needed as Sugar Ray Leonard started the final phase of his career. Brash, cocky, but not abrasive, Hector understood like no other fighter how to maximize his growing stardom. Considering his own return to the ring, Leonard, not one to verbalize praise effusively, welcomed the comparison. "I spoke to [Hector]," said Leonard. "I told him that people are always asking who's going to take my place. I told him he could, but you can't take my place unless you straighten up. He said he already has."

Hours later on the Atlantic City boardwalk, Hector made his presence known, this time by defacing an expensive hotel mural for which Hector and his entourage had to face Don King. To avoid punishment, Hector blamed it on his entourage.

Just when it appeared that Hector was on the verge of something spectacular, he had reverted to his immature ways. As often as Hector had told himself he was growing up, he was still making rash decisions. Academically, Hector had been kicked out of seven schools, but in situations where he had to rely on instinct, Hector outsmarted the toughest of characters, and he was fiercely loyal. He never forgot his friends, which was why Pee Wee Rucker was fighting on all of his cards. Although Rucker was an excellent amateur, he had not had the same type of success at the next level. But his friendship was enough for Hector, who made sure that Rucker kept fighting with him.

"He was a caring young man," said Weston. "He just had to be Macho. Living in the New York City streets, life was a struggle. He still had to be the Macho Uptown Man. Naturally being who he was, he didn't trust many people. But he was a real nice kid."

★ ★ ★

Melvin "Tank" Paul, a sensational amateur, a three-time Louisiana State Golden Gloves champion, and U.S. representative at the 1978 World Amateur championships in Yugoslavia, was up next. If his 222-32 amateur record was any indication of his identity as a professional, Paul should have concerned any fighter.

Hector prepared to face Paul at the Copa Room of the Sands Casino Hotel in Atlantic City on October 30, 1982. Both camps agreed to fight at 135 pounds. The fight was promoted by Jeff Levine of Round One Productions, Top Rank, and Cedric Kushner Promotions. Televised on CBS, the fight card also included Youngstown's lightweight Harry Arroyo, a name that would soon be discussed as a viable opponent for Hector. On the same card, stablemate Pee Wee Rucker faced Norberto Figueroa.

Flaunting a pink robe and matching trunks, Hector warned Paul when he walked in the ring: "Hey buddy, look out."

Giles, working with Harold Weston at the Garden, maintained a two-month gap between fights, possibly so that Hector, now 17-0, did not go astray. Paul, at 133.5 pounds, was undefeated in sixteen fights and, squarely built, he looked every bit his "Tank" moniker. Hector, who came in at 132 pounds, knew Paul was one of his last hurdles before earning a world-title shot. To offset Paul early on, Hector would double up on the jab, move inside, and land a perfect jab and straight left combination. Employing head movement was more necessary against Paul, who was quick and sturdy. At the end of the first round, Paul landed a straight right on a vulnerable Hector and then capitalized again in the second with a straight right to Hector's chest. Frustration set in temporarily for Hector over the first three rounds because he could not fight the fight he had hoped for.

But Hector spilled out at the end of the fifth with a seven-punch combination that overshadowed Paul's single punch landed. Hector also raked Paul with a right hook to the neck. Paul landed his two best punches—a straight right and left—to start the sixth but Hector, in the midst of an impressive second half of the round, ripped off a gorgeous right hook to the head, followed by two more scoring blows going into the seventh. The good news was that Hector, constantly analyzing and making changes, was seeing his hard work pay off; the bad news was that he could not dent the rock-solid Paul. Paul returned to form in spurts in the seventh and the beginning of the eighth, but watched as Hector, now emboldened, unpacked his uppercut on two occasions and was still throwing five-punch combinations.

Fighting ten rounds may have benefited Hector. In other performances, Hector had overwhelmed his opponents, but this effort was workmanlike, fought in layers. A clear back-and-forth ensued as Hector landed a jab, straight left, and vicious right hook in the ninth, causing Paul to stumble. Both fighters ended the fight exhausted, but it was Hector placing a perfect uppercut in the round that left the final impression on the judges. The fight felt closer than it appeared as only Paul Cavalieri (8-1-1) gave Paul a round. Judges Harold Lederman and Frank Cappuccino scored a shutout for Hector.

"You were the better man tonight," Paul told Hector after the fight.

"I don't doubt you," Hector responded.

Despite being ranked seventh by the WBC and unranked by the WBA, Hector, who was getting comfortable with Levine, knew that he would have to cross paths with King, whom Billy Giles loathed. As far as the pecking order, Giles would not cater to King, as so many had done before him. "But I'll be number one and they'll have to fight me," said Giles. "The public will make them."

That confidence was also ingrained in the Macho Man, who often encouraged a childish banter everywhere he went. *Yeah buddy!* was his famous saying, and he had yet to grow out his famous spit curl that most people identified him with. But things were not always smooth sailing between Giles and Hector.

Through his New York ties, Hector became good friends with boxer Iran "The Blade" Barkley, who saw firsthand how Giles interacted with Hector. "Sometimes it was bumpy with Giles," said Barkley, a middleweight prospect at the time. "But when it was time to take care of business, he would stay on top of Macho. Macho would then stay focused and be serious. After training was over, Hector would go back to being humble and have playful moments. He was like a real, funny guy."

After the Melvin Paul fight, Giles's concerns about having to deal with King were bound to be realized, as King had recently signed both Sammy Serrano, the WBA 130-pound champ, and Bazooka Limon, the WBC champ. But before Hector could even think about a title shot, he had to wait for Serrano to defend against Roger Mayweather and for Limon to defend against Bobby Chacon. Anyone who was familiar with Hector knew that none of those four opponents gave him cause for concern.

Not a month passed before Giles put Hector back in the ring, this time against Greg "The Candy Man" Coverson, who hailed from Kalamazoo, Michigan. Despite an impressive record of 29-0, Coverson, five years Hector's senior, had not fought topflight opposition. Having started his career four years earlier than Hector, Coverson clearly had an advantage experience-wise but came into the fight as a 4-1 underdog. Coming into the bout, Hector was ranked No. 3 by the WBC; whereas Coverson earned a No. 10 ranking in the lightweight division by defeating Davey Lee Armstrong a month earlier. Both fighters came in a shade under 132 pounds. Channeling the brash Aaron Pryor, Coverson pointed at and stared down Hector prior to the opening bell at the Showboat Hotel & Casino in Las Vegas. If anything, the posturing pissed off Hector, who became more animated with his pre-fight preparation.

The showmanship, however, took a more menacing turn toward the end of the first round, as Hector hovered over a fallen and hurt Coverson. After an unusually passive back-and-forth where Hector landed an upper-cut on the break, he then unloaded a straight left on Coverson that picked up speed so that Coverson felt the absolute brunt of it. It was the type of punch that opponents do not get up from. Yet, to his credit, Coverson beat the count and had to maneuver around a swarming Hector, hell-bent on destruction. Still searching for that knockout, Hector, who showed how methodical and focused he could be against a good opponent, scored knockdowns in the second and eighth rounds on his way to a unanimous decision. Judges Chuck Minker had it 98-91, Dave Moretti scored it 98-90, and Dalby Shirley saw it 99-89, all in favor of Hector.

"He had a maturity in the ring that belied his age," said boxing journalist Steve Farhood. "He turned pro as a teenager, but I don't remember the maturity as much as I remember the pure speed and skill level. If you took that away from him, he had the tricks and the moves. But his pure speed combined with the southpaw style and the command of being center stage made him the total package."

By the time 1983 came around, Hector was nearing a complete transformation. Boxing had brought him some financial security, but also a sense of self. Fighting was in his blood, prompting Giles to famously state, "Michelangelo was born to paint pictures, Hector Camacho was born to knock guys out."

After being approached by and then maintaining a relationship with wealthy businessman Bob Uchitel, a friend of Jeff Levine and founder of Multivisions, Hector recognized that he could cultivate a following in Alaska, which is just what he did when he signed to fight No. 6 rated John Montes on February 12, 1983, at Buckner Fieldhouse in Anchorage. With the backing of Uchitel, who would later invite Hector and all his friends to stay at his expensive out-of-the-way hideaways, fighting in Alaska did not seem so unconventional. Hector trained hard, and the excitement was palpable. Montes, 22-1, had traveled to New Mexico four months earlier in a decision loss to Kronk Gym stalwart Hilmer Kenty.

Managed by Benny Giorgino, Montes was struggling with a bad ear infection before the flight to Anchorage, landing him in and out of the hospital. "The doctor told me, 'There is no way you can fight,'" said Montes. Only later would Montes learn that Giorgino was paid $10,000 to keep him in the fight. With a week to go before the fight, Montes had not sparred and had only informally worked out with his father.

"I told Benny, 'I'm not ready to fight,' and that I wanted to fly back home and forget about it," Montes recalled. "He told me I could still beat Hector if I put my mind to it."

The fight went on without a hitch.

CBS commentator Tim Ryan, who worked the fight with Gil Clancy, looked beyond Hector's recklessness and embraced the complex fighter who presented so many diverse faces: the happy-go-lucky Hector, the vindictive ring Hector, the charismatic Hector, and Hector the entertainer. Anyone who remembered him from that time agreed that Hector was blessed with a special quality.

"We got to be quite fond of Hector," said Ryan, who called several of Hector's bouts for CBS. "As a broadcaster, you don't want to be tied to one fighter over another in the same way you don't want to favor a team. So I was very aware of being arbitrary. You just want to describe the event. But Hector was such a likeable kid."

Before the fight, the promotion started off perfectly. CBS had coaxed Hector into getting on a dogsled at the local Fur Rendezvous Festival to boost ratings. Always eager to entertain, Hector jumped right in and began "mushing" the dogs. Holding the reins with his right hand and raising his left fist in the air, Hector was a promoter's dream, and it was easy to see why. The Macho Man did not just show up to hype a fight; he took center stage and never looked back. When Ryan asked how Hector's experience had been as a "musher," Hector flashed his Hollywood smile and said, "It was like driving a Cadillac."

"Here's this Puerto Rican kid from New York in ice country," said Ryan, "in the middle of winter. We brought a camera up there, promoted by Uchitel. He wanted to help sell tickets, to show off Hector. So he wanted Hector to drive a dogsled . . . the very idea was priceless."

It did not take long for Hector to acclimate himself to the Alaskan weather and people. As he joked with Ryan—saying he called the dogs "Mush, Mush"—there was a clear sense that the fighter belonged in Anchorage and that the people there felt lucky to have him.

But the happy mood quickly shifted the night before the fight. Called over in the middle of the night from their hotel room, Ryan and Clancy found Hector hanging from a hotel window. "There were three or four corner guys—and I don't know what it was—but Hector got high and threatened to jump out the window," said Ryan. "One of the guys called us over and said that Hector wanted to talk to Gil [Clancy]. He was nervous and scared. I was next to Gil and they wanted him to stop him."

Ryan had developed a rapport with Hector, but it was Clancy who knew Hector from the early days in New York through Harold Weston. Like Ryan, Clancy could see past Hector's flaws and focus on his good traits.

"Hector was crying and sobbing and Gil was trying to talk him down," said Ryan. "It was like a cop on a suicide attempt—a real scene. Gil was calm and authoritative, like a father. He told him that he was going to be a big star and that people [loved him]. Gil successfully talked him from doing it, and they came over and shooed us away, saying 'He's okay.'"

When Hector woke up the next morning, the team behaved as if the incident had never happened. "That next morning Hector didn't say anything to us," said Ryan. "Nothing like, 'Thank you for helping me' or anything."

The flurry of activity never reached John Montes (and Jerry Villarreal Sr., who was with Hector, denies it ever happened). Montes had his own personal problems to deal with, yet he was familiar with Hector in the ring and had pegged him stylistically. "From looking at Hector, I saw a fast but kind of a smaller guy. My thing was that I watched him fight Louie Loy, and he didn't impress me," Montes recalled. "I saw speed and that was it."

Televised on CBS, the fight also featured Harry Arroyo in a tune-up. Both Hector and Montes entered at 134.5 pounds, and Hector was looking to extend his streak to twenty consecutive victories. Hidden in a black wolf-fur coat worth several thousand dollars, with MACHO stitched in mink on his back—presented to him by Senator Ted Stevens and Uchitel at a press conference before the fight—Hector bounced around the ring to a mixture of boos and mostly applause from the four thousand fans in Buckner Fieldhouse.

Although Montes had downplayed Hector's abilities before the fight, that tune changed once the fight began. Relying on his signature move by illegally pulling on the neck with the right glove to secure Montes and then raking him with an uppercut, Hector landed the punch and blocked the referee, Davey Pearl, from witnessing his method. Pearl counted Montes out, and the fight was stopped at 1:13 in the first round. Camacho fans stormed the ring. Handlers pulled Hector aside to avoid him getting involved in a fracas. Knocking out a fighter who had never been stopped and doing so as a lightweight spoke volumes.

"When I got hit, I went out. I have never been so stunned in my whole life. Davey Pearl was the referee and he did nothing about the punch," said Montes. "Hector grabbed the back of my head. Davey should have disqualified him when he did what he did. But it happened so fast. To me all I wanted was to go back home."

Even though the bout was over, the fighting continued as Giles went over and nailed Giorgino as payback for an earlier incident during a press conference. "Billy went over and punched their manager in the face, but to Billy's credit, he deserved it," said Jerry Villarreal Jr.

Even though Montes was upset about the way the fight went, he did not appear concerned about Giles's quick post-fight KO. "When the manager cold-cocked Benny," said Montes, "in many ways, I was happy he got hit. I was glad he socked him in the face."

After the fight in Anchorage, things were happening so fast that Hector had no time to reflect—on anything. Having been consumed by boxing, it was nearly impossible for Hector to balance being a father, good son, boyfriend, and boxer. Lee was gone, and Giles, "the champ maker," had become, by all accounts, quite enamored with himself and his shaping of Hector. Only time would tell what kind of fighter Hector would become.

Hector Camacho lands a right uppercut against Johnny Sato during their fight at the Sands Casino Hotel in Atlantic City on August 28, 1982. *The Ring/ Getty Images*

It's Macho Time! Hector poses at a fight in New York in the early 1990s.
The Ring/Getty Images

A young Hector and his friends frequently gathered in the plaza outside of the Lady Queen of Angels Catholic Church in Spanish Harlem. *Courtesy of Christian Giudice*

Hector stands next to John Montes before their showdown at Buckner Fieldhouse in Anchorage, Alaska, on February 12, 1983. *Courtesy of John Montes*

Showcasing his blazing speed, Hector Camacho lands a hard left against Rafael "Bazooka" Limon during their fight at Hiram Bithorn Stadium in San Juan, Puerto Rico, on August 7, 1983. Camacho won the WBC super featherweight world title by TKO in the fifth round. *Sports Illustrated/Getty Images*

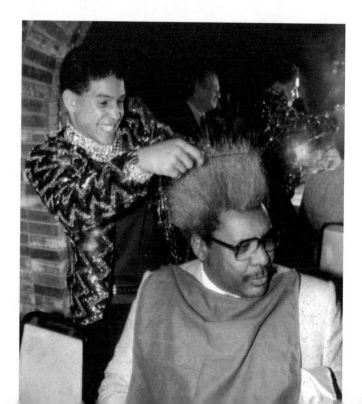

Always the jokester, Hector shares a playful moment with Don King. The two separated soon after. *New York Daily News/Getty Images*

Sam's Famous Pizza was a Spanish Harlem hangout. Hector's girlfriend, Kisha Colon, lived above it. *Courtesy of Hector Camacho Jr.*

Broadcaster Tim Ryan embraces Hector during an interview following his victory over Louie Burke in Atlantic City on January 19, 1985. *Courtesy of Tim Ryan*

Hector Camacho keeps Jose Luis Ramirez at a distance with a jab during their WBC lightweight world title fight at the Riviera Hotel & Casino in Las Vegas on August 10, 1985. Camacho won his second world title by unanimous decision. *The Ring/ Getty Images*

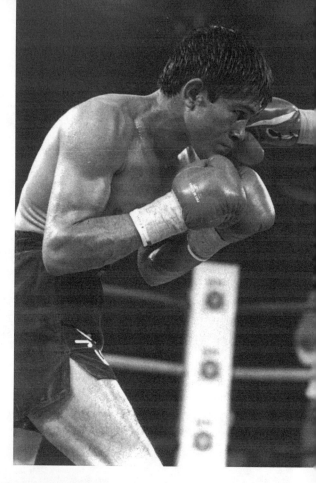

Dressed to impress, Hector Camacho sits ringside at Julio Cesar Chavez's fight against Lonnie Smith at the Mirage Hotel in Las Vegas on September 15, 1991. Camacho's showdown with Chavez took place one year later. *Allsport/Getty Images*

Hector Camacho looks to throw a counterpunch in his fight against Edwin Rosario at Madison Square Garden on June 13, 1986. Camacho retained his WBC world lightweight title by a controversial split decision. *The Ring/ Getty Images*

Hector enters the ring in full Native American headdress before his fight against Vinny Pazienza at the Convention Hall in Atlantic City on February 3, 1990. *The Ring/Getty Images*

Facing
Bazooka

8

At twenty, Hector Camacho was getting closer to a championship. His visits to see Junior were less frequent, but when he did see him, Hector would give him hugs and kisses all day long. Hector was nothing like the father who had abandoned him. For those close to him, seeing how Hector treated his son was heartwarming. He did not push him into boxing but rather allowed him to share his platform as a mini-Macho boxer.

"I felt genuine love from him," said Junior.

Joining Junior and his father was Hector's girlfriend Kisha Colon, who had begun to play a major role in his life. Her family lived above Sam's Famous Pizza Place, a neighborhood hangout on East 116th Street. Everybody who knew Kisha at the time said that she emitted a positive energy that Hector needed. Though they were headed down different paths—Kisha looked to a career in law, Hector pursued a world title—they shared a lot.

"I remember the first time I met him in 1979/1980," recalled Kisha. "It was at the neighborhood pool and he approached me to ask for suntan lotion. Then he asks me, 'Aren't you going to put it on for me?' in this cocky way. I was thinking how full of himself this guy was. I didn't know him as any up-and-coming boxer. I did not put it on him."

At the time, Kisha was a sophomore at Cardinal Spellman High School in the Bronx. Her mother worked for a lawyer named James Levien, who would later play a major role in Hector's career. Having spurned his advances at the pool, Kisha did not realize how relentlessly the young boxer would pursue her. Soon, Kisha began working at a local Key Foods supermarket, and Hector became a regular customer. At the time, he was also dating Maida.

"[Hector] would come by with an open bag of chips and a soda, hoping to get a discount," Kisha recalled, "then come up with this lame attempt to pay for it. I found it charming. He was good-looking, very charismatic. I remember he had this great sense of humor. And there was something that drew you to him. He was always the center and the guy that everyone wanted to be around."

Meanwhile, as he waited for a title fight, Hector prepared for a ten-round showdown at Phoenix Civic Plaza with the tough Irleis "Cubanito" Perez (25-0, twenty-one KOs) on April 3, 1983. Jeff Levine and Steve Eisner co-promoted the bout. A Cuban who resided in Las Vegas, Perez, twenty-four, had not fought anyone of note heading into the fight. Conversely, Hector, who had twelve knockouts, had just registered his most impressive one-punch stoppage of Montes in Anchorage. Despite the precedent he had set for young fighters, Hector did not take anyone lightly, and Perez, at five feet eight and a bona fide lightweight, proved to be a stylistic nightmare.

"I have been training for a monster for four weeks," Hector told a reporter before the fight. "This is the way I train for everybody, but this guy ain't nothing."

Despite planning to train in Palm Springs for the bout, Hector suddenly had to make new arrangements when they caught Billy Giles there with his girlfriend. The Macho team had always held tight to the promise of never bringing girls to camp.

"We get to Palm Springs, and we open the door to the room and Billy is there with his girlfriend," said Jerry Villarreal Sr. "Hector hits my pocket and says, 'No way. Let's go back to Detroit.' And that's what we did. Everything was set for us, but Billy was letting the success go to his head. He didn't even know we left."

Hector had earlier brought Perez in to spar with him to prepare for his 1982 bout with Greg Coverson. The relationship quickly soured, however, when Perez abruptly exited camp. Camp conflict was nothing new for Hector, as his sparring sessions were purposefully intense and challenging, but there was enough conflict between the two fighters to foster lingering bad blood between them.

Hector and Perez made weight the morning of the fight at 134 pounds and 135 pounds, respectively. Hector was ranked as high as No. 2 with the WBC and No. 7 by the WBA. Meanwhile, Perez was ranked No. 20 by the WBC and No. 11 by the WBA. Hector came into the bout, which was televised by *CBS Sports Sunday*, only needing to earn the decision to affirm his standing and situate himself for a title fight.

Sauntering to the ring to the tune of the Village People's "Macho Man," Hector looked comfortable in front of the more than twenty-five hundred fans in attendance at the Phoenix Civic Plaza. In the first round, Hector opened up his offensive arsenal, making Perez look a step slow. Doubling up on the jab and then placing a straight left, Hector wanted to come out fast—and if he did not want to dictate the pace, he wanted to send a message to his former sparring partner. By the end of the round, the message had been delivered. Still, Perez had a quick enough jab and a long enough reach advantage to create more problems for Hector than some previous opponents had. CBS analyst Sugar Ray Leonard suggested that Hector use more body and lateral movement to get inside against a taller fighter. Hector struggled to get inside and offset Perez's jab and reach, but Hector was more active and landed more impactful punches.

Too big and strong to be offset with flurries, Perez was rejuvenated and stalking in the sixth, closing out rounds on his terms. Often when a fighter becomes energized in one round, he may pull back to preserve energy in the next. Perez, however, did not lose confidence or pull back as he cracked a defensive Hector, crouching in the corner, with a right and a left hand to start the seventh.

Two major factors contributed to the sudden shift in momentum: Hector's lack of conditioning and his inability to land combinations against an awkward, taller fighter. By the ninth, fans were booing as the clinching Hector emerged, and in the tenth—a round that some critics thought Camacho had to win—he only landed four punches to close out the fight. For such an entertaining fighter who had won the applause of the world's best, watching debris enter the ring from angry fans must have been disheartening. Still, Hector won a unanimous decision: Robert

Cox scored the fight 99-94, Mike Munoz scored it 99-97, and Joe Garcia scored it 98-93.

Former welterweight champion Carlos Palomino, who watched Perez train at his Westminster Gym, recalled a much different fight. "I actually thought [Hector] lost that fight. Perez was a tall, lanky southpaw who was five feet eleven, 135 pounds. Hector was used to having so much more speed than his opponents, but Cubanito was right there with him; plus, he had the advantage in height and reach."

After the decision was announced, Hector responded to the naysayers: "He was aggressive. He fought a good fight. He kept up the pressure. But I thought I outsmarted him. I fought with a lot of defense. He was not easy to hit. I expected this type of fight." Hector also noted that he fought a "scientific" fight—an unusual way of describing such a performance, which was anything but. He was not a finished product; he still had a lot to learn in the ring. So when a new opponent presented new wrinkles, it wasn't easy for him to adapt instinctively.

Instead of protesting the disputed decision, a classy Perez said, "He's a future great. I wasn't as sharp, and next time I will be sharper." Later Perez added that next time, he would also bring his own judge and referee. The headlines the following day were not as forgiving: "Camacho Wins as Crowd Boos" was the headline in the *Arizona Republic*; "Camacho Wins by a Hair" in the *Hartford Courant*; and "Crowd Unhappy with Unanimous Decision for 'Macho' Camacho" in the *Reno-Gazette Journal*. For their efforts, Hector earned a $150,000 payday to Perez's $75,000 purse.

Hector did not allow the lukewarm response to the Cubanito bout derail his championship plans. All fighters experience difficult moments, and Hector was no different. He looked to Giles for guidance. Through Giles's connections at the Garden, Hector had developed into a Felt Forum mainstay and a CBS heartthrob. Having integrated all of Robert Lee's intricate lessons into his repertoire, Hector was transforming from a blinding fast prospect to a more well-rounded fighter. No one could outbox him, overpower him, out-quick him, or, by any means, outsmart him in the ring. Casual fans loved what they saw because of his energy, flair, and talent, whereas hard-core fans saw glimpses of greatness evident in legendary fighters who had come before him.

If there had been any flaws that had emerged over those first twenty fights, they were Hector's penchant for allowing bigger fighters to use their strength to body him and push him to the ropes and his tendency to rely on his God-given talent and resort to leaving himself open on the inside during exchanges. Neither of those idiosyncrasies affected him much, however, because he could take a punch. Although he could not walk through punches like some of his predecessors, Hector could take punishment, hold, and recover without any residual effects.

Only ten years older than Hector, Giles was more of a friend than a moral guide for the young fighter. Having helped shape Hector's career path, though, Giles had made the right moves by putting a range of capable opponents before him. Unfortunately, there were also reports that Giles fed Hector's drug fetish instead of stanching it.

Indeed, even as Hector approached his zenith, he was still struggling to shake old labels. One feature story referred to him as a "former inmate of Rikers Island," then later praised him for staying "unaffected." Hector, equally fragile and demonstrative, got comfort from neighborhood friends who would accompany him to his fights. He loved his old barrio—the streets, the colloquial language, the jokes, the sounds, and, clearly, the warmth and familiarity of home. It was hard for him to distance himself from a place that brought him so much joy.

Being able to joke with Tito Cuevas or Edwin Gonzalez about things that eluded older friends like Giles, in his thirties, and Jerry Villarreal Sr., in his late forties, proved cathartic. No one but Tito and Edwin could evoke the same laughter from Hector. No matter what role Tito and Edwin played, Hector wanted them along for the ride. One story seemed more outrageous than the next, and Hector often found himself in the middle of difficult situations. Once while staying at the Holiday Inn in Southgate, Michigan, Hector, whose beloved Cadillac Eldorado had been stolen earlier in the evening, noticed that his Corvette was being broken into outside the hotel as well.

"Tito was there. Hector comes running out of the hotel in Speedo underwear with these guys trying to take his Corvette. So Hector and Tito get in the car and chase these guys into Southwest Detroit," said Jerry Villarreal Sr. "They're running stop signs. Next thing I know I see

Tito on the side of the road. Hector told him to tell the cops he was in 'hot pursuit' of the criminals. While Hector is in hot pursuit, he hits a car . . . [and] wrecks his Corvette. When I get there, Hector is sitting on the side with his Corvette. They take him to jail in his Speedo underwear with no I.D. When I get to the station with Tony Kidd, Hector is sitting on top of the desk in his underwear, holding court, promising the cops, 'If you guys come to New York, I'll give you tickets to the fight.'"

With a flair for the dramatic, Hector got himself into and out of scrapes that could have damaged his family and his career. His personality was the key. "Next to [Sugar] Ray Leonard and next to Ray Mancini and Alexis Arguello, Hector is potentially as appealing as anyone in the game," said CBS analyst Tim Ryan. "He has the personality, the style, the good looks. And he has the story."

When it came to finding a common link between Sugar Ray Leonard and Hector, not everyone was willing to oblige. "I never compared the two," said boxing analyst Larry Merchant. "Sugar Ray Leonard was a star when he started because of his Olympic gold medal. His first pro fight was on national TV. It's like comparing one type of apple to one type of orange, if you understand. Leonard had a running start and he defined that level of greatness."

Even Hector pushed back against the comparison. At one point, Leonard came out and famously said, "I thought *I* was cocky. Camacho surpasses me by three or four levels. But when Camacho brags, he's not trying to convince you of anything; he's just telling you what's going to happen."

Hector responded, "I'm not the next Sugar Ray. I'm the next Macho Man." Most fighters this side of Roberto Duran would have basked in the glow of Leonard's praise, but not Hector. Though respectful toward Leonard, Hector let reporters know that he would be his own man.

As Hector blossomed, Don King became ensconced in legal disputes with Bobby Chacon, delaying Hector's title shot. Initially, King claimed, Chacon had signed options, the first one to defend his WBC super featherweight title against Hector for $210,000. Disputing and ignoring King's claim, Chacon moved forward with West Coast promoter Don Chargin and fought—and decisioned No. 1 contender Cornelius Boza-Edwards for $500,000 in a bout the WBC refused to sanction. Chacon attempted to sue the WBC for stripping him of his title, and King sought damages from NBC for breach of contract. In the process, King sent Chacon a counteroffer of $450,000 to defend against Hector, but to no avail. After the second offer was refused, WBC president Jose Sulaiman ordered the WBC title vacated. Restless, Hector was forced to bide his time, although many believed he could have easily catapulted past any of the champions after his fifteenth bout.

Still living on 115th Street and Lexington with his mother, his siblings, and a niece and nephew, Hector was on the verge of becoming a potential all-time great, according to experts, but he still felt the pull of Harlem's streets, which were all he ever knew from the day he arrived as a four-year-old fleeing an abusive father. One can only imagine how emotional it must have been for him, on July 1, 1983, to hear the title fight between himself and Rafael Limon officially announced for August 7 in San Juan, Puerto Rico, at the heralded Hiram Bithorn Stadium.

Far from Puerto Rico, Hector wanted to be accepted by native-born Puerto Ricans as one of their own. In his mind, it was unfair to classify him as an outsider. In New York, he was beloved, and the Macho label had been ingrained in the culture. He saw how little boys' eyes gleamed at his shiny Eldorado or how little girls chanted his name and knew his record by heart. But fans in Puerto Rico were not entirely sold.

Before fighting for the championship, Hector was content. At a moment's notice, he knew, he could call for Junior or bring the Cadillac to go pick him up. Hector still played basketball at Jefferson Plaza and hung out at the local haunts. When Hector needed to de-stress, he looked for friends like Henry Rosa, Freddie Guerrero, Freddie Villanueva, Scooby, or Ramon Ruiz or he went to the local pool with Kisha. The enticing sounds emanating from the Lion's Cage on 103rd Street or the threads at Garmany Ltd. were enough to satiate a man on the verge. There would be time after the title fight to hit up more upscale clubs such as The Palm Trees in the Bronx or Broadway 96, or even take a trip to one of his favorite spots, Great Adventure in Jackson, New Jersey. Although he preferred hanging out with close friends, Hector felt comfortable mixing in any crowd, but he was extremely conscious about identifying who was being honest and forthright. He was not one for artifice.

Surprisingly, Hector may have felt most comfortable by himself. Neighborhood acquaintances from the 1980s recall seeing Hector alone in the corner of a club dancing by himself for hours at a time. Alone with his thoughts, Hector did not have to be anyone but himself.

As his fame increased, so did the demands for his attention, which made an already restless kid even more anxious. And Hector knew that at some point, he must decide whether to leave his home for a better life or to stay in Spanish Harlem. No one knew what Hector pondered late at night when he was alone, but even as a young boy, he had wanted to bring a world title back to Spanish Harlem.

Now one man was in his way: Rafael "Bazooka" Limon. Having faced fighters like Bobby Chacon, Alexis Arguello, Cornelius Boza-Edwards, and Frankie Baltazar, Limon was set to make $50,000 for the fight, and on the downside of his career, it may have been his last big payday.

Although the fight, which was scheduled for August 7, landed at the Hiram Birthorn Stadium in San Juan, Harold Weston tried initially to bring it to Madison Square Garden, but there were too many obstacles to overcome, most notably that the Garden was not available on the fight date.

For the Macho team, the path to the bout led directly through King, whom Giles had vowed never to work with. Typically in this situation, Hector, ranked No. 1, would logically face No. 2 ranked Rafael Solis for the vacant belt. But King engineered it so that No. 3 ranked Limon—a King fighter and an easy matchup for Camacho—and not Solis would get the title shot. Solis accepted $150,000 in step-aside money. King's matchmaker attempted to justify the decision: "[Solis] is in our camp too, and he's agreed to step aside."

Meanwhile, WBC president Mauricio Sulaiman deemed the super featherweight crown an "interim championship," trying to justify the decision to jump Limon to a title shot. Everyone, including the combatants, ignored the "interim" label and understood that whoever left the ring with the belt would be crowned the legitimate champion. No one, especially not Sulaiman, who would benefit greatly from having Hector on his side, was going to try to enforce the interim tag.

Starting training camp in early July, the Macho team stayed at the Palace Hotel and trained at the Benito Ortiz Gymnasium in Barrio Obrero.

Sparring with Boo Sawyer and other fighters, Hector was devoted to his daily regimen of four-mile runs each morning, followed by afternoons of sparring, and then 45- to 60-minute warm-down sessions to close each workout. There were distractions—girls called his room day and night—but Hector was happiest with Kisha around. Hector may have strayed from his singular purpose of boxing later on, but not for Limon. There was too much riding on this fight. Hector finished his training camp on August 5, predicting that the fight would not go beyond five rounds.

Comparisons could be made between Hector's bout with Limon and Wilfred Benitez's 1976 showdown with Antonio Cervantes when he was seventeen years old and won the welterweight title. Young Benitez prided himself on movement and his brilliant defense, whereas Cervantes was an aging champion who was past his prime. Although Hector was more offensive minded in 1983 than Benitez was against Cervantes in 1976, both Puerto Rican fighters were relying on youth and boxing intellect to befuddle their opponents. The only difference separating the fighters was that Benitez had initiated his career in Puerto Rico, where he was beloved, and Hector still had to prove himself there. As outspoken as Hector was in some interviews, he deeply wanted to be looked at in the same light in Puerto Rico as Benitez and Wilfredo Gomez.

"There was a general sense that [Hector] could have been one of the best of the best of the best," said boxing analyst Larry Merchant. "Whatever that meant to whomever defined it."

What tools did Limon possess to destroy the rhythm of a boy wonder who thought like a veteran and adapted like a boxing genius? As a veteran of sixty-one bouts over more than a decade as a professional, there was nothing that Limon had not seen in a professional ring. When Limon fought Alexis Arguello at the Felt Forum in 1979, he used illegal tactics to disrupt the composed Arguello. For a couple rounds, Limon succeeded in aggravating Arguello. Arguello was a classic boxer and a fierce puncher, but he did not move very efficiently.

Hector was a different kind of fighter. His grace and speed made up for his flaws, but speed was only part of a package that included incomparable defensive instincts, precision punching, a menacing jab, sharp angles that rarely put him in harm's way, and a willingness to stretch the limits of what the referee allowed. That left Limon with only one option—to make it a rough fight from the beginning. If successful, Limon could attempt to land his powerful punch that led to thirty-five previous knockouts.

"Lots of lateral movements, avoiding parking myself in front of him," said Hector about his strategy going into the championship bout. "He'll never know what I'm up to in the ring because I'm going to keep him confused. Limon's best weapon is his punch when you're squarely facing him. But I don't plan to be there. He won't be able to touch me."

Ten thousand rabid fans packed into Hiram Bithorn Stadium in San Juan, Puerto Rico, on August 7, 1983, for the bout between Hector Camacho and Rafael Limon. Even though Hector was still trying to prove himself worthy, fans came with the hope that Hector would take down his Mexican foe. Only five years removed from another Puerto Rico vs. Mexico showdown when Wilfredo Gomez devastated the Mexican knockout king Carlos Zarate in five one-sided rounds at the nearby Roberto Clemente Stadium, Hector understood that to be placed alongside these great fighters, he had to win in an entertaining fashion. Benitez was riveting; Gomez was nearly unstoppable; but Hector borrowed Benitez's genius and Gomez's wonderful movement and added a little flash to make him possibly stand out even more than those fighters. The way he smiled, whether it was a mischievous grin or a soft smile infused with charm, Hector invited people in. To add to the charm, he was brutally honest in the process.

"I enjoyed his company, not just as someone I interviewed, but in a personal sense," said writer Steve Farhood. "When Hector walked into the room, he was the star. It's a quality that a lot of good fighters rarely have. Duran had it, yes, but Hector was more outgoing. He did not have the same cachet as Duran had yet, but you could sense it was coming."

Waiting for his day in court, Chacon, still part of the narrative—as many believed a Chacon–Camacho showdown would be more competitive—provided his analysis: "I'm looking at one more fight, two at the most. Camacho seems to be hot. I'd like to try him. My experience would even out the good legs he's got. I don't think he's at a good spot yet. He's learning, but he hasn't fought anybody. He's built his name on nobodies." No one put much credence in Chacon's harsh critique since he had signed a contract to fight Hector and then backed out of it.

As for Bazooka, Chacon added, "I think Limon has an excellent chance if he's in shape. Hector hasn't been hit yet. Bazooka's gonna land some shots. Camacho will use his speed to box Bazooka's ears off. I'd like to see Camacho get a good test. I'd like to see Bazooka give him hell."

Just like any other young fighter, Hector felt anxious heading for the arena on the biggest day of his boxing career. Having warmed up in his dressing room for more than an hour, Hector wanted desperately to get on with the fight. Other difficulties emerged as Hector had to wait for guards to clear his path before heading to the ring. He bounced down the aisle, his hands on Jerry Villarreal Sr.'s shoulders, Jeff Levine leading the way. Don Thibodeaux and Billy Giles laughed as Hector, decked out in a form-fitting sequined Puerto Rican flag driving cap, conducted an interview with a reporter. After the chaos subsided from the dramatic entrance, Hector, in a leopard-print robe, shimmied and did his patented flurries to ignite the crowd. A mass of people waited to see history unfold. It was not a passing of the torch, but Hector had the potential to step in where the last Puerto Rican idol, Wilfredo Gomez, had left off.

Sadly, it was almost as if Limon did not exist as he waited in the ring. Standing in the corner to avoid the sun's glare, Limon shook out his arms and waited patiently for the hysteria to die down. All eyes were on Hector. If there had been any doubts about how Puerto Rican Hector really was, there was nothing but pure, joyful adulation for him among the crowd as fight introductions were announced.

As the fight started, Hector nearly chased Limon back to his corner. It wasn't a full-on sprint, but, after a brief meeting in the middle of the ring, Hector, overanxious, followed Limon, landed a straight left, and slipped as he attacked with two uppercuts that barely landed.

The pressure—and tension—of such an overwhelming moment beats down on any fighter, and Hector was no exception. Early on, Hector missed his jab purposefully in an attempt to get his timing down. Almost as an afterthought, he ducked under Limon's wide-arcing punches with ease, as if he could predict each one's exact trajectory. Instead of staying and countering, Hector glided away. Neither fighter relied on straight punches: Limon loved to hurl wide telegraphed hooks to the body, while Hector threw his in succession, reaching from his knees with sharp uppercuts. Each rat-a-tat-tat became more impactful as the fight progressed.

Hector's punches were crisper and more precise in the second round. He was one of the few guys in the sport who could hurt an opponent moving backward and, although he did not hurt Limon that way, he was able to land a right hook. Since Limon was normally off-balance, Hector's punches only accentuated that imbalance. Fighting back, Limon was throwing punches, and his wide-arcing shots were glancing off Hector's arms and sides.

A quiet round concluded with Hector using his jab to lead into a left uppercut and right hook; however, in the third, the young fighter started to take more risks. Hector needed Limon to come forward and he obliged. Working behind a stabbing jab, Hector timed the stalking Limon by unleashing a right uppercut that stunted his momentum. Then came the tricks. Limon had seen them before, but now he was part of the spectacle as Hector stabilized his head with his left glove and deposited a right uppercut.

As tough as any fighter, Limon walked right through it, and with nineteen seconds remaining in the third round he suffered an unabated straight left. Always studying his opponent, Hector recognized that in his southpaw stance, Limon left his right guard extremely low. Hector capitalized on the opening. If Limon was hurt, he would only have to survive briefly and then have at least a minute to recuperate. But Hector was not finished. With three seconds left in the round, he landed a vicious straight left to Limon's neck that sent him reeling to the canvas. Immediately, referee Richard Steele entered the fray and administered an eight-count as Limon walked back to the corner. Hector's knockdown punch landed directly over a weakly thrown right hand. But those two final punches were identical and capitalized on Limon's porous defense. When Limon got hit with the knockdown punch, his descent was swift, but he was quick to rise. His team of handlers surrounded him in his corner. A collective cheer came from Spanish Harlem as "Little Man" neared a world title.

Hector was energized. Instead of rushing to finish Limon in the fourth, Hector attacked with a direct, punishing jab. Each power punch affected Limon, and his attrition, both physically and mentally, was apparent. Reflective of his inner strength, Limon recovered to have his best round of the fight. But, as Clancy noted, Limon was still fighting in "slow motion" compared to Hector, and as the Mexican stalwart ramped up his offensive attack, he left himself open for counters. On the inside, Limon walked into a crunching right hook and was also stopped in his tracks by a straight left. Having physically rebounded from the knockdown, Limon no longer feared Hector, but he knew he could not hurt him either. As in the previous round, an invigorated Hector came alive within the last 20 seconds. Brilliantly pinpointing exactly when to punch, Hector read Limon perfectly and knew every little nuance to his style. Whether Limon was merely coasting out of each round, or had no answers, Hector understood when to attack. Stealing the momentum again, he nailed Limon with a jab and left hand with 16 seconds remaining and then tattooed Limon with a straight left that not only shocked Limon, but sent him reeling into the ropes. Steele provided the only barrier to preserve Limon's health as the round ended.

When Hector landed a body shot that paralyzed Limon in the fifth and sent him doubling over on the canvas, everyone knew that a new chapter in the 130-pound weight class was beginning, and the flamboyant star named Hector Camacho was at the forefront. Rubbing his forehead along the canvas, Limon writhed in pain. Only seconds had passed before he was raising his hands to assure Steele that he was physically capable to go on. In an odd reaction to a knockdown, Limon got up and walked away from Steele and to the other corner almost as if to say, "Follow me." Sensing blood, Hector waited for the respite, cut off the ring, and pushed Limon against the ropes.

The crowd anticipated every punch that finally came in rapid-fire succession. The jab helped position Limon, but the following three uppercuts thrusted from his knees helped Hector establish a rhythm. A quick two-punch combination opened Limon up for three more uppercuts, with Hector whiffing on the final one as the brave fighter was already descending over the top of the bottom rope.

It would have been easy for Limon to keep his reputation intact and be counted out, but, still conscious, he wriggled under the bottom rope and jumped into the corner, hands up to show he was clear headed. After unleashing six more punches, Hector watched as Steele stepped in at 2:52 of the fifth round and grabbed Limon to officially end the bout. Hector Macho Camacho was the new WBC super featherweight champion. He jumped in the arms of his friend Carlos "Sugar" De Leon, and his family, friends, and handlers rushed the ring. Hector started to cry as he pulled his mother close to him.

When the fighters finally embraced, Limon had some advice for the new champion. "Limon told Macho, 'Kid you're going to be a great champion," Jerry Villarreal Sr. recalled. "'Just be careful how you pick your friends. Make sure you have good people around you. Everybody wants to be around a winner, but when you're like me at the end of your career, nobody will want to be around.'"

After a chaotic end to the fight, CBS commentator Tim Ryan sat down with Hector to discuss his plans. Hector, with his Puerto Rican driving cap turned around, appeared comfortable and content.

"I keep telling you that I'm going to be a three-time champion," Hector told Ryan, "because I am the Macho Man. And I am going to dominate the game. It's *my* time, it's Macho Time."

Puerto Rican fans placed Macho and his mother in a convertible and paraded them through the city. When they returned to the hotel, hundreds of people waited for the party.

Hector would go on to call out Wilfredo Gomez, Rafael Solis, Bobby Chacon, and anyone else in the division—as well as heavyweight Larry Holmes. Limon, subdued, told a reporter that the body shot was the one that hurt him. For five rounds, Hector, with his speed, movement, and combinations, had reduced Limon to a plodding, broken fighter. He had knocked him down three times, and almost a fourth. Endorsed by Leonard and many others, Hector combined a tactical beauty with calculating aggression. Limon could not touch him. If a spectator settled in to watch Hector, it was impossible to turn away, especially since at this stage in his career he took dangerous risks.

King's machinations combined with numerous lawsuits and court dates leading up to the fight had left fight fans perplexed as to who the real 130-pound champion was and who deserved to fight for the title. Chacon and his lawyers even went as far as to attempt to have the fight stopped. To Hector and his team, Chacon's persistence—two petitions in state courts pending when the fight occurred—was aggravating, but not a threat. Networks clamored to showcase Hector. Promoters salivated at his marketing potential.

"He was a trailblazer," recalled former welterweight champion Carlos Palomino.

But after Hector won the title, whether the euphemism used was "interim" or "vacant," Sulaiman and the WBC were not going to let him go. Years earlier, Sulaiman had gone so far as to create an entirely new 122-pound division to fit the dynamic young Wilfredo Gomez into his plans, but Hector presented a new reality—a self-promoting champion who was entertaining and spoke English. In Sulaiman's eyes, the future promised a crossover star in the Latino community.

"I have never seen such an extraordinary performance—so sensational, so full of speed in his hands," gushed Sulaiman. "It was terribly impressive. Camacho could become a brilliant fighter, without limits."

Those who remember Hector coming up in the sport knew that he deserved the joy and good fortune that his fists had brought him. "Guys like Hector were not fighting for themselves," said the Garden's Harold Weston, "but for people they love and care for. He was fighting for his son and his mother."

A photo of Hector turning his back to Limon after one knockdown made all the newspapers. An image of Maria, clinging to him for dear life in the center of the ring, did as well.

A couple weeks later, at a publicity event, Hector stressed that even amid the lights and the growing fame, he still just liked to be alone. He took his purse money and fulfilled part of the bargain that he had made with his mother as a precocious seven-year-old boy when he promised to buy her a house in Bayamon, not far from the stadium. Things were changing quickly for the family.

"He was such a good boy," said Maria. "So young. That first check he sent to me. If it was someone else, they would have spent it."

As for Maida, the newfound fame did not immediately equate to a better life for her and her son, but she didn't complain. "Hector was a great father and would take care of Junior," said Maida. "With child support, it was great. We were satisfied with a little bit of money. I wanted a place to sleep, to make sure school was paid for, and that there was food on the table."

To add to the euphoria, everyone on the team received a new Cadillac Eldorado, and the party continued for days.

Meanwhile, Hector had finally won over Kisha, and she began to play a more involved role in his life. As she followed her boyfriend's lead, Kisha flashed her smile from her ringside seat. Even then with Hector on the cusp of something great, she could not help but bristle. Of course, she loved the moments when Hector was focused before a fight; what she could not grasp, however, was the partying.

"I was part of his circle at that time," said Kisha. "There was a huge parade in Puerto Rico. It was a big deal. I was never someone who was going to jump up into the ring with him after the fight. I didn't feel that was my place. But I was in the background. Often, I just stayed alone in my hotel room."

A month after the championship victory, Hector helped move Kisha into her dorm room at Marymount University in Arlington, Virginia. Hector had been involved with many girls, but Kisha was educated and clearly had a plan for her future. Deep down, Hector too wanted to succeed academically, but the "Macho Man" could not reveal that publicly. In his mind, there were too many obstacles such as time and patience.

"He looked so sad and worried when he moved me in," said Kisha. "He was worried about what might happen to me. He turned to my mother and said, 'Are we just going to leave her here?' And I thought how sad it was that Hector did not really know how college worked." Kisha added: "I was hoping that him seeing me getting my education would motivate him to get his GED, but it did not."

Hector had other plans. Displaying a style and aggression that belied his age, he was about to become the face of the sport. "Presence," recalled Sugar Ray Leonard. "He had presence. The way he carried himself. . . . [Hector] walked into that ring with authority and I saw something . . . I just saw something. Not just physically, but mentally, spiritually. He walked into that ring like 'I'm going to win.' When he displayed his heart, when he displayed his talent, when he displayed his speed, I just knew this kid was going to be a star."

A Champion's Grind

9

Not only was Hector able to buy his mother her dream home, he also got to return to Spanish Harlem as a local hero. Everything that he had promised himself after his eye-opening stint at Rikers had come true. With the championship belt around his waist, Hector knew how to appreciate his good fortune.

Yet despite his increased celebrity, Hector reinforced his media image as a "ghetto street kid" during an HBO interview with Larry Merchant. "Out here I walk down the streets and I see a guy beating on a guy with a bat, I say, 'Jesus Christ. Hit him again.' That's our attitude," said Hector. "We grew up with that roughness."

Merchant homed in on how there was a fine line between being aggressive and being dirty. Hector did not back down. "There's nothing fair in war," said Hector. "You get rough, I'll get rougher. I'll let you know that I'm the boss." He continued: "If you got money and you walk down the street, if I know you got money, and you know you got money, if you know you're gonna pass through there and let me take your money, I'm gonna take it."

To many, Hector's words were shocking. To those who knew him, it was Hector being Hector.

Hector's attitude did not stop President Ronald Reagan from inviting him to the White House, where Reagan compared the Oval Office to a kind of fighting ring. "I have the T-shirt from when Camacho went to visit Reagan," said Ismael Leandry, who would later work as a manager for Hector. "He told me that the president said, 'Hector you are like an artist in the ring. I like your personality!' There were forty-one secret service men—and Camacho."

★ ★ ★

It was easy for Camacho to enjoy the moment, but it didn't last long. He returned to the ring to make his first title defense on November 18, 1983, against Puerto Rico's Rafael Solis. Conflicts between Jose Sulaiman and the International Boxing Federation (IBF) president (then the USBA/International) Bob Lee halted initial talks to stage the fight in a more lucrative fight town like Atlantic City. Instead, Sulaiman settled for Coliseo Roberto Clemente in San Juan, Puerto Rico—Solis's backyard.

As brash as Hector was, Solis did not back down from anybody. He would not be intimidated or overwhelmed by Hector's wild antics. The pre-fight feud that developed between Hector and Solis was real. In fact, during one confrontation in a bar in Puerto Rico, Hector glared at Solis, who was surrounded by a host of burly cohorts, and challenged him.

"Hector had the biggest pair of balls you have ever seen," said Jerry Villarreal Sr. "He looked like James Dean leaning against a pole or a tree at the time, leaning back with a toothpick in his mouth, telling Solis and his guys that he was going to fuck them up. 'C'mon you motherfuckers. You brought all these ugly motherfuckers here. You know I'm going to fuck you up in the ring. Tomorrow, I'm going to kick your ass. And these big motherfuckers can't get in to help you.' I was like, 'What the fuck? Can't you see we're outnumbered here?' There were like six of us and thirty of them. But that was Hector."

The fans are with Solis, but the money is on Macho was a sticking point for Hector. From the time that the fight was announced on October 6, 1983, Hector could not stop comparing his Puerto Rican roots with Solis's. When he came to Puerto Rico to fight for the 130-pound title against Rafael Limon (Solis knocked out Benny Marquez on the undercard), Hector got caught up in the magnitude of the fight. Now, for his

first title defense, Hector had more time to reflect—and he remained adamant about keeping the title: "The title is mine and will always be mine,"
he said. His main goal in fighting Solis was to reinforce the notion that he
was the best fighter in the world.

Solis, ranked No. 1 and trained by Julian Delgado, had not had many
recognizable opponents that would concern Hector. Still, style-wise, Solis,
or "The Whip," a five-foot-ten hard-hitting southpaw, presented problems for most fighters; having dropped three of his first twelve bouts, he
had then gone on to win twenty-one of his next twenty-four bouts and
had registered eight knockouts in his last eleven. The other bouts were a
no contest, no decision, and a draw. Without any signature wins on his
record, Solis had still done enough to catapult him into a position for a
title shot.

While training in San Juan for the fight, Hector adhered to Billy Giles's
instructions and employed Jeff Levine as his business manager. Trying to
project a more mature image, Hector even brought Kisha to Puerto Rico.
"I was a kid then," said Hector referring to past transgressions. "I got
class now. I make money. I'm around good people and I got a good life."

Still, hometown Solis fans treated Hector as an intruder. The camp
received death threats and had things thrown at their van, and Jerry
Villarreal Sr. was concerned enough to have his sons turn their Macho
shirts inside-out to avoid any backlash.

The fight took place in the Roberto Clemente Coliseum and was televised
on HBO as a Don King Production. Hector was getting $200,000; Solis
settled for $50,000. Leading up to the fight, Hector, who weighed in at
129.5 pounds, trained at the Bairoa Gym, but it was difficult to simulate
Solis's five-inch height and eight-inch reach advantage.

Although Hector looked loose in his pink robe and slick black trunks
dancing to Michael Jackson before the fight, he allowed Solis, 129 pounds,
to gain momentum in the first round, feeding off the raucous crowd of *his*
fans. When Solis raised his hands at the end of the physical round, he
showed Hector that he didn't fear him. As the fight progressed, Solis tried
to bait Hector and derail his focus, but the champion landed a clean hook
to close out the second round. Over the next two rounds, Hector walked

into Solis's lead lefts and had to address the awkwardness of getting inside on the bigger fighter. Because Solis was so lanky and long, Hector could not get inside with the same ease as he had against Limon.

"Hector was so wise, intelligent, and fast," said super bantamweight legend Wilfredo Gomez, who was ringside for the fight. "He didn't hit hard, but he was so technical. He was skilled like a technician. Solis was not a special boxer. The tricks [Hector] used . . . you couldn't even imagine them. It happened so fast."

Away from what was happening in the ring, Hector became preoccupied with a disturbance in the crowd, near his family. Employing more head movement, he was still getting hit by more punches than he bargained for. Solis beat Hector to the punch as the fourth round ended, and the pro-Solis crowd reacted accordingly. Thriving off a visceral disdain for Solis, Hector landed a right hook in the fifth that caused an alarmed Solis to chase him recklessly—and later walk into a counter left that sent him down. After falling to his knees and rising by the count of four, Solis took an eight-count from referee Octavio Meyran to avoid any further damage. Reports noted that after the knockdown, Solis glanced over at Maria and Hector's sister Racquel and smiled at them, inciting Hector even more. Solis's supporters, including Solis's mother and girlfriend, stirred the proceedings from the beginning, deliberately standing in front of and blocking the view of Camacho loyalists.

The commotion, according to Maria, had nothing to do with the view of the ring. "I was wearing beads," she said, "and his mother tried to grab my beads. Macho looked up from the ring, and warned me, 'Mommy, she come and hit you. Don't touch her.' He got crazy. But my daughter Racquel pushed her, 'You don't touch my mother.' And then I took my beads off, and I challenged her."

Despite clinching and stalling tactics, Solis walked into one final left that stopped him at 2:02 of the fifth round. Hector's controversial comments in the Merchant HBO interview resonated: "If you walk down the street and show me your money, I'm gonna take it." He embodied that vicious mindset as he glared at and cursed Solis after the knockout punch. Bloodied and three teeth poorer, Solis had fought valiantly over the early rounds. Surprisingly, Solis had also hurt Hector with a left in the round. Until then, all three judges scored an even fight, 38-38. Hector was not accustomed to challengers who kept an even pace.

"I knew this was going to be a tough fight," said Hector. "He was fighting in front of his mother and fans."

Amid the boos and the hecklers, Hector took offense at the theory that he was the inferior Puerto Rican. He loathed the cadre of followers who lined up to support Solis. Defiant, even in the end, Solis was willing to do anything to incite Hector: Nothing was off limits. Deeply sensitive, Hector had one final parting shot. It was not a scintillating performance, but he finished the job with a passing grade.

"I'm Puerto Rican, but if you don't want me," said Hector. "I'm Macho . . . forget it."

On the surface, some journalists may have glossed over Hector's objections to unfair treatment. "He got really emotional when he heard that [narrative about being less of a Puerto Rican]," said Gomez. "He was Puerto Rican just like anyone else."

Whenever he fought another native-born Puerto Rican, Hector felt judged unfairly for having left the island. When he and his family first left Puerto Rico, they had no choice. Hector's father had been abusing them. Then, when Hector became famous, he embraced his roots, returning as a world champ. Not many Puerto Ricans who were forced to leave were fortunate enough to return home on their own terms. So when he returned to Puerto Rico and the red carpet that had been laid out for him before the Limon fight had been pulled, it was heartbreaking. But Hector rarely showed his feelings, and so his frustration morphed into resentment.

Hector probably felt a similar resentment toward his father, who had failed him miserably. As a teenager, Hector did not publicly scorn his father, and friends have claimed that he even sought him out. When it came to his own son, Hector tried to do better. During training camps, although Hector was inaccessible physically, emotionally he was available. Even when he was away, he would call Junior and Maida to make sure they were okay.

Living in his father's famous shadow and suffocated by the notion that he was merely an extension of him, Junior needed to find himself. Maida, meanwhile, yearned to have positive male role models for her son. Once she started dating a man named Julio, a new dynamic began to emerge, and she had to distance herself from Hector. Coming in through Junior's window at three in the morning after going to clubs was no longer an option for Hector.

Maida was also worried about the pressure on Junior to live up to his father's name, and so she moved them to Madison Avenue, far enough away to create a new life. Just as decades earlier, Maria had moved from Puerto Rico to escape her then husband and Hector's father, Maida tried to create distance between Hector and Junior. One family fled from abuse; the other fled trying to escape the shadows of a famous father. Along with the new life came a new identity for Junior. Instead of "Macho's son," Junior now went by Hector Luis. Indeed, Junior was figuring out how to be a different kind of man than his father. He was learning that he didn't have to be Macho like Hector, and it was liberating. *I can be myself. And I know who I am.*

"Away from my father's name, I was funny Hector Luis, the good baseball player," said Junior. "I finally got the chance to be myself. I felt free."

But he could never truly escape his father. There would always be rumblings on the street that his father was driving around in one of his sports cars looking for him. When his father called to say he was coming over, Maida sent Junior out to meet him. She did not want Hector interfering with their new life.

As Junior was finding his identity, his father, the fighter, was concerned about losing his.

Kisha had become a major part of Hector's life. Despite difficulties and busy lives—Kisha with her studies, Hector with his boxing career—the couple managed to continue their serious relationship, but it was difficult to navigate both worlds.

"I was very worried," said Kisha. "I remember so clearly. Before fights were the best times. Hector was getting enough sleep. . . . He was in good shape, and positive. But after the fights, it was always crazy and they would party hard. A lot of times . . . I would be asking myself, 'Is it ever going to be like it was before?'"

Meanwhile, Billy Giles and Hector would team up for one final bout on May 20, 1984. It had been seven months since Hector defended his title against Rafael Solis. Managerial, weight, and personal problems had not only stalled his career, but also destroyed the momentum he had coming off his championship victory a year earlier. Defending his title once in a year must have been disappointing for a fighter who prided himself on being active. Now, with Giles's blessing, Hector was considering a move up to the 135-pound weight class.

Rumors of future bouts with lightweights Livingstone Bramble and Ray Mancini were pervasive, as the team's relationship with Don King was no longer a fluid one. Before officially making the bold move through the media to leave the division and relinquish his 130-pound super featherweight crown on July 6, Hector signed to fight a nontitle bout with Panama's Rafael Williams in Corpus Christi, Texas. After his seven-month spell without a fight, he returned to the gym for six weeks to train for the May return. Williams, 19-1 and twelve knockouts, was not a world-class opponent and not as dangerous as Solis, but his height and reach were ominous. With only a handful of wins against world champions, Williams, from Colon, Panama, was only now venturing outside of Panama to get fights. His only blemish had come when he suffered a unanimous decision loss to Livingstone Bramble in January.

Through his relationship with Josephine Abercrombie, a boxing promoter and heiress to a Houston oil fortune, Jeff Levine was able to get Hector and Pee Wee Rucker an opportunity to train on her lavish six-thousand-acre Abercrombie Cannonade Ranch near Gonzales, Texas. It was not long before the rambunctious champion was getting kicked out of the training camp before the fight for shooting BB guns out the window of a Lincoln Continental. After word got out, Hector and Pee Wee were soon surrounded by law enforcement officers at their hotel.

"When I got back, I heard the news that they got evicted," said Jerry Villarreal Sr. "They had the sheriff there and I know they were thinking, 'We don't like your kind around here.'"

The fight with Williams was held at the Coliseum in Corpus Christi, Texas, and was televised on NBC *SportsWorld*. More than five thousand fans were in attendance to see what shape Hector was in. He weighed in at 135 pounds; Williams weighed in at 133.75 pounds.

People again looked to Sugar Ray Leonard to validate Hector, and he did not hesitate to anoint him. Someone needed to take the mantle that Leonard had so definitively captured in his prime, and Hector, inside the ring, was making all the right moves. "He had that personal radar," said Leonard. "In other words, he's in the corner and his opposition is throwing punches at him and he just moves slightly to the left and slips the punch. Very few fighters have that. It's even hard to articulate what it was. There was a list of guys who had that camera, that videotape in their head. They felt the punch coming."

Once the fight started, Hector accentuated his body work and tried to minimize Williams's six-inch reach advantage. After getting inside Williams's wide punches in the first round, Hector landed multiple hooks to the head. Because he was so long, Williams needed space to get punches off. Even when he applied feints, Williams got nailed by Hector's left and right hooks.

In the second round, Hector missed several punches and lacked intensity. But, since he was so intent on going to the body, he was able to eventually place that pulverizing left hook. Fortunately for Williams, who rarely worked behind a jab, he was not facing Macho, the nineteen-year-old phenom, but rather Hector, a boxer trying to work on timing. Some fighters are awkward and hard for any opponent to fight, but Williams was unusual in his reliance on a sort of bolo punch that reminded Panamanians of one of their featherweight idols, Eusebio Pedroza, a rough-and-tough champion in his own right. Williams dropped punches on Hector's head like a hammer and landed a wound-up bolo punch and right hand as the second round closed out.

A hostility emerged between the fighters in the third round, and a tepid fight transformed into a physical one. Referee Dick Cole proactively scolded Williams for what appeared like a string of low blows. The round was marred by such warnings and by friction between the fighters. Adding to the tension, Williams screamed at Hector as the men headed back to their corners, eliciting a slap in the head from Hector as the round ended.

Usually, it was easy to assess Hector's performance by the percussive feel to the round. At his best, Hector mixed punches, keeping his opponent off balance with his unpredictability and piling up points with blistering combinations. But then there were times, as in the fight with Cubanito Perez, when Hector met a fighter who stylistically hindered him from establishing those norms. Williams, with his height, reach, and unconventional punching style, created problems that frustrated Hector. But what separated Hector from other champions was his ability to read a situation and adapt. So in the fourth round, instead of getting frustrated, Hector tripled up on his jab, moved inside, planted his glove on Williams's head, stepped back, and landed a nice jab and follow-up straight left. What followed was another mixed bag that Williams was unprepared to respond to.

With the low blows becoming more of an issue, Williams had a point deducted in the fifth round but eventually hurt Hector in the same round with a straight right hand. For the first time, the champ was forced to clinch. Williams gained momentum by jarring Hector, marking the first time that Hector had been so agitated by a punch since the Solis fight. A guy so skilled and talented usually did not have to concern himself with getting hit by too many big shots, but Hector, by his own account, had been hurt by Blaine Dickson, Tomas Diaz, Rafael Solis, and Williams. And yet he had never been knocked down.

In the last minute of the sixth round, Williams forced Hector into retreat mode with four punches that made him stumble. Although not dazed, Hector was fending off punches rather than attacking, and he waited for Cole to break them up after he absorbed two more right hands. Often when a fighter asserted himself, as Williams did in the sixth round, Hector intuitively knew he had to respond sharply. Giles preached to him in the corner to work behind the jab, and a spirited Hector landed a sharp left.

"Macho, Macho!" The crowd's chant gained steam.

Hector obliged his adoring crowd by hurting Williams with a big left to his neck that sent him bouncing off the ropes. Going into the seventh and final round, Hector shocked Williams by landing four uppercuts. Cole stepped in at this point to admonish Hector for holding and hitting, but Hector was undeterred. Instead, the champion landed a dangerous right hook with 46 seconds remaining that jolted Williams's head back. Concerned about Williams's condition, Cole stepped in to stop the bout as Hector landed three more uppercuts in the fray. Critics claimed that Cole was too quick with the stoppage. Going into that final round, Hector was ahead on all scorecards. If anything, Williams looked stunned early in the round when Camacho sent him reeling, but when the fight was stopped at the 2:19 mark, the controversy was warranted. In fact, since Cole hesitated before the stoppage, it almost seemed as if he was preparing to send Williams back out for battle before he waved it off. Williams had been battered with clean hooks throughout the round, but he was neither hurt nor helpless at any juncture.

★ ★ ★

No one knew it was coming, but Giles had stood in Hector's corner for the last time.

"In the beginning, when they first started working together, they were all hootin' and hollerin'," said Jerry Villarreal Jr. "But when they started to make money, well that's when things got negative. Macho used to tell Billy, whose nickname was Bill "The Thrill," to 'stop being so fucking greedy. Just sign for the fights. I want to fight whomever.' But whatever Don [King] offered, Billy wanted more. But Billy felt he had the baddest dude around. The only thing bigger than Mach during that time was Sugar Ray Leonard."

Before the Williams fight, Giles kicked Tony Kidd, a mainstay on the Macho team, out of the camp. In his place, Giles brought in a guy only known as "Juice" to work the fight. Pee Wee Rucker, fighting on the card, never let that go. He loved Kidd dearly. Giles's pushing Kidd out of the corner marked the beginning of when things started to unravel.

Leaving Billy 10

Hector Camacho had a unique ability to detach himself from emotionally charged incidents that would devastate some people. Confidants suggest that he rarely spoke about his emotions, and though he showed anger and laughter, he rarely shared his pain. Often, his smile deflected the hurt. But he could not tolerate betrayal.

Billy Giles and Hector loved each other—or so Hector thought. He recalled when he and Giles had nothing, and they, along with Pee Wee Rucker, would wake up at the crack of dawn to take in the clean air of Belle Isle in Detroit. Or the turbulent but memorable sparring sessions when he and Giles took over the Kronk Gym and Emanuel Steward tried desperately to match up Hector with a worthy opponent. Or even the collective laughter when Hector used his spinning back-kick to knock down a hotel door. The more Hector rewound to those moments, the more troubling it became to try and refocus that now-blurry lens.

Even with Robert Lee by his side, Giles had referred to himself as "The Champ Maker." In Giles's mind, he had built Hector from the bottom up, which is not entirely inaccurate. He had shaped Hector's career so that the fighter faced challenging opposition when he was just getting started, reinforcing his confidence. Instead of padding his record with a litany of nobodies, Giles negotiated fights with very capable fighters—Louie Loy, Johnny Sato, and Melvin Paul to name a few. If Giles had chosen an easier path, Hector may not have transformed into the dynamic fighter he had become.

"Billy did not give him cream puffs," said Jerry Villarreal Jr. "He wasn't getting him bums. Macho was beating everybody. I have never seen anyone so confident. He was just beating these guys up."

The trouble started in July 1984, when Hector and Giles agreed to relinquish the 130-pound title two months after the victory over Rafael Williams. By doing so, they maneuvered out of a contract with King and avoided giving him the final options they owed him. Giles also felt that the team could secure big-money fights at lightweight that were no longer available at super featherweight.

At the time, Hector still owed King two defenses, but he felt slighted by the smaller purses. When confronted, King reacted harshly: "I own you. You belong to me motherfucker." Hector, who had signed away all of his endorsements to the promoter, told King to fuck off and left his office. If Hector, who then felt cornered, relinquished the belt, the contract with King immediately became null and void.

That summer, Giles announced: "It's official. An ex-champion at twenty-two." Still speaking for Hector, Giles claimed that the fighter could face either Aaron Pryor or Livingstone Bramble at 135 pounds.

During that time, Hector discovered that Giles had not been forthright with his behind-the-scenes handling of money. Having hired attorney Raymone Bain to investigate the case, Hector had evidence that Giles had started misappropriating money from Hector's purses to pay his taxes. Enlisting Bain to oversee his finances, Hector was able to trace the money back to Giles. When he got wind of the truth, Hector, hurt, reached out to his mother.

"Mommy, what should I do?" asked Hector, stunned.

"Leave him," said Maria.

When Hector, Maria, and Giles sat down to discuss the allegations, they all became emotional. Giles promised to change, but Maria would not budge. She urged her son to let Giles go.

Showing little emotion, Maria looked back retrospectively on that emotional encounter: "Billy talked to me to go back to Macho," said Maria. "'Talk with Mommy,' said Macho. I said, 'No.'"

But Giles pressed, "Please give me a chance, Maria. I will be nicer with Macho.'"

"No, you do something wrong with Macho, and you will keep doing it," Maria responded.

Maria started to cry, then Macho followed suit. It was difficult to say goodbye to a man who had had such a huge impact on Hector for so long.

"Macho told him, 'See what you have done to my mother? You hurt my mother.'"

"I am sorry Ms. Camacho," Giles uttered one final time.

"Go away from my son, go away from me. Please Billy, go."

Maria never saw Billy again.

Giles, feeling trapped, went after Hector in the media. First, he claimed Hector was "drowning in drugs, and he will never make it back." Then he alleged financial issues: "When he took my money, it was okay," Giles argued, saying that he constantly gave the fighter money early in his career. "Then when he started making money, he didn't want to pay me. He was trying to beat me out of my money."

Giles, who often addressed reporters wanting answers about Hector as "we," did not back off of his comments.

"[Hector] had his demons," said Jerry Villarreal Jr. "But that was wrong of Billy to [go to the press]. Maria and Hector let him go and Billy wanted to get back at him."

Whether what Billy said was true or not did not matter in Hector's eyes. Giles broke the code of the streets about keeping sensitive information in-house and not exposing it to the public. After being burned by Robert Lee, Hector didn't expect that Giles had it in him to do the same. Both breakups were over money, but Giles took something personal and made it public.

Lonely and feeling betrayed, Hector turned inward in an extreme, unhealthy way. But by the beginning of 1985, he began to deal with that grief through the press. "I've been burned twice," Hector told an *Inside Sports* reporter. "I thought [Robert Lee] and Giles were honest. I let them take over my business. I didn't know what I was worth then. But I've been through school now, I've learned, I know what to do. It's hard to find sincere people in boxing. Jimmy [Montoya, who became his adviser after Giles] doesn't treat me like a child the way [Lee] and Giles did. But I know half of it was my fault for being so freehearted—they took advantage of it.

I have Jimmy as an adviser now. But I've got the final say-so about what I do; nobody makes decisions but me alone. If I make a wrong decision, what the hell. It won't be the first time I fucked up."

"At one point things couldn't get no worse," Hector told a *Boston Globe* reporter. "Giles got power hungry, and Don King and Madison Square Garden didn't want to deal with him and here I am on hold. I wanted to fight—I was winning, so why not fight?—but I had to dismiss him because of the job he was doing. It hurt; he was like a big brother."

What did not reach the press was that Giles was misappropriating the money and filing his taxes with Hector's Form 56. Instead of having Giles arrested, Hector and his team decided to let him go, since there was so much history between them.

"We got together and we talked about the good times," said Jerry Villarreal Sr. "Hector told [Giles] they would split the money (from the misappropriation of the taxes scandal) and he would let Giles, who was about to go to jail anyhow, off the hook." This was confirmed by Hector years later through the press when he said, ". . . the breakup came because of certain things I found out but didn't press charges on."

By not pressing charges against Billy Giles, Hector saved himself legal hassles and rid himself of Giles on his own terms.

First, it was Lee, then Giles. The two men who had helped craft Hector's career were now gone: Who could Hector turn to? He leaned on the Villarreal family during these hard times, but he also did some major soul searching.

In response to the attack, Hector turned inward and away from the ring. Over the next several months, he figured out what his life without Giles, the leader of the Macho team, would look like. During that long layoff, Hector lost himself—and almost lost his will to fight. How could he love a sport that only introduced him to what he considered immoral individuals? Even when he appeared to be doing the right things, Hector felt the changes he was making were not substantial enough. When he started his professional career, he knew that he would have to deal with fame, but the more famous he got, the more he had to deal with disloyal people. And if Hector did not properly weed those people out, his stress level increased dramatically.

"Hector has always liked being by himself," said Maida. "He never trusted friends. He hung around and was in sports, but he was always more to himself. That's who he was, and he's always been like that. He was a loner."

"When Hector was breaking ties with Billy," said Harold Weston, "it really hurt him. Billy was not proper. He took it really hard when that happened with Billy. He needed a friend who understood him."

But there was more. What Giles brought to Hector was irreplaceable in the fighter's eyes. This was more than a spat between fighter and manager/ trainer; instead, to Hector, it felt as if Giles deliberately destroyed what they had built together.

"Billy always wanted to take the credit, but he didn't deserve it," said former trainer Robert Lee. "Billy got caught taking money, and tried to make himself look better. If Hector got caught up with drugs, it was because of Billy."

So Hector escaped.

Finding his own way to combat the depression, Hector bought plane tickets and traveled aimlessly to vacation destinations where he would isolate himself in his hotel room. The self-destructive pattern continued as he headed to Detroit.

When Hector returned to Detroit, he holed up in the Villarreal household and stayed away from everyone for a weekend. At some point, curled up under his blanket in the back bedroom, he asked himself how he had gotten to this point. Who was to blame?

Things were so easy, at times, in the projects, hanging on the corner, rollerskating, playing "dare" games with friends. But when money was involved, relationships deteriorated. Beneath the Macho exterior, Hector was as impressionable as any other kid his age. And yes, he was still a kid. A kid without an education. A kid who never had a consistent father figure to tell him right from wrong. A kid who constantly encountered people who wanted a piece of him. A kid who felt betrayed and alone.

"He was hurt and he went into a depression," Jerry Villarreal Jr. recalled. "My mother took care of him. He was supposed to go to New York, but no one knew where he was. He just disappeared."

Although Jerry Jr. was young, he did spend time with Hector and looked up to him. His father, Jerry Sr., was still part of the team and understood what had happened with Giles—and its lasting impact.

"We had a room for him and Kisha," said Jerry Sr. "When he was having problems and wanted to get away where no one would bother him, he came here. There was always someone looking for a handout or some kind of help. When you don't have a dime, no one wants to talk to you, but when you have twenty cents, they're asking, 'Can I get one of those dimes?'"

Jerry Sr. continued: "When we fought in Atlantic City, oh my God, half of Harlem was there. And nobody bought tickets. The leeches were all over the place. That was part of success. Everyone wanted to be around a winner. Sometimes it was a burden."

Having suffered through depression herself, Kisha understood what her boyfriend was experiencing. She had seen Giles and Hector grow closer over time. Kisha also saw the unforgiving side of the sport. "He needed good friends, and he didn't have that," said Kisha. "Around that time, Patrick [Flannery] moved back to Queens, New York, and he was not around as much. [Hector] was pretty down. I know about being depressed, and he was depressed. He asked me, 'Are these people around me just for my money?' And I was like, 'Yes!' But he didn't see it that way."

Reports confirmed that Hector, as a free agent (before he brought Jimmy Montoya on as an adviser), missed several big paydays by pricing himself out or by going to great lengths to avoid any King involvement.

To stay active, Hector sometimes engaged in philanthropic pursuits. At the end of 1984, he fought an exhibition run by Joel Levine to help raise money for a Soviet Jew being held prisoner. A month later, Hector helped Jimmy Montoya put on a fundraiser in Mexico City for the victims of a natural-gas explosion. Contrary to what some thought, it was not always about Macho. There was more to the man.

But while Hector disappeared from the professional scene, the boxing world moved on. People were no longer salivating over Hector's other-worldly skills. He was seen as an enigmatic character who made rash decisions. As Hector experienced this emotional overhaul in 1984, the lightweight division began to reshape itself.

Jose Luis Ramirez (WBC) and Livingstone Bramble (WBA) would insert themselves as champions in the fall and summer, respectively. One of Hector's major missed opportunities was a showdown with Bramble that had hard-core boxing fans salivating, but New Jersey promoter Dan Duva believed the boxer priced himself out of that fight as well, whereas Hector blamed Duva for not securing the date and letting King step in with a title fight between Edwin Rosario and Jose Luis Ramirez.

Hector also had to pull out of a scheduled 130-pound defense on July 22, 1984, in Las Cruces, New Mexico, against Louie Burke. Later, Hector blamed it on the fight's promoter not coming up with the agreed-upon $500,000. Charlie "Choo" Brown was then signed to replace Hector. Other reports claimed that Hector had sabotaged the bout himself. Although he was set to fight the winner of that bout in September, it never materialized, as he went into a personal tailspin.

But in January it was clear that Hector was finally coming out of the personal haze and returning to form. Jimmy Montoya, who had by then replaced Billy Giles, was taking over as the dominant voice in the camp.

"I remember that I was in Vegas in the casino and one of my guys came up to me around three a.m. and said, 'Camacho is looking for you,'" said Montoya. "He looked at me and said, 'You're my new manager.' But then I told him, 'Before I do anything, I want to talk to Billy Giles.' Then, I called Billy at three a.m. and told him, 'I got this kid here.' And he immediately said, 'Take him and give me money.' I paid him off after that first fight. That was it."

Hector let his distance from Giles be known. "I don't worry about it now," Hector told the *Philadelphia Daily News* in January 1985, referring to the breakup with Giles. "People will forget about him. *I'm the star.* If it wasn't for me, he'd be working at Wendy's."

Once the cycle of distrust and deception died down, Hector came to trust Montoya. In his mind, Montoya had passed all the necessary tests.

Through his relationship with Montoya, King got back into Hector's good graces. Able to thrive in the ring as a trainer and be serviceable outside of it, Montoya negotiated with King and eventually signed a contract where Hector would earn $2 million for five title fights. The contract allowed Hector to be more active, which was a blessing, but conversely, Hector would no longer have the autonomy he felt he needed.

All of these changes were happening fast for any fighter. Not one to hold a grudge, Hector made an exception when it came to Giles, whom he viewed as a hypocrite. In the end, Hector had trusted Giles completely and was spurned. Lesson learned, Hector quickly began to tighten his control over his career.

"I don't know what happened, but when I got [Hector], he had been messing around with drugs," said Montoya, who trained two other world champs, Juan Meza and Richie Sandoval. "I said, 'I don't give a shit about the money, but I care about you. If I catch you messing around with drugs, I'll get rid of you.'"

According to Montoya, Hector embraced that idea of having a no-nonsense trainer and was content to move forward with a new team out of Los Angeles. At the time, Hector was not in a good place psychologically, but that quickly changed as Hector (24-0, fifteen KOs) got ready to fight Louie Burke (19-1, twelve KOs) on January 19, 1985, at the Imperial Ballroom in Atlantic City, New Jersey.

No one considered Burke, who was trained by Angelo Dundee in Miami, a dangerous opponent, although he proved a durable one. In Miami, Dundee had set up Burke with suitable sparring partners, hoping to simulate Hector's speed and movement; unfortunately, most fighters in the world could not cope with either.

"There was no way to get the same speed," Burke recalled. "He was phenomenal. Once in a lifetime speed."

Conversely, Montoya had to integrate Hector into a system already in place with his other fighters. It is never easy to bring a proven commodity in to a new, more structured system, and it took a while for Hector to recognize he did not call the shots anymore. Needing to get acclimated to a new atmosphere and training regimen, Hector tried to negotiate with Montoya.

"I will come around at 4:30 a.m. to pick you up to run," said Montoya.

"I usually get up around 10 a.m. to start my workouts in the afternoon," Hector responded.

"That's okay. I'll pick you up at 4:30."

"But that's too early, too early."

"I can pick you up at 4:30 and you can run by yourself, okay?"

"Yeah."

But when Montoya went to get him, Hector was still sleeping. "I told him to get the fuck up," Montoya said. "But once he saw that there were seven or eight guys waiting for him in the car, he liked that. He liked to run with the guys. On the fourth day we ran, we saw Sugar Ray Leonard and that gave him more incentive to run. He listened to me. I loved him and he loved me. It was like father and son. I told him 'No motherfucker will beat you if you do what I tell you to do. You're doing good with drugs. You're clean and in good shape.'"

Figuring he could work with the drug issue, Montoya turned his attention to the camp hangers-on. Montoya felt that to get the best out of Hector, he needed to get rid of everyone. Hector still had his relapses, and Montoya had to flush his weed down the toilet on one occasion and chide him for racing his sports car on another. Still, the transition to Montoya went relatively well. Hector had been searching for a male role model to fill the gaps left by legions of immoral, corrosive people who only wanted a piece of him.

"I got rid of the leeches," said Montoya. "I banned the dope addicts, all the guys he was paying just to yell for him. When I was done, we had six guys. Before that, he had twenty guys around him."

While ditching the negative influences, Montoya indulged Hector's needs for extravagant outfits. Hector would sketch the outfit he was looking for, and Montoya would send it to a guy to make it for him.

Things were running smoothly. Then, a month before the fight in December 1985, Hector was summoned back home to settle a near-fatal street dispute. After calming the situation, he returned to camp with Montoya. A year earlier, Hector might not have made the trip back to Los Angeles.

Back in the ring at the Imperial Ballroom in Atlantic City, Hector Camacho stared at Louie Burke. Weighing 136 pounds (the contract allowed for an extra pound), Hector was fighting at his heaviest weight and was seeking to put the layoff behind him. Ranked No. 5 by the WBC, Hector, twenty-two, sported his classic leopard trunks under his beloved fur coat. Style mattered.

"He was an entertainer, loud and cocky with the camera," said Burke. "As I prepared, I didn't care for him. I wanted to shut him up."

As the match began, Hector, calculating and aggressive, whipped off six jabs followed by a straight left and then hammered Burke's head back with two clean shots amid a ten-punch combination. Burke, flailing, took more punishment throughout the round. At one discouraging point for Burke, Hector landed three right-hook counters. As blazingly fast as Hector was, his rustiness was evident. At times, he looked slow on his feet, and he tended to clinch in the first round, which was unheard of, rested on the ropes, and avoided sharp angles. Still, he opened up his attack confidently and landed four- and five-punch combinations—a positive sign for any post-layoff fighter.

"I considered myself quick," said Burke, "but he was a different level than everyone else. I couldn't believe how he put his punches together. I never saw combinations where he punched you with [such] power and speed. He punched you while he was still moving."

Some opponents would have found the early intensity demoralizing, but Burke forged ahead. He went down early in the second from a straight left hand. Trying to catch himself with his left glove, Burke was unable to keep his balance. Referee Larry Hazzard whisked Hector to a corner and gave Burke an eight-count. After the eight-count, a vintage Hector, seeing an opening, attacked Burke with a barrage of fifteen to seventeen punches before the round ended.

As blood formed on the bridge of his nose, Burke landed glancing punches on Hector, who had punched himself out. Burke, to his credit, stayed upright, lasted the round, and even landed an uppercut after the bell, which brought a stare from Hector.

"I ran into a straight left as I was coming forward," said Burke about the knockdown, "but I felt I could throw punches forever. I knew I had to wear him out. I could be relentless. But I ran into a lot of shots. He would draw you in and his speed didn't diminish his power."

Whenever Hector questioned his own conditioning going into a bout, he used the first couple rounds to attack his opponent relentlessly. Keen boxing observers were aware of this tactic—it was Hector's way of showing that he was not properly prepared. Unfortunately, this proved detrimental in many fights when his refreshed opponent gained his second wind while Hector was losing his. But although Burke was tough, he had little power and less movement. It was unlikely that Burke would have truly tested Hector at any stage in the Puerto Rican's career.

Despite Burke having moments in the third and fourth rounds, Hector dissected him, setting him up for the fifth and final round, during which Burke's eyesight became blurred. After another dazzling Hector combination, Hazzard intervened to give an eight-count after a barrage of punches. Not long after, Hector scored an uppercut that caused Hazzard to step in again to administer one final standing eight-count. Burke retired on his stool after the fifth round.

"His pop at 135 was to be respected," recalled Junior. "He had power. He had some tough fights like Burke, and he stopped all of them. His power was his speed, and he could generate good uppercuts as he would explode up."

After winning the fight, Hector sat down for a post-fight interview with CBS commentator Tim Ryan. "I was in the process of telling the TV audience, 'It's nice to have you back . . .' But then Hector started to tear up," Ryan recalled of the interview. "Will you be my friend?" Hector asked Ryan. The question came from a place so innocent and sad that it proved difficult not to feel a deep sympathy for the fighter. Hector continued: "I need friends."

As Hector cuddled into the crook of Ryan's arm, his air of vulnerability replaced chants of "Macho Time" or playful banter like "Yeah buddy!" Few athletes had ever made themselves so vulnerable. What slowly unfolded was a touching and heartbreaking admission that, despite being surrounded by friends, family, and a host of cornermen, this young fighter felt alone. At that moment, the "Macho" show was over, and life's problems weighed in.

Neither Ryan nor Gil Clancy were shocked at the turn of events unfolding on national TV. What did shock Ryan was how quickly the interview shifted from boxing to Hector's mental health. It was easy to forget that beyond the flash, he was a real person with real deficiencies, just like anyone else.

Witnessing the incident from the perspective of a relatively new trainer, Montoya claimed that Hector felt overwhelmed because of an earlier incident with a fan. But in that telling post-fight moment, Hector made the decision to shift away from the happy-go-lucky star who craved attention. For many viewers, the act humanized him.

"Hector was a big-hearted guy," Montoya recalled, "and that was the problem with him. He was on a radio show and a guy called up and called him a 'dopehead.' Macho replied, 'No, no, no, man.' But that had a lot to do with what happened. [Hector] wanted to be clean. He always told me, 'I'm hooked. I'm hooked.' He was mentally hooked. I told him we would get him out of that bullshit."

A downtrodden Hector showed a mixture of sorrow and resignation. All throughout his life, Macho had needed help but would not ask for it. His pleas often came in the form of long, stream-of-consciousness, rambling interview responses late at night to various sportswriters. Crying on Ryan's shoulder felt safe. Doing the same thing in front of a close friend or camp hangers-on did not. Hector had a reputation to uphold and after exerting himself physically and emotionally, the only thing that seemed natural was to release the emotions that had been pent up for so long.

What Hector didn't say was, *It's been a tough month and the stress has hit me so hard that I have struggled to stay afloat.* As his words came out, Hector looked down and sighed. His world seemed to be crumbling. He didn't want to focus on boxing anymore. Instead, he held tightly to Ryan, a friend. Inside, Hector was screaming for help. He trusted Ryan. He trusted Clancy. Both of them had witnessed him at his worst. Clancy remembered saving Hector from himself in Alaska, where he saw firsthand how his drug habit affected him. To everyone else watching, seeing Hector call for help was shocking and out of character. To Clancy and Ryan, the display was just an extension of what they had seen in Alaska.

Here was Hector, the equivalent of boxing's Elton John, unloading everything *after* his fight. Where was the joy? The ebullience? Nowhere. He needed help and rest; he needed someone to step in and change the way he was living his life.

"He was like a little kid," Ryan recalled, "who was emotionally spent. It was heartfelt, and we felt like we made a difference. I said something like, 'Nice job in the fight.' I wanted to get him to go to commercial. I just remember how emotional it was and how it stuck with me years later."

Both incidents had a profound effect on Ryan, who lost touch with Hector over the years. He never approached him about the breakdown or any other traumatic incident. "If Hector was in normal mode," said Ryan, "he would have never let that happen. You saw a troubled guy. We were well aware that he had a problem."

Most fighters can detach themselves from the proceedings immediately after the fight. They view the sport as a job, and once the final bell sounds, they punch the clock and the fight is over. It was usually easy for Hector to do that, although occasionally it took time to disengage from the Macho image.

"I really enjoyed conversing with Hector," Burke recalled. "When we were fighting, he was all show. And it sold tickets. His adrenaline went up. He made the act part of him. But he wasn't a bad guy. After the fight, we became good friends."

"When that happened after the fight . . . I remember [Marty Cohen, an old friend,] talking to Hector, and saying, 'It doesn't matter if they love you or hate you," Jerry Villarreal Sr. recalled. "It only matters if they fill the seats. And after that Hector was like, 'I'm going to be me.'"

After the Burke fight, Hector took a mandatory drug test administered by the New Jersey State Athletic Commission. The results would not be announced until several months later.

After beating Burke, Hector easily pounded out a twelve-round unanimous decision over Roque Montoya at the Memorial Auditorium in Buffalo on April 29, 1985, for the NABF lightweight title. Since the Montoya fight was for a title, albeit a minor one, King promoted it as the co-feature of the WBA heavyweight title fight between Greg Page and Tony Tubbs.

Roque "Rocky" Montoya (14-6-2), weighing 134 pounds, was a Mexican national champ; Hector, weighing 135 pounds, came in with an undefeated record of 25-0. In his maroon-and-yellow trunks—and beginning to make his spit curl a true fashion statement—Camacho did not waste time. First, he beelined for Montoya and threw four consecutive left hands, which sent Montoya retreating. Shifting to his right, Montoya became flustered when he moved directly into Hector's comfort zone.

Without hesitation, Hector set up the body work with a dominating straight left hand. By the second round, he had Montoya doubling over from fierce hooks to the body, which he followed with a hook to the head. As committed as he was to body work, he was just as focused on applying his tricks behind referee Luis Rivera's back. Rivera warned Hector in the third round for holding and hitting, but it was imperative that Rivera step in, as the fight had become even more physical.

In one more confrontational exchange, Hector held Montoya, landed two uppercuts, and had to quickly clinch a charging Montoya. Then, they both clashed heads on the inside. Two aspects were evident in the fourth round: first, Hector was brutalizing Montoya and was able to effectively leverage some of his punches; and second, Montoya—who had previously fought two top-notch opponents, Tony Baltazar and Gato Gonzalez, before fighting Hector—was unfazed by the onslaught. Still, he could not sidestep a big left hand from Hector thrown with ten seconds remaining in the round.

Clearly bothered by another slicing left in the following round, Montoya actually benefited from facing a slightly unconditioned version of Hector. Exploiting this lack of conditioning, Montoya won the sixth with straight right hands as Hector breathed heavily. Hector countered effectively in the seventh and then sent Montoya to the canvas in the eighth round with a five-punch combination. Rivera came over to administer the count, and Montoya gathered himself at eight. In a fury, Hector pushed Montoya down again, but it was ruled the second knockdown. Hector would hurt Montoya one more time in an exciting round where he dropped him twice and blistered him on two other occasions. Physically spent, Hector did not have the strength or energy to muster that type of beating in the ninth, instead executing a series of left hooks, right hooks, and counters in the tenth. Comfortably ahead, he relied on a sharp jab in the eleventh, but he allowed Montoya to regain his confidence with a series of right hands that had only nicked Hector to that point. That confidence never wavered as Montoya stole the momentum heading into the final round.

Hector's hero, Muhammad Ali, was in attendance, and he maintained a running conversation with Hector at the beginning of the final round. Petering out in the late rounds was not unusual for Hector, but he rarely gave up rounds to a fighter so far removed from his class. Preserving his energy for the second half of the round, Hector still could not avoid a slicing right hand to close out the fight. Winning by a landslide—judges scored the match 120-107, 118-111, and 119-107—Hector exuded praise for his opponent. He was shocked at how motivated Montoya was to fight him.

"He's one of those tough Mexican fighters," said Hector during the post-fight interview. "He came ready. He knew he wasn't going to out-point me, so he knew he could only beat me by knocking me out—and boy he was trying to knock my head off."

Hector added, "My timing was good because my jab faked him out and I took advantage of it, but he was keeping me outside real good and he was trying to leverage me. He fought a great fight; he was so tall I had to reach in, and I kept taking that step back and [tried] to land that uppercut."

Traveling together on the same plane after the fight, Hector invited Montoya to come to party with him at his condominium in New York. Montoya's manager politely declined the offer, but Hector took off the gold "M" necklace from around his neck and gave it to Montoya.

"He told Montoya, 'You fought a great fight. This is something for you to remember this fight,'" said Jerry Villarreal Sr. "Montoya was in awe. That was something he would never forget. No one knew about those things."

After only fighting once in 1984, Hector was now on his third fight of 1985, a good sign for someone who struggled to find clarity away from the ring. Earning a reputation as a fighter who took down the best Mexican boxers in the world, Hector, who had beaten an over-the-hill Limon, was now facing Jose Luis Ramirez (90-5), not far from his prime. More important, in two of the most high-profile fights of his career, Ramirez knocked out a high-powered puncher in Edwin Rosario and outdueled Alexis Arguello, knocking down the Nicaraguan legend during a contro-versial split-decision loss.

Jimmy Montoya had a connection to Ramirez's trainer, Ramon Felix. He was well aware of Ramirez's power and strategized accordingly. Montoya knew how tough Hector was but, as a trainer, he recognized the pitfalls of overconfidence and stressed a couple of fundamental points for Hector to adhere to. "I told him that Ramirez had a punch," said Montoya, "and that we were going to box, stay on our toes, and when Ramirez jabbed, we would double jab. I would also have him slip to his right and throw his left hand."

With Patrick Flannery as a camp assistant (and later hired as a camp coordinator), Hector would be held to high standards, and there would be no deviating from the game plan. Of course, Flannery, a bodybuilder who once had to throw a teenage Hector against a wall to get his attention, did not always have enough firepower to offset his pupil's creative methods of engaging in mischief. (In one bold move, Flannery shipped Hector's beloved Corvette out of town in a crate.) In the hotel in the week prior to the fight, Flannery attempted to keep Hector out of the casino by hiding his clothes. It only worked momentarily.

"He went out stark naked in the hall," Flannery said. "He went all the way up to the elevator before I caught up with him and threw him a pair of pants."

Despite Flannery's inability to dissuade Hector from heading to the casino, he did manage to coordinate a training camp that Hector agreed was the best he had ever experienced. A prepared Macho was a dangerous thing, and he appreciated the discipline just as he appreciated what Flannery, the teacher, had done for him at Manhattan High School when no one else seemed to care. In a different role, Flannery soon established his own rhythm and unique approach, managing logistics, planning meals, and taking care of financial duties. More important, Flannery had to keep an eye on the feisty young fighter during press conferences, where Hector sometimes disrupted the proceedings. Though earning $500,000 for the fight (to Ramirez's $400,000), Hector felt that he deserved at least $1 million paydays. As the well-oiled training camp rounded out, Hector knew that he was capable of a virtuoso performance.

Pure
Perfection

11

Hector was back, and Don King orchestrated the terms between him and Jose Luis Ramirez. King initially secured a June 6 date for the fight to occur on the same card as Michael Spinks and Jim MacDonald at the Riviera Hotel and Casino in Las Vegas. King called the event "D-Day Dynamite." However, at a press conference a month before the fight, Hector announced that he would be bowing out due to an ankle injury he had suffered playing pickup basketball. King, who already had a syndicated TV deal with the Lexington Broadcast System, would later replace Camacho–Ramirez on the card with a cruiserweight bout between Carlos DeLeon and Alonzo Ratliff. Hector's relationship with King, though, had clearly frayed.

"When Macho established uncertainty, it hurt the promotion," said King. "I don't deal with uncertainty. Camacho is much too important for me to challenge for a crown at less than 200 percent. I took Hector off the card because I love Hector."

Less diplomatic, Hector focused on self-preservation and did not hint at any regret about disrupting King's initial plans. "I can't run and in the gym I favor my leg," said Hector. "Who should I think about? Don King and the TV guys and fight this guy on one leg? It's my butt, not Don's hair."

Well aware of his worth and content to play out their personal soap opera through the media, Hector verbally jousted with King and never backed down from his demands. Hector easily separated the animosity he expressed through the media from the business side, however. Before the Ramirez fight, Hector had signed a five-fight deal with King (negotiated with the help of Montoya)—a Lamborghini and the $500,000 purse for Ramirez lured him back.

"Get me a Lamborghini and a bonus!" Hector demanded "[Don] thought it was a Corvette or some $30,000 car. When he found out it cost over $100,000, he started playing with his hair."

In typical fashion, King ended up using Camacho's purse money from the fight to pay for the car.

Able to salvage the original June 6 card at the Riviera Hotel and Casino (and find a replacement for Hector in Manuel Hernandez to fight Ramirez), King then confirmed August 10, 1985, at the same venue for Ramirez vs Camacho. In an article detailing King's difficulty negotiating the Ramirez–Camacho championship bout with HBO, journalist Richard Hoffer referred to Hector as a "spangled street urchin" and as a "135-pound Muhammad Ali."

Hector had arrived at the Riviera Hotel and Casino more than a week before the fight. Not only did he escape Patrick Flannery's grasp to have a little fun, he also was making a noticeable impression on journalists and fans alike with his flashy outfits and outsized personality. Just two days before the fight, Hector was playful as usual, mussing Don King's hair, popping balloons, and mischievously starting fake feuds between rival heavyweights on the same card. The act got *Sports Illustrated* to dub him "the 1980s version of Dennis the Menace." King chose the 5,600-seat SuperStar Center at the Riviera to stage the lightweight title fight, which would be televised on HBO. Ramirez had wrestled the WBC lightweight crown from Edwin Rosario in November 1984 with a fourth-round knockout after recovering from two early knockdowns. With a gaudy record of ninety wins and seventy-four knockouts, Ramirez had boxed since age fourteen and could hit with either hand. But the narrative surrounding the fight revolved not around Ramirez's power but rather Hector's speed.

Even though Hector had experienced some gaps in his career, there was little evidence that he had lost any speed as he moved up from 130 to 135. Although Hector was officially 3-0 at 135 pounds, he had been facing legitimate 135 pounders even before he beat Limon for the super featherweight crown. All along he promised his critics that he would win three titles, and, by abandoning his WBC 130-pound belt, he was well on his way to winning his second.

To prepare for Ramirez, Montoya started the camp in New York and then brought Hector back to his gym in Belle, California. Montoya stressed speed, boxing acumen, and caution. Whenever Hector veered from the strategy, Montoya reeled him back in. Mentally, Montoya had mapped out the blueprint years earlier when he brought Refugio Rojas to face Hector. He knew exactly how his version of Hector would perform for him. On the other hand, the persistent Ramirez came forward and blistered opponents with his straight left. Compared with the growing reputation of his fellow countryman, Julio Cesar Chavez, Ramirez was a hit with the Latino community and knowledgeable boxing fans but considered a nonentity in other pockets of the boxing world. He lacked Chavez's aura, Salvador Sanchez's stamina, and Ruben Olivares's charisma.

Drowned out during the pre-fight leadup by Hector's need to tell everyone in earshot about "Macho Time," Ramirez seemed even more subdued as he entered the ring with lead trainer Ramon Felix the evening of the fight, evoking eloquence and class in his resplendent velvet red robe. HBO broadcasters Barry Tompkins and Larry Merchant attempted to describe Hector's ring attire as he came down the aisle with Montoya. Tompkins took one look at his pointy robe of the Puerto Rican flag and deemed him the "Good Witch of the West." Beneath the extravagant $800 robe was an even more glitzy purple jacket and matching trunks. It was a show, and the people were there to see the entertainer perform. In that regard, Hector did not disappoint.

In Montoya's mind, a respectable win over would Ramirez put Hector in prime position to revisit his original path of greatness, but his fighter needed to look impressive. As much as people talked about Hector's unique style, the outfit and how he wore it made him a striking figure. The comparison with the outrageous act of a professional wrestler may have been apt in some circumstances, but in wrestling, attire usually reflected the wrestler's identity, either good or evil; for Hector, the costume was merely an expression of his tastes. Hector was still that same kid dreaming of jumping off the top rope, wearing an El Santo mask, and landing solidly on his opponent. He heightened fans' expectations with his entrance and then capitalized on that intrigue by dancing and putting on a show.

"He loved outrageous clothes. They were pleasing to his character. That was Macho," said Montoya. "From the very beginning I had his clothes made. I made him the Puerto Rican robe for Ramirez. It was beautiful. Everything that Camacho wore that had sequins was mine. He loved wearing sequins."

Occasionally, Hector would become secretive about his next ring costume. He would sketch it on a pad and then cover it up so Junior could not see. "No one could touch or see his outfits," said Junior. "I remember the only time he got mad at me, he was like, 'Did you fucking touch my outfit?' His style was unique, and it didn't come from anywhere. That was just him."

An 8-to-5 favorite, Hector shimmied and perfectly timed his dance routine to the sounds of "Ain't No Stoppin' Us Now." He looked reenergized and prepared to win his second title. To stay loose, Hector danced for two hours before the fight. Once the fight started, he never stopped. Alternating chants of "Mexico" and "Macho" filled the outdoor arena. Camacho, 134 pounds, and Ramirez, 134.75 pounds, had no issues making weight. Referee Mills Lane looked directly at Hector in the center of the ring, affirming that he would not tolerate anything outside the rules.

"Hector and Jose were friendly," said Montoya. "But there was a sense like *this is what we gotta do*. He told Ramirez to his face, 'I will beat you,' but he didn't do it in a hard way."

Hector looked polished in the first round. As soon as Ramirez set and prepared to punch, Hector skirted away. In the first round, Hector tripled up on his uppercuts and hooks, and they were coming in at a ferocious pace and backing up Ramirez. Hector was fearless. Each time Ramirez punched, Hector responded with one or two counter shots. Emboldened, he even jumped in with running right hands. Finally, he established a pattern of targeting the body early and then moved to the head.

This version of Hector was as aggressive as he had been in two years. His performances against Burke and Montoya had not generated that level of speed and intensity. The Riviera and Vegas brought out the best in Hector. After the first round, Ramirez's corner calmly told him to "take it easy," but Ramirez recognized what was happening. Emphasizing his speed, counter right hook (which landed flush), and straight left, Hector used the second round to build off what he established in the first three minutes. To accentuate the disconnect, Ramirez had only landed a handful of ineffective punches in those first two rounds, a far cry from his usual output.

Between rounds, Montoya told Hector, "You can win this fight easily." The comment spoke volumes when Ramirez picked himself up off the canvas in the third round as Hector chopped him with a wicked straight left. Hector used a short right hand to stabilize Ramirez for the big punch. Getting into a mode where he would dip in and mimic throwing a brief flurry and then pull away, Hector gave Ramirez a host of different looks. Seeing the impact of the straight left, Hector pounced on the wobbly Ramirez but only had to give him a slight nudge as he hit the canvas. Up by the count of five, Ramirez still had to stay away for the remaining 1:54 of the round. Camacho smothered the lightweight champion so aggressively that he almost fell over. Referee Mills Lane inexplicably came in to give a warning during a sequence where neither Hector nor Ramirez needed one. Hector threw his hands up in frustration. A stream of blood exited Ramirez's nose as he returned, disoriented, to his corner. One final left from Hector closed out a perfectly orchestrated round where Hector had made a very good fighter seem pedestrian.

"Camacho came back after the knockdown and said, 'I want to knock this guy out,'" recalled Montoya. "I said, 'Just do what I fucking tell you to do.' I did not want to trade with Ramirez. I told him, 'Keep boxing and move side to side, fake, and then throw your left.' I did not allow him to take chances."

With the blood still consistently streaming in the fourth round, Ramirez walked into a deadly combination where Hector ignited the sequence with a right hook, followed by a straight left, a jab, and one more stinging left hand. The Macho vs. Mexico chant continued in the background as Ramirez's handlers stressed, "Camacho is getting tired." A sharp two-punch combination in the fifth represented a thing of beauty for Hector, as his entire offensive arsenal was on display. But Montoya wanted results without putting Hector in peril.

"Fight your fight. Don't get brave, box this guy," Montoya said. That was precisely what Hector was doing. Having connected on 138 of his

399 punches over the first five rounds, Hector was accurate and productive; Ramirez, who landed 55 of 183 punches, was not.

Pitching a shutout, Hector applied pressure and that staple chopping left hand—which Ramirez could not defend against—at the halfway point of the fight. Ramirez was having more success, but only in small increments.

In the seventh round, Hector continued his boxing clinic by switching up speeds with his jab (three jabs and a right hand) and moving swiftly into Ramirez's power zone and then coming back out. Then, he sidestepped to the right so when he wielded and released his chopping left hook again it came in at an angle. Ramirez had no chance to even reach him. It was masterful. Hector's decision to mix in rangy uppercuts rendered Ramirez's offensive attack nonexistent. He negated any offensive look from Ramirez. Ramirez had only one option: move in headfirst.

Witnessing Hector's performance, Montoya proudly urged him to "keep this guy off balance" between rounds. Only he and Hector noticed a small cut that emerged, so minor that the broadcast team did not pick it up. Montoya wanted to preserve his fighter and may have taken too cautious of an approach when he said, "Don't take any chances!"

Hector did not blink. He just kept moving to his right, made a stutter step, and shifted back to his left. He was reminding Ramirez: "You can't touch me." It no longer mattered if Ramirez landed a piercing blow: it was too late. Hector was too fresh and too quick to allow any significant turn of events to occur.

In the eighth round, Hector stayed inside and ripped an uppercut that forced Ramirez to drop his head. Hector then raked him with a right hook and one more for good measure, as the once dangerous Ramirez offered a weak right hand. Mexican fans must have been sad to see their fighter reduced so definitively. For Camacho fans, it was reassurance that Hector's genius had not diminished from inactivity and drugs. Montoya had stressed over and over that his fighter was clean and, as Hector's purple shorts shimmered in the Vegas sky, there was no longer any doubt. To close out the eighth, he pulled out a short left hook—a new addition to his arsenal—to offset an incoming Ramirez. It was hard to believe that Hector was doing the same things with the same effectiveness as he had been doing in rounds one and two. He looked ahead blankly as Montoya congratulated him before sending him out for the ninth.

"You're doing great," said the trainer; in the other corner, a Ramirez handler swabbed a bloody nose, later confirmed to be broken. For the first time, Ramirez landed punches toward the end of the ninth when he worked behind his jab. But just when Ramirez was gaining confidence, Hector sapped his energy with a straight left hand. A round later, Ramirez landed his best punch of the fight—a straight left hand with forty-five seconds remaining in the tenth round. Trying to follow up, Ramirez stalked in the eleventh in a rough round involving a tackle and clinching. As the crowd got restless, Hector landed one final uppercut and a right hook to close out the fight in a quiet twelfth round. Everything that Hector promised before the fight, with the exception of a sixth-round knockout, he had delivered. As the bell sounded, he put his arm in the air and hit Ramirez's glove. Victory was his by a wide margin—the judges scored the match 118-111, 119-112, and 119-109.

"Hector used defense, knowledge, and speed to beat Ramirez easy," said Puerto Rican journalist Rafael Bracero, who covered the fight. "He proved that Ramirez was not a boxer on his level."

After averaging nearly seventy-three punches a round over the first nine rounds, Hector pulled back to fifty in the championship rounds. In the process, Hector threw three hundred more punches than Ramirez; and although some punch stats are deceiving, these were not. Hector dominated.

"I'm a hard puncher and I proved it," Hector told HBO's Larry Merchant in an interview after the fight. "He's a strong fighter and he proved it. It was a great fight. I thought I would knock him out in the early rounds, but he was in excellent condition and determined."

With his family and cornermen in the background, the Camacho train was raring to go. Hector stressed that he did not want to play himself "cheap" and knew that if he did not get a knockout, he was prepared to fight twelve rounds. Then, Hector released any pent-up frustration that he may have been holding in: "I'm the best fighter pound-for-pound in the world!" he said. "Bring 'em on! Bring 'em on! Mancini, I don't respect your opinion. Come on, baby, so I can knock you out! And Pernell Whitaker, you can get some, baby, you can get some too . . . Bramble . . . Larry Holmes . . . All y'all niggas!"

And one more thing: "Yeeeeaaah Buuudddddy!"

Stand and Deliver

12

After the fight, Hector smoked weed and celebrated in a hotel suite with family and friends. At that point, he could not possibly know how much the racial epithet he threw out in his post-fight interview would follow him over the next couple months.

"I remember going up to the suite and I opened the door to the puff of smoke," said Jerry Villarreal Sr. "I asked Maria why Macho was smoking and she said, 'He needs to calm down.'"

Fighting Ramirez liberated Hector. The Ramirez fight was his masterpiece, his master class of boxing, possibly the finest moment in a career defined by glorious highs and severe lows. It was a way of moving forward and a moment of absolute glory. No one could take it away from him; he was back.

If the comparisons with Sugar Ray Leonard had cooled with controversy and inactivity, his dominance over Ramirez reignited that flame. Surprisingly, Hector and Leonard did not bond over boxing analysis; instead they discussed family life and bantered lightheartedly about who was the better fighter.

"I remember that I was not too happy with myself being retired at the time," said Leonard. "I just saw something in a kid who turned out to be an incredible champion."

But as harsh as the pressures and misfortune that Hector had encountered were, Leonard did not always see him as a victim. "No, I went through a period of darkness myself with drugs and alcohol," said Leonard. "And nine times out of ten, this happens to all inner-city kids. You grow up with nothing and then you become something."

While on vacation less than a month after the fight, Hector received bad news. Having failed a post-fight urine analysis after the Burke fight because of traces of marijuana, Hector received a ninety-day suspension starting August 26, 1985. Thirty-eight other boxers were also suspended, but Hector's suspension, enforced by the New Jersey State Athletic Commission, would not have any significant impact on his future plans since he did not have a fight scheduled during that time. Only a handful of the other boxers' names were made public, and Bob Lee, acting chairman of the New Jersey State Athletic Commission, confirmed Hector's failed test.

The news did not seem to derail Hector and Montoya, who worked well together. Next up was Freddie Roach, "The Choirboy." Before signing a contract to face former lightweight champion Edwin Rosario, Jimmy Montoya wanted Hector to fight a tune-up. But there was also talk about a newcomer on the scene by the name of Julio Cesar Chavez, nicknamed "J. C. Superstar," a super featherweight champ who was making everyone take notice.

Montoya pushed back on a showdown with Chavez, suggesting that Chavez was too inexperienced as both a fighter and a commodity to warrant a superfight with Camacho.

In several interviews, Hector confirmed that he and Chavez agreed that they would fight when the money was right, but there was also a sense that Hector had moved into an elite class by beating Ramirez, whereas Chavez was still developing. In retrospect, Montoya might have miscalculated, especially if he was setting up a big payday with Don King: Hector was in his prime; Chavez was reaching his.

Always focused on money, especially because family members and friends were pressuring him, Hector hounded Montoya about fighting Chavez. "Hector told me, 'We can get rich together,'" Montoya recalled. "I told him, 'If you produce, the money will come.'"

Hector's 135-pound title fight against Jose Luis Ramirez had been the first fight of the five-fight contract Hector had signed with King. But the relationship with King began to deteriorate again because, according to Hector, King could not produce that same $400,000 purse regularly, and instead he offered Hector upward of $250,000 for a title bout with Sergio Zambrano. King's constant need to decrease purses made Hector defensive and threaten to sign with Bob Arum.

"When I signed with Don, it was for five fights for $2 million, with nothing under 400 grand. Now he wants me to fight for 225 grand? I can't do that. I'm too big for that," said Hector. "A week ago I got a check from Don for 10 grand, and I called and said, 'Forget it man.'"

King claimed that the purses dwindled because the networks lowered the price they would pay fighters. Spurning King, Hector opted for a smaller purse and a smaller stage. Instead of defending his title against Zambrano, Hector signed to fight Freddie Roach in a non-televised, nontitle bout held on December 18, 1985. Several Montoya fighters were added to the card. Even though Hector had the contract with King stipulating that the promoter would promote his next three bouts, Montoya, reading the contract, found a loophole and affirmed that he would handle any nontitle ten-round bouts, meaning that he could work directly with his good friend, West Coast promoter Don Chargin, one of the nicest guys in the sport.

So Montoya set up the bout with Roach through Chargin, who did not get along with King but needed a boost financially. By working with Chargin, Montoya could help his friend and keep King out of the proceedings. Additionally, Montoya could get Roach a nice payday. "I wanted to do it for Don [Chargin]," Montoya recalled. "He needed money at that point, and Freddie [Roach] came to me about getting the fight with Camacho."

The fight, which pitted the undefeated Hector against the 39-9 Roach, was held at the Arco Arena in Sacramento. Having separated from former trainer Eddie Futch, Roach was being trained by his father. When it came time to prepare for a fighter as fast as Hector, nothing came easy. "I tried to find guys who were fast," said Roach. "It was all about speed, speed, speed. But when I got to the fight, they all seemed slow compared to Camacho."

The bout wasn't without controversy. In preparation for Roach, Hector had bought a new outfit to mark the occasion. However, by the time Hector got to his dressing room, the trunks were gone, and he was infuriated. Without a brand-new outfit to show off, Hector felt betrayed and looked to Roach's camp for answers.

"He came over and they blamed me," said Roach. "They thought I stole the trunks. I told them, 'No way. If I stole the fucking thing, I would be wearing it right now. So don't worry about that. I didn't steal his clothes.'"

The incident made the newspapers. The mystery was never solved, and before the fight, Hector, whose stolen outfit had been estimated to be worth $2,700, reluctantly wore an ordinary pair of white boxing trunks with "Bronx" stitched into them. Roach recalled the replacement outfit: "[H]e came out in a fancy robe, but he had to borrow somebody's shorts who fought right before us. . . . [They were] white and gold shorts with blood on them. It wasn't quite what Hector Camacho was used to."

Both fighters entered the ring at 137.5 pounds. The fight itself proved one-sided, as Hector's speed overwhelmed Roach's toughness. No one expected Roach to be too competitive against Hector, who was still an elite fighter. Roach was defenseless.

On the downside of his career, Roach had dropped three of his last six bouts. Camacho would be his last big name. "From the beginning, Roach was catching a lot of shots," said Jerry Villarreal Sr.

At one point, Roach felt the brunt of a vicious uppercut, but Roach knew what he was going up against. "I didn't want the referee to stop the fight," Roach recalled. "I told him, 'I'm not hurt. He hasn't hurt me. Let me go one more round.' He tells me, 'No, there's two left.' The card girl goes walking by and I point up to her to show him there's one round left. I was happy that he didn't stop the fight. He couldn't hurt me, but he just outscored me so badly."

Although Roach had trained for Hector's speed, like so many fighters before and after him could attest, nothing would prepare him for how quickly the punches came in. "[Hector's] speed was another level," Roach recalled. "I even bit him at one point, and he stopped and turned to me and said, 'That's not gonna work.'"

Hector went on to win a unanimous decision: 99-90 on two scorecards and 99-89 on the third. For Roach, still standing, pride was all that mattered. "I told the ref that this was going to be on record for the rest of my life," Roach recalled. "I didn't want to be knocked out by anybody. I didn't want to be embarrassed."

Before he left the ring, Roach went over and thanked Hector for giving him the opportunity to fight him. "Roach held his own, but Hector was one of a kind," Montoya recalled. Hector also praised Roach's toughness.

After the Roach fight, Hector and Montoya separated. They would work together again in some capacity, but their relationship would change dramatically over the next couple of months. Hector started to settle down in Clewiston, Florida, while Montoya had too many responsibilities with two other world champions in Los Angeles to switch gears and follow Hector. The relationship between a fighter and trainer is fraught with complexities, and the one between Montoya and Hector was no different. Distance, however, was not the only issue.

"Out of the ring, he was my friend," said Montoya. "He was a happy-go-lucky guy, who gave kids money and was a good human being. He was a guy who used to tell opponents, 'I'll let you hang around for eight rounds, but if you fuck with me I'll take you out in six or seven.'"

Montoya was the third trainer in five years with whom Hector had parted ways. Hector's team members and Montoya cited different causes for the breakup. Montoya noted that he had been upset about the state of Hector's camp, months prior to the June 13, 1986 fight against Edwin Rosario, and decided on his own volition to move on. Conversely, members of Hector's team claimed that Montoya wanted to work with Hector for that fight but that Hector had already made other plans to move forward with another trainer.

"It was very hard," said Montoya, who felt obligated to all of his fighters, most of whom were on the West Coast. "I knew that if [Hector] went back to Florida, he would fall into that same trap. After we left each other, he was never the same."

Indeed, something happened to Hector over the next six months. Still taking drugs despite the ninety-day suspension, and now stuck in a psychological rut and facing financial difficulties, Hector impulsively reached out late one night in January 1986 to a man so far removed from his radar that the initial contact felt like a prank call: Marty Cohen, whom Hector had met in 1983 after a Michael Dokes fight. Cohen, a financial adviser and WBC vice president, had been recognized in the boxing world for his work resuscitating Dokes's career and had developed a reputation for getting fighters out of difficult situations. Possibly looking for guidance, Hector asked Cohen for his business card when they had first met.

Hector's call to Cohen was not a social call, but rather a plea for help. "Hello, who's this?"

"It's the Macho Man. You know, Hector."

"Hector?"

"Yeah, Hector Camacho. I want you to manage me."

"Forget it. I don't manage fighters anymore. I don't want to be your manager."

"You don't want to be the manager of the Macho Man?"

"No."

"Do you want to make a lot of money?"

"I don't want to make a lot of money."

"You're crazy."

"You're crazy."

"Well, then would you give me advice about how to hold on to my money?"

"Well if I can help you, I'd be happy. But don't offer me any money, because I don't accept any monies from anyone, because then I'm in no way obligated and you're in no way obligated to me. Goodbye."

That initial conversation led to a bond between the two completely different characters: Hector, a high-wire Puerto Rican boxer always on the brink of euphoria or a breakdown, and Cohen, a wise older Jewish businessman enjoying his final go-round in boxing. In some ways, both men needed each other, and they grew close. Cohen entered Hector's life when it was fragmented, and Hector needed someone to bring order to the chaos.

Cohen and Hector, "boxing's odd couple," spoke to *New York Times* journalist Phil Berger about the newfound friendship. What Hector did not need was someone else in his life who wanted a free ride, and Cohen emitted a comforting honesty and directness. Soft-spoken and open-minded, he proved the ideal replacement for Giles, who had little financial acumen. Hector listened intently to Cohen's advice about managing money and, using his connections, the eighty-eight-year-old Cohen arranged for Hector to purchase a Fort Apache training base from a friend who had held a summer camp there. Cohen was flabbergasted at the low asking price of $35,000. Idyllic and tucked away behind luscious corn stalks, the old campsite was located a hundred or so miles north of Miami in a quiet fishing village called Clewiston. As much as Hector loved Spanish Harlem, he would finally have the privacy he yearned for.

"He just needed to get away. He needed a new start," said Junior. "Clewiston gave him that privacy."

After assessing Hector's finances, Cohen concluded that the fighter had only saved a small percentage of his earnings. The champion's extravagant needs, impulsive spending, and trusting nature had exacerbated his financial instability.

"I'd have to say [his financial situation] was horrible," Cohen said. "This young man has earned $5 million since the time he turned professional [in 1980]. I found that of the $5 million, all that he had was approximately $200,000, and none of that in cash flow. He had a $110,000 condo in New York and a home he purchased in Puerto Rico for his mother. That was it."

In many ways, Clewiston turned out to be a gem and a curse. Ultimately, Hector got the privacy he needed, but seclusion was not always ideal for a guy who could never slow down. Hector searched for shelter from his mounting personal problems. Over time, he would have his own ring built for training purposes to the left of a garage in front of a blue, plywood barn, which he would adorn with the apt title: "WBC Lightweight Champion of All the World." In his garage he would park his all-terrain vehicles, sports cars, and motorcycles. The makeshift gym would include a punching bag, speed bag, space for jumping rope, and a mirror. His vision for his Clewiston hideaway began to take hold.

"I just want to live out here and do my own thing," Hector said. "I want to shoot my guns, ride my motorbike. Here, I've got peace of mind, and that's the best thing that's happened to me in the past few years."

Cohen joined a circle of support that included Patrick Flannery, Kisha, Jerry Villarreal Jr. and Sr., Junior, Raymond Muhammad (a friend), and a revolving door of trainers, sparring partners, and family members—including Hector's mom Maria and her husband Ruben, Hector's brother Felix, and Cohen's wife Lillian—who would come and stay or work for him.

Purchasing the Clewiston retreat was vital, but Cohen also helped Hector incorporate Macho Camacho Inc. and talked Don King into nailing down future opponents for a lightweight unification series. What really benefited Camacho was Cohen's relationship with King. In the early stages of his own career, King looked to Cohen for guidance. When Cohen came along, King still owned title options from the contract he had signed with Montoya. Hector desperately needed someone to intercede.

In Cohen's mind, for the relationship to work, Hector had to live by two basic tenets: (1) say "no," and (2) send any "schemers" his way. As the relationship progressed, Hector called Cohen his "guardian angel" and developed a strong affinity for him. Cohen did not seek him out, and this was crucial. At eighty-eight, Cohen did not need anything from Hector and seemed genuinely interested in helping him. With Cohen's guidance, Hector exerted more control over his career and at some point decided against naming an actual manager. Cohen did not have any clear agenda and did not request a salary. He only asked Hector to cover his accommodations, and Hector obliged, as he wanted Cohen to feel comfortable amid what felt like a hodgepodge crew of businessmen and Spanish Harlem drug dealers.

Clewiston was just a pit stop for Hector, who professed to be extroverted and reclusive—a social butterfly, but insular. Hector loved being around people, but only if he felt 100 percent in control of the situation and was the center attraction. Maybe he felt that bringing people to him in Clewiston would grant him that level of control.

After beating Roach, Hector experienced a lull—not an especially long one, but lengthy enough to afford him a respite from the sport and its pressures. But it was the second layoff that Hector took in three years. From 1984 to 1985, Hector was inactive for eight months; then, after beating Roach, he stayed out of the ring for another five months. In early 1986, everyone wanted a piece of him: family, journalists, and friends all wanted something, be it time or money. He spent time with Junior and Kisha, who provided a bastion of support.

Everyone loved Kisha and the sense of calm she exuded. She understood what being a boxer meant to Hector and accepted the fact that he was in high demand. As understanding as she was, she had set her sights on law school, which presented a dilemma. Hector wanted to start a family with her eventually, but she was not prepared to give up her dreams to settle down with him. She loved him, but his lifestyle burdened her, as it would have anyone who was searching for balance.

In the summers, Junior was always around. Despite the emotional strife that Hector had experienced in 1985 and early 1986, Junior had always been a beam of light that never faded. Run-ins with the law, drug issues, and family conflict weighed on Hector, but the thought of Junior nearby always soothed him.

"I take him to all my fights," Hector told a reporter from *Inside Sports*. "He loves it. I don't see him as often as I want to, but I'm sure when I'm away he misses me as much as I miss him. I don't know if he understands exactly what I do, my career and all. But he's smart in school. I want him to be good in school, like I wasn't. He means everything to me—I want him to have everything."

Three months after decisioning Roach, Hector signed to fight Edwin Rosario on June 13, 1986, in Madison Square Garden. Young heavyweight Mike Tyson was slated for the undercard. In March of that year, when the fight was signed, Hector and Rosario were only two of many great 135-pounders who graced what was widely considered the deepest division in boxing. Along with Rosario, the number-one challenger, Hector could have picked from a number of formidable challengers: WBA champ Livingstone Bramble, Cornelius Boza-Edwards, Pernell Whitaker, Meldrick Taylor, Greg Haugen, Jose Luis Ramirez, and the IBF champion Jimmy Paul. The only division that compared to the lightweights was the stocked middleweight division that boasted of a champion named Marvelous Marvin Hagler.

Boxing fans were well aware of Edwin "Chapo" Rosario, whose claim to fame was his vaunted power and pressure style. Debuting in March 1979, Rosario had already won ten professional bouts by the time Hector made his professional debut. Conventional wisdom in the boxing field suggested that Rosario was a very good fighter: no one would have debated that notion; however, Hector was a spectacular fighter heading toward legendary status if he stayed the course and remained disciplined. For many fight analysts and boxers, salivating over Hector's skill set was normal, and they still considered him on a path to greatness. In fact, he had not done anything to make the boxing world think otherwise. If an opponent wanted to sit back and box him, Hector either bested him with speed or waited for the opportune time to attack. If a fighter wanted to get inside and brutalize Hector, he first had to get past Hector's veritable force field of jabs, thrown at varying angles and speeds.

In addition, Hector was an entertainer, which was unusual for such a technically brilliant fighter. It was hard to pigeonhole him as a technician; his vast repertoire was more reflective of a stylist capable of attacking at any moment. He knocked out guys with one punch, but he also accumulated stoppages as a result of his speed. Because he loved being in the ring, people loved watching him. Alexis Arguello had respect; Roberto Duran had cachet; Hector Camacho had presence.

"Hector gave you vibrancy, energy, a boyishness, there was an impish quality about him," said boxing journalist Steve Farhood. "All of those were evident in his pro debut. He even had that boyishness when I covered him later on. The bigger the stakes, the better he was." Farhood and his colleagues had seen enough of Hector to see the substance beneath the flash. Those who did not have the same access may have only seen one side of the great fighter.

As brash as Hector was, Rosario was just as reserved and soft spoken. In addition, social class distinguished the fighters. Rosario was educated, while Camacho lacked the grace and maturity to circulate in a similar social class. Hector sized up guys like Rosario as one-dimensional, limited personalities lacking the ammunition to handle an entertainer who had the hype game down to a science.

"Hector was a business mastermind," said Puerto Rican sports journalist Rafael Bracero, "and Rosario was the contrary. He looked at Hector as the enemy, and personally insulted him. Camacho looked at boxing as a business, and when the show finished, it was over."

Puerto Ricans loved Rosario's straightforward attack style, but also thoroughly enjoyed Hector too. Fans traveled from far and wide to see Rosario, the fisherman so steeped in the country's tradition and the culture. As a small-town boy from Toa Baja, Rosario was widely considered more refined. Facing Macho presented Rosario with an opportunity to make amends for the carelessness he displayed in his fourth-round knockout loss to Jose Luis Ramirez, which he suffered on

November 3, 1984. Since then, Rosario had won his last four bouts, three by knockout.

It would have been logical for Hector to keep Jimmy Montoya at the helm as he faced Rosario. Montoya only needed to re-create that same magic that brilliantly guided Hector past Ramirez. Yet Hector may have viewed Montoya as dispensable, and Cohen may have persuaded Hector that paying Montoya to do something that he could master on his own was wasteful. Montoya, based out of Los Angeles, tried to persuade Hector to train there, but Hector had other plans and wanted to stay in Clewiston for camp to be close to his family and friends.

Eventually, the trainers made a most unconventional switch, one rarely seen in championship bouts: Hector would train with Puerto Rican ex-fighter and trainer Felix Pagan Pintor, who had previously trained Rosario, in Clewiston, Florida, while Montoya, without Hector's knowledge, would join the Rosario team in the month preceding the bout.

Before making a final decision, Montoya had gone to Clewiston to monitor Hector's progress at the training camp, and he did not like the lack of discipline he saw. What rankled him most was the reality that he no longer would be running the camp or reclaim the title as No. 1 trainer.

It was unclear what sparked Hector's change in mindset, but either he wanted more autonomy to call the shots, which he did not have with Montoya, or he felt that he could work with the nucleus already established in Clewiston.

There were few subtleties when it came to Montoya. It was hard to compare him to the ultra-strict Mexican trainers, but Montoya liked things done his way. And he balanced that intensity with a soft, affectionate side, allowing himself to joke around with his fighters. What he witnessed in Clewiston was unacceptable. His voice and instructions were diluted by Pintor, a trainer for whom he had little respect. The only advantage retired professional Pintor possessed over Montoya was ring experience. Pintor had been close with Rosario and his family since the early days. Pintor knew the little nuances surrounding Rosario and what mentality he might adopt come fight time, but he was not recognized as a topflight trainer yet.

To this day, Montoya bristles at the thought not only of the conditions of the ring and training camp in Clewiston, but also the lack of respect. "Pintor did not know shit," said Montoya. "They were training at 11 p.m., eating at night. I left camp." The other problem was that Pintor was the No. 1 cornerman," Montoya recalled. "I was his second. It couldn't be that way. I had to be the main voice. Macho was listening to both of us. It wasn't that Camacho wasn't listening to me, but Pintor bullshitted him that he knew how to beat Rosario." He added: "I was pissed off at Pintor being the head trainer. I knew what I had. I had the perfect fighter."

Even though the state of the Clewiston camp angered Montoya, other unspoken tensions emerged when Montoya's underling Rudy Mata left Montoya to go work with Hector. Later, Hector admitted to a journalist that "[Jimmy and I] never did break up. I just didn't hire him for that fight."

Hector rarely spoke about Montoya's ability to get him in an ideal condition and mindset. In Hector's most brilliant performance, against Ramirez, Montoya had built the perfect strategy. Not wanting Hector, as talented as he was, to freelance or stray from the game plan, Montoya advised Macho to stay cautious—not because he did not trust his fighter, but because he knew that Ramirez could hurt his opponent at any point in a fight.

Hector would adopt a different mindset against Rosario. He would have to. He could still double up on that jab and move away to his right and then to his left at his heart's content, but he would have to be more offensive to offset Rosario's pressure.

Before joining the training camp, Pintor—who had a falling out with the Rosario team, specifically lead trainer Manny Siaca, who had a falling out with the Rosario team, and was forced out of the camp—received a phone call.

"Hello, Pintor, do you know who this is?"

"No."

"I'm Macho. Hector Camacho, Macho Camacho."

"What the hell!"

"No, this is Macho Camacho. You're going to train me to beat Rosario. I know they kicked you out of the camp. I can make you a big name."

Was this a joke? "I couldn't believe it," said Pintor. "I did not believe that Macho Camacho was calling me to train him to fight Rosario, but it was true. I told him, 'Be honest.' Rosario was like my son, but I had to leave. If this was for real, I would go talk to Rosario's father and mother."

Pintor wondered what he had accomplished to that point to be sought out by the world's top fighter to face his country's most beloved one. No one was closer to Rosario than Pintor had been, so the intimacy factor may have been tantalizing for Hector. What made it more surprising was that Pintor had worked with Rosario since his amateur days. Manny Siaca was Rosario's lead trainer, whereas Pintor was relegated to the background. True to his word, Pintor went back to the Rosario family to discuss his options. Even though Hector had promised big money to train him, Pintor needed to see where the Rosarios stood on the matter. Only then would he make his decision. To this day, their assurances paid dividends.

"When I went to see Rosario, he was not there," said Pintor, "so I ended up talking to his parents. I told them about Camacho's proposal. They listened and soon gave me their blessing. They knew boxing was a business. But it meant a lot to me. 'Don't worry about those guys,' they told me. 'Make your own name. I know Edwin is like your son. Don't worry about that. Edwin's fighting Camacho, you go and do your job.'"

Hector and Pintor quickly developed a rapport despite their short time together. Knowing full well that this single opportunity could enhance his training resume, Pintor did everything he could to fulfill Macho's expectations. Sometimes he had to go beyond the call of duty. When Maria lamented about her son's refusal to eat healthily before a fight, Pintor put on his chef's hat. Even though Pintor harbored regret about working opposite a fighter whom he cared deeply for, he still enjoyed every moment with Hector.

"Everything I asked him to do, he did," Pintor recalled. "He was one of the best fighters I have ever seen. He trained completely, no games. He ate everything I made too."

Along with monitoring Hector's weight, Pintor wanted to provide him with a unique lens through which to study Rosario. Who better than a former sparring partner and trainer? Only time would tell how impactful Pintor's approach was.

"I knew everything about Rosario from being his sparring partner," Pintor recalled. "He was a helluva puncher. I knew Rosario, so I kept Macho moving. He was in good condition. We even went to the forest. I gave him an ax to chop down trees. He liked to cut. I would say to people, 'Camacho doesn't like to work? He did when he came to work with me. He's crazy, but when he has a job to do, he did it well.'"

Pintor's decision to motivate the lumberjack in Hector resurfaced when the fighter joked for the cameras by slamming the ax into the tree and saying: "This is what I'm going to do to Rosario."

The lines had been drawn.

Popular sports journalist Rafael Bracero traveled to Clewiston before the fight to interview Hector for a documentary. Taken aback by his welcoming personality, Bracero got intimate enough with Hector for him to admit his drug use, which was still a source of concern.

"He told me he was using marijuana since a young age," said Bracero, "and that he was accustomed to it. I told him that it could hurt his relation with the people. But he told me that he was born into an environment that was very different, that he had to deal with that from 'scratch' and a lot of people his age were doing it. It was a custom of the habitat."

Deep down, Hector felt that he would have to go to great lengths to enrage Rosario. In Manhattan to announce the fight, Hector made the rounds and explained at length how he was the "Puerto Rican Michael Jackson." He sat alongside Marty Cohen, who expressed his gratitude for working with such a devoted fighter.

"I checked him out completely," Cohen said, "and I'm sure this kid is clean. If I didn't think so, I wouldn't have anything to do with him."

Macho needed Cohen desperately at that stage but thought he could thrive without Montoya. If he had not been facing a vicious stalking puncher like Rosario, then maybe Pintor would have been enough to replace Montoya. However, Hector needed a taskmaster, and Pintor did not have the experience nor the relationship with him to take any authoritative stance. Even though Pintor stressed how respectful Hector was, there were rumblings of a less-than-tightly-run training camp, and that only Hector made the key decisions.

As the controversy surrounding the camps began to swirl, another relationship began to reemerge. Like many Latin fighters in the 1970s and 1980s, Don King was always on call. It did not matter that King was the same guy who had told Hector he "owned" him; King had contacts that no one else did. So with Cohen emerging and King reentering the picture, Hector felt comfortable with the team that he had cobbled together. Hector held a press conference in part to clear up any misconceptions about his relationship with King.

"Everything you heard about me leaving Don is bull," said Hector. "With Don, everything is first-class. I'm here to stay."

By all accounts, Hector never badmouthed King behind his back. He confirmed that they had mended their relationship and looked forward to the big showdown. "It's been four years since I fought in New York," Hector said. "We're going to turn this city upside down."

The fight itself was set for June 13 on boxing's biggest stage, Madison Square Garden. Camacho wanted desperately to dictate the pace of the pre-fight hype. After a hostile meeting with Hector at a bar in Puerto Rico, Rosario recognized that Hector lived by a much different set of guidelines. Rosario did not take the bait.

"Camacho came in with smiley eyes and happy," said Rosario. "He had to be drunk. He was arguing with drunks and old people. That's something I would never do, stand on a corner and argue with drunks. I'm a gentleman. I was going to invite him to my friend's seafood restaurant, but I noticed he was a low-class person."

Rosario's suggestion that Hector was low-class was aimed at his own target audience, *his* Puerto Rican people. While Hector resorted to childish pranks, Rosario maintained his cool. Hector responded with insults in English, which Rosario, who spoke only Spanish, was not equipped to handle. But for the first time, Hector, even on his own turf, witnessed firsthand how native Puerto Ricans saw him as an outsider. Hector had seen the animosity that Rafael Solis spewed in their earlier fight, but that rivalry did not carry the same panache as Camacho vs. Rosario did. Having gone to Puerto Rico to promote the bout, Hector realized he was engaged in something closer to a superfight, facing an iconic Puerto Rican figure in Rosario, who was a great fighter compared with Solis.

This realization and the perception that he wasn't a true Puerto Rican once again hurt the already fragile Hector deeply. In his mind, he was just as Puerto Rican as anyone else. Ebullient and free-spirited, Hector represented a different breed of fighter who flaunted his clothes, freely shared his opinions, and tried desperately to enliven any event with his vivacious nature. *What time is it? Macho Time. Yeah Buddy!* Because Hector was so good in the ring, people overlooked his childishness and immaturity; much of the time the act was fun and worked wonders for boxing promotions. Hector knew how to play the game, unlike some fighters. The theory that he was *only* a street boy pissed him off, but the notion that he did not belong in the same category with Puerto Rican fighters because he was not of the same fabric was demeaning and hurtful, an offense that Hector could not brush off. *Sure, I spent most of my life in New York, but that doesn't mean I'm not as Puerto Rican as anyone else, does it?* When his people started to invalidate him as a Puerto Rican, the insults felt like harsh excoriations. He had no problem with people disliking him, but Puerto Rican fans were crueler, and Hector could only try to refute their attacks by expressing his frustrations through the media.

After winning the vacant WBA lightweight crown from Ramirez in May 1983, and then defending it twice against Roberto Elizondo and Howard Davis Jr., Rosario only celebrated briefly with his new belt before Ramirez knocked him out in the fourth round of his third defense. Rosario blamed the loss on poor conditioning and hand problems.

Now Rosario would share center stage with another great young 130-pounder in Culiacan's Julio Cesar Chavez, who would defend his title against Refugio Rojas that evening, while Mike Tyson faced Reggie Gross. Although Rosario—and Chavez—were growing, Hector, or the Harlem Heckler as he was recognized early on, was the draw.

With Montoya gone and the savvy Cohen at the helm, Camacho was guaranteed $400,000 for the Rosario fight and 40 percent of the television and live-gate receipts. In other reports, Cohen had negotiated a $100,000 signing bonus. Experiencing a clear uptick in his purse and order in his financial situation, Hector valued Cohen. More important, he had already signed on to face Cornelius Boza-Edwards for the same amount, provided he beat Rosario. Cohen had definitively brought a level of stability to

Hector's life. He had also stabilized the link to King, which ensured—win or lose—that Hector would stay put in the more lucrative lightweight division. Having made his way into Hector's inner circle, Cohen was there to stay.

★ ★ ★

Five years earlier, on August 21, 1981, fans waited patiently for the superfight between featherweight legends Wilfredo Gomez and Salvador Sanchez to occur. Instead, what they got was a one-sided beating that belied the odds or the competitive nature of both combatants. That fight featured the wonderfully creative and sublimely conditioned Sanchez against a brilliant mover and puncher in Gomez. Most people gave Sanchez credit for not letting a competitive chess match ensue because he was so mentally and physically prepared. The truth was that Gomez had become so enamored with the limelight that he treated the matchup as a tune-up and not a championship, and he paid dearly. At no point was Gomez actually in the fight. For the wonderful Puerto Rican fighter, the rude awakening started early and never got easier as he got knocked down in the first round and never recovered. Sanchez's beating stayed with him for decades, and the great Mexican champion passed away in 1982 before a possible rematch could occur.

It is not fair to say that Rosario replaced Gomez and that Hector replaced Sanchez, but the situation was eerily similar. "They were different styles—Edwin and Hector," said Pintor. "Edwin was a puncher. Hector had good power, but not the same power. He had skills, and skills beats power."

Outside the ring, it was also a war of diverging styles. As the fight neared, Hector made what could have been his biggest miscalculation. Hurling a napkin at Rosario during a press conference was child's play, but sending a pair of lacy red panties to Rosario's hotel room as a gift in a box addressed from the Governor of Puerto Rico, Rafael Hernandez Colon, ventured into uncharted territories. Hector gave a kid off the streets $20 to deliver the gift, stay to observe Rosario's reaction, and then report back to him. Later, in rare form, Hector wistfully regretted the decision.

In Rosario's mind, there was hell to pay.

Rosario did not shy away from perpetuating the story line, and Hector, as usual, never shied away from confrontation.

"I am the natural Puerto Rican, not him," Rosario said. "The people are behind me."

Meanwhile, just hours before the June 13 showdown, Jerry Villarreal Sr. went over to Rosario's dressing room to watch his trainer wrap the gloves. "I get in there, and I'm like, 'What the hell?'" said Jerry Sr. "Here's Montoya working Rosario's corner!"

Jerry Sr. went back to Hector's dressing room to break the news to Hector, knowing that if he waited until fight time, the revelation would be too emotional.

"Hector, you're going to like this one," said Jerry Sr.

"What?" asked Hector.

"Your boy Jimmy Montoya is next door with Chapo."

Although Hector was not one to show how emotionally invested he was in a trainer, this move by Montoya hurt him. "He went crazy, absolutely crazy," said Jerry Sr. "To the point where we couldn't get him in a rhythm before the fight. We couldn't calm him down. It took him out of his zone. It wasn't so much that Montoya could give Rosario an edge. It was a mental thing. It really messed with his head."

Whether Montoya really wanted to hurt Hector—which he later said was not his intent—his actions left Hector conflicted as he entered the ring. Another friend had betrayed him, and Hector could not control himself. The timing was awful, and the shock created both anxiety and resentment. This combined with a less-than-stellar training camp left Hector at a severe disadvantage when he appeared in the ring with his entourage.

Even though there was history between Rosario and Montoya, there was no discernible bond between the two men. "I knew Rosario because I used to get all of his opponents," said Montoya. "I made all of his clothing. I always dressed him. I helped with his training. I was with Rosario a week before the fight. I never told him to fight a certain way. I didn't want to get Camacho hurt. They used me to psychologically screw Camacho."

The gambit paid off, as Hector was out of sorts. When he first worked with Montoya, Hector compared their connection to "Batman calling Commissioner Gordon" from his Machomobile. How times had changed.

★ ★ ★

On June 13, thousands of Puerto Ricans stormed Madison Square Garden for the fight. Billed "Friday the 13th: The Resurrection," the fight was televised on HBO. Hector was 28-0 with fourteen knockouts and was making the first defense of his WBC lightweight title, whereas Rosario, who trained in Albany, New York, and earned $150,000 for the fight, had twenty-three victories in twenty-four fights with nineteen knockouts. Broadcasters Barry Tompkins, Larry Merchant, and Sugar Ray Leonard called the fight. Leonard, especially, heaped praise on Hector. Coming in at 135 pounds, a bulked-up Macho came in one pound heavier than Rosario.

Managed by Jim Jacobs and Bill Cayton, Rosario looked primed and ready for the showdown that, according to him, Hector had avoided for two years. When entering the ring, Rosario appeared confident, spurred on by Montoya and the rest of his team. Montoya led the charge before the fight:

"What time is it?"

"Chapo Time!"

"What time is it?"

"Chapo Time!"

Hector had not yet entered the ring, so he was out of earshot. Still, it must have been odd to see a man who most people associated with Hector for so long turn around and utter the revised catch phrase.

But it was business.

After a memorable ring walk down the aisle flanked by his mother, Marty Cohen, Ruben, and Junior leading the way holding a toy torch, Hector stepped aside to let his son mimic his characteristic flurry. It was a moment that Junior would never forget. He looked up into the stands and thought for the first time, *I want to be my father.* Recognizing that this was the biggest fight of his entire career and on his home turf, Hector entered the ring in style. He had paid $8,000 for his glittering robe, which he unveiled in front of more than ten thousand fans. Hector had started his career at the Felt Forum, but it had been four years since he last fought at the Garden. This time, he was headlining.

Hector opened the fight by—surprise—going to the body with a left hook. Rosario beat him to the punch but got baited into a more dangerous predicament when Hector pulled his head down with his right glove and nailed Rosario with a straight left, while Rosario instinctively pulled his head up.

Bang. Check one off for the Macho Man. With twenty seconds remaining in the first round, Hector, content to move laterally from right to left to right, jammed a straight left hand between Rosario's high guard after coaxing him to get within range. Visually, the punch shot back Rosario's head, but Hector's body work dictated the pace of the round. In between the first and second round, Pintor implored Hector to "move, move all the time. Get the body now; he's already hurt."

It was not unheard of for Hector to showcase his diverse array of skills over twelve rounds and limit his opponent to being a one-dimensional fighter. He blended movement, right and left hooks to the body, a consistent jab, and a straight left. But he did not evoke that same level of confidence and spirit in round two as Rosario inched his way inside, landing single shots. When Rosario landed the first significant right hand, it arrived as a right cross. Rosario threw it with speed and power, and the combination alarmed the usually composed Hector, who felt uncomfortable trying to escape Rosario's pressure, especially when that pressure left him vulnerable against the ropes.

Jose Luis Ramirez was also a pressure fighter, but he did not possess the foot movement to trap Hector or cut off the ring. Rosario did, and in that second round, Hector had to reset after being hit by right hands on two or three different occasions. Before the fight, Rosario had promised that he would re-break his hand "on top of [Hector]." Most fighters never got the opportunity to fulfill their pre-fight promises, but, in the second round, Rosario started to see the openings. Still not reaching his ideal output of landed right hands, Rosario watched as the slick Hector topped off a nice combination with a straight left and then possibly stole the round with four consecutive jabs followed by a second straight left. Hector's decision to ramp-up his offensive intensity late in the round may have been a game-changer. Meanwhile, before the third round, Rosario listened intently as his trainers urged him to throw "both hands," advice that Rosario took to heart.

Their movements were based on a style similar to a choreographed dance: wherever Hector went, Rosario shuffled with him. Rosario shoved Hector into a psychological corner where breaks were not allowed. But for Hector, the most devastating part was that if he did take a break—a few seconds or more—he risked getting hurt. Those realities made him uneasy. During his first twenty-nine fights, Hector set the guidelines that fighters adhered to. Against Rosario, he set some, but Rosario did too. And it did not help that Villarreal and the other cornermen could not get Hector to let go of the perceived betrayal by Montoya. "I had to tell Macho, 'Fuck Jimmy [Montoya],' He's trying to antagonize you," recalled Jerry Villarreal Sr.

Right hands rained down on Hector in the first thirty seconds of the third round. Since Rosario released them from such a high point, he did not have to go through any particular motion: each one formed directly from his guard. Even the quickest fighter in the world did not have much time to react. More important, the punches never arrived in a straight line; they were always crossing Hector's guard, which presented another problem from the southpaw's point of view. Hector moved away from Rosario's right hand, but still showed he was susceptible to those straight rights and the crosses. Before the midway point of the round, Hector traded his straight left and took a counter right in return. He did not want to trade with Rosario, but at this point, had no choice. The Hector who fought Ramirez would not have allowed an opponent to get so close, but this Hector was less fluid with his foot movement and put himself in peril.

Hector for some reason was not quick on his feet. Taking advantage, Rosario landed one right hand after another throughout the round. Whether he was trading with Hector or backing him against the ropes, Rosario was winning individual battles. He learned from these three minutes what he was capable of, and that set the tone for the next two rounds. As he walked back to his corner, Hector's body language revealed as much. He had swept the first three rounds on all three judges' scorecards, but after the third, things began to change, and a different attitude emerged in Rosario's corner when his trainer said, "He's ours. We're winning."

Lashing out to start the fourth, Hector landed a left hook followed by a right hook to the body. The same pattern, however, persisted from the previous round: Rosario chased; Hector retreated. Referee Arthur Mercante, determined not to let illegal tactics interfere in the fight, aggressively scolded Hector on two occasions. Then Rosario took the initiative. Hook to the body. Straight right, left hook. These punches all led to one of the most influential shots of the fight—Rosario's right hand with forty seconds remaining in the round. Immediately after the punch, Hector started to paw at a cut above his left eye—having never been cut before, he reacted wildly. Seeing the blood and sensing something amiss, Rosario punctuated the round with one more right hand for good measure with twelve seconds remaining. Arms down and despondent, Hector readied himself for what was to come. Pintor's only advice was "Stay away from those right hands." Moving to his right, away from Rosario's power, was obvious, but there seemed to be a lack of communication or cohesion in Hector's corner, whether that lack of direction was a by-product of hiring a new head trainer for the first time or of Hector's need to run the show was unclear.

Then in the fifth, something occurred that many experts point to as the climactic moment in Macho's career. Everyone in attendance recognized what was happening. Still aware of the cut eye, a pawing Hector looked concerned. In his mind, attacking early was vital, but Rosario just walked through his straight left. Unacknowledged by the analysts was a short left hook that Rosario used to stabilize Hector, who eventually moved away rapidly to his left. As Hector stood with his back to the ropes, Rosario threw a soft right hand. In return, Hector threw a left hook but did not pull it back in time to block an incoming punch. Conscious of this flaw in the midst of battle, Rosario shattered Hector and spun his head with a left hook to the neck that caused him to catch himself as he stumbled toward the canvas. Either shocked or instinctively avoiding a counter, Rosario quickly jumped back and observed the damage. Calculating, Rosario pounced on Hector again to land a right and left hook (and missed on an uppercut) as the hurt fighter covered up. In typical fashion, Hector tried to corral Rosario by clutching his arms, but having clearly prepared for the clinching, Rosario slithered away, thus making the tactic completely useless.

Slipping away for the time being, Hector moved to his left. All of his fears were exposed as he instinctively knew that two minutes still remained in the round. How would he survive against a killer hell-bent on revenge? Trying to stay composed, but tasting his own blood, he understood that getting trapped against the ropes meant the end for him, so he tried to escape to open spaces. In that open space, Rosario released and missed a knockout uppercut but followed it up with a jolting right hand that jammed Hector's head back. Losing his bearings, Hector completely dropped his guard and retreated, leaving himself open for another right hand. The ring had always been a safe haven for comfort from the repercussions of how Hector lived his life outside the ring, but Rosario changed all of that with one punch.

Struggling, Hector refocused through combat. Rosario was the first fighter in his career who expressed—through violent measures—that it did not matter who he was in the ring. What mattered was how he would survive against a more destructive force. And as Hector continued to shuffle around the ring without throwing anything in return, he must have thought about who he was and if he wanted to be in the ring anymore. Scoring with two right hands and a left over top allowed Rosario to manage the pace as he continued to stalk his prey. With 1:15 left in the round, Hector had just weathered one more right hand and decided he had to fight back. Summoning the Macho from Spanish Harlem, he threw a straight left that signaled that he still had fight left in him. But Rosario quickly stripped him of that bravado with a left hook and straight right that left him reeling across the ring. Soon Hector, who had just experienced the worst round of his career, started walking to the wrong corner.

"When the fight started, the fans were chanting for Hector," said Jerry Villarreal Jr. "But as the fight went on, the fans turned on Hector and they were all for Rosario. We had a bunch of people from California who liked Hector who came to the fight. Everyone who had a Hector Camacho T-shirt on, the Rosario camp was beating them up."

A doctor put an arm around him to guide him back to the corner. In a moment of defiance, clearly in crisis mode, Hector tried to push him away. Surrounded by officials looking to assess his well-being, cutman Don Thibodeaux stepped in and discouraged them from stopping the fight.

"You ok, Hector?" they asked.

"Yea, he's alright," Thibodeaux confirmed.

According to Jerry Villarreal Sr., Thibodeaux was like a "horse doctor" and was able to stem the cut by "getting a finger full of the shit" that he had mixed, shielding the camera from his little manipulation, getting the vital coagulant on the eye, and applying pressure.

"He stopped that cut like it was never there, pure magic," said Jerry Sr. "That could have been a big factor since it was his first cut and Hector was panicking. I told Camacho, 'Quit your whining. You cut yourself worse when you were shaving. We got the cut under control.' He never mentioned it again, because it never ran down his face anymore."

For Hector, not only the cut but the level of adversity he faced was foreign to him.

"He was dancing, but not because he wanted to," said Jerry Sr. "Hector, being who he was, hung in there and came back out in the next round, and didn't do too much punching because he was still hurt."

Pintor tried to downplay the moment by stressing that Rosario was tired and that Hector had to box more. But the damage was evident as Thibodeaux pressed on Hector's eye; Hector's strained look reflected his deepest fears.

"I remember looking up at the jumbo screen, and every time I looked, Rosario was landing or my dad was moving," said Junior. "Everything was happening so fast."

Feeling more alone and unstable than ever before, Hector revealed his response in the first minute of the sixth. Rosario shuffled, kept his guard up, and fought with purpose. Hector moved to his right, pushed a sharp jab, and avoided brawling. Renewed but not restored, Hector landed body shots and brushed off Mercante's warnings against low blows. Signaling his comeback, Hector raised a right hand as he went back to the corner. Going into the seventh round, Rosario had landed 41 percent of his punches, but his corner still urged him to throw more combinations and to "be smart . . . he's hurt."

Hector burst out of the seventh and struck first, but he could not sustain that same energy throughout the entire round. No one could. A lethal combination of Rosario's resolve and Hector's exhaustive movement left the champion doused physically—and mentally. During his fight with Ramirez, Hector had had the luxury of working against a plodding fighter who could not accelerate to another gear. But Rosario's conditioning, percussive movement, and awkward punching style (he kept his guard in a position to always be able to punch) forced Hector to stay in harm's way, whereas against Ramirez or another slower mover, he would easily shift his weight and disappear. Or he would actually turn his back and walk away, glaring at his opponent so as not to lose sight of him. Regaining some confidence, Hector stopped Rosario's forward movement with a perfectly landed left hook. The punch reflected one of the few times that Rosario actually reconsidered wading in to attack. Halfway through the seventh round, Hector posited a left to the body, followed by a straight right, and closed out the flurry with a hook over Rosario's guard. Aggressively seeking the body, and actively taking the lead, Hector connected more than previous rounds, but he also allowed Rosario to land that right hand more as the round ended. Much to Rosario's chagrin, Hector still believed he could catch him and close out the show.

With only five rounds remaining, Rosario pulled out his uppercut in the eighth, which he landed cleanly on two occasions, but it was the ninth that got everyone's attention. Most would later agree that this fight caused Hector to rethink his fight strategy, but, if anything, his performance in the ninth round evoked a moment of passion and bravery. As Rosario dipped his head to the left, Hector timed him with a straight left, his best punch of the fight. Then, like a cobra unfurling, Hector scored on three punches and, out of necessity, Rosario tied him up. Rosario, reputed to have a weak chin, appeared hurt and started moving backward as Hector shuffled after him in ambush mode. But Hector was not finished as he sent Rosario, flustered and unstable, back to his corner with a right uppercut.

Yet Hector could not finish Rosario; when he had the opportunity, he tried too hard to force the action. Few fights were defined by such momentous shifts. It was unusual for two great fighters like Hector and Rosario to create such an interesting ebb and flow.

After a nondescript tenth round, Thibodeaux, who took over for Pintor as the main corner voice, made it clear that Hector had no choice, "Need next two rounds big kid. You need 'em. I'm telling you, you have to have them." Hector stared blankly ahead as Pintor tried to implore him to "punch with him against the ropes." Then he addressed him one more time: "You win these two rounds! You hear me champ." With seconds left, Thibodeaux made one final plea: "Go all out. Five- and six-point combinations. OK, baby?"

In the other corner, Rosario's cornermen relied on a completely different narrative: "Now we have to work a little bit. Use the hook and then the right. We have to knock him out." Whatever happened over the next two rounds was moot in the sense that both men—after ridiculing each other as uneducated and cowardly—had earned each other's respect. Those who to this day stand in Rosario's corner discuss the eleventh round as evidence of a definitive Rosario victory. As Rosario slammed one final left hook to Hector's neck and then capitalized again with forty seconds remaining in the round with a right hand that stunned Macho again, the harsh effects drained Camacho fans. Junior closed his eyes to the abuse. To the Rosario loyalists, the left hook confirmed what they already knew about *their* fighter. *Their* fighter had not only been the aggressor, but also landed the bigger punches.

From his fans' perspective, Hector had started off strong, weathered some huge right hands and hooks, and showed heart and composure by winning some of the middle rounds. Some of the punches landed would have knocked out most opponents, but Hector and Rosario were both from a different class of fighter. The puncher vs. the stylist story line had not changed. Neither fighter could afford to lose the final round, and when Rosario took the lead at the start of the round, it seemed like whoever made headway should be declared the winner.

"I told him, 'Hector, listen, you've got guts. But don't get too close. If he gets you, he gets you, but don't get too close to him,'" said Pintor.

Rosario emerged early with a right hand, slight uppercut, and another right hand. Returning fire, Hector landed an uppercut and two hooks. But after trading during a hard round to judge, neither fighter had imposed his will on the other. If anything, Rosario, still the aggressor, may have landed a couple more punches. When the bell closed out the fight, Hector, no longer the vivacious showman, just walked away; Rosario put his gloves up and hit Hector's, and then was hoisted on handlers' shoulders. It was not a Macho reaction to the end of a fight, but he was exasperated by what the man in front of him had forced him to do.

"He had nothing for the twelfth," said Jerry Villarreal Sr. "He just started to hang on. We told him, 'big finish,' and to 'dig deep,' but he was hurt. There was not much strength left and he was still fatigued from the eleventh. Chapo was no joke."

The punch count revealed an accurate account of the fight: Hector threw more punches (825) and landed only 24 percent of them. Conversely, Rosario was more judicious with his punches (490 total), but landed 35 percent. Yet the fans reacted harshly when Hector was awarded a split decision: Tony Castellano and Stewart Kirshenbaum both awarded the fight to Hector (115-113) and Luis Rivera scored it 114-113 for Rosario. More telling was that only six of thirty-one journalists polled had Hector winning the fight.

The scoring left a lot to be desired. Castellano and Kirshenbaum gave Hector rounds six through ten. Rivera gave him all those rounds except the seventh, which he scored as even. Neither Castellano nor Kirshenbaum awarded Rosario a 10-8 round in the fifth or eleventh round; Rivera scored them both 10-8.

While fans became irate, Hector calmly responded to Larry Merchant's questions in a post-fight interview. "It was the most I ever got hit," said Hector. "It was a close fight and I admit it. But I was the more skillful fighter and I proved it." Later he added, "That guy was hammering me with things I never got hammered with." When asked about what he was thinking the moment that the cut formed on his eye, Hector said, "Hell yeah this is a fight."

The difficulty of the fight shocked Hector, reflecting how good Rosario was and how focused he was during training camp. Rosario, through a translator, echoed fans' sentiment when he said, "I beat him all the way." Later, in the dressing room, Hector shifted gears and berated journalists in the press room for being critical of him.

Hector lost something that night, but not in the same way that Robert Duran lost something in the rematch with Sugar Ray Leonard or Alexis Arguello lost something valuable in his first fight with Aaron Pryor. This was different. Hector's air of invincibility, which he had relied on, was gone; Rosario took it, forcefully. What bothered his loyal fans was that Hector fought to near perfection against Ramirez and had to rely on a survival mode against Rosario to squeak out a victory. Those contradictions infuriated those who expected Macho at his best. Hector had to decide either to devote his life completely to a sport he loved and abandon all his vices in order to maintain his greatness, or to continue down a path where he could dabble in both worlds and still be very good, but not elite. The decision to change his style was merely a by-product of that primary choice. In order to stay relevant in boxing and still enjoy his reckless lifestyle, Hector felt that he had to prioritize defensive over offensive tactics. He preserved himself by fighting only occasionally and becoming primarily a stick-and-move fighter and integrating more offense only when his opponent appeared vulnerable.

"I told him from the beginning to avoid those hard shots," Pintor stressed. "Then there was that one shot in the fifth round. I had to keep him moving. He had good preparation going into the fight . . . and that helped him recuperate. He got cut, but Hector was intelligent in the ring and he knew what he was doing."

Macho weathered the storm, but the damage was done.

For Hector, it must have seemed like forever since Junior was sparring in the middle of the ring at the start of the fight. *Look how cute he is.* Nothing was cute anymore as Kisha compared Hector's face to a Cabbage Patch doll.

As Jerry Sr. and Hector tried to sneak out of the building to escape the melee, Hector encountered an unpleasant reality: A score of disgruntled Rosario fans were right there waiting for him. They hatched up every insult they could. Villarreal and the team feared the worst. All Hector could do was fight back and colorfully repeat how he beat Rosario's ass.

"Hector didn't give a shit who it was," said Jerry Sr., who was getting jabbed in the back by the Puerto Rican fans as they walked away. "He always spoke his piece. He was too tough."

After the fight ended, a new jingle rang out.

"What time is it?"

"Time to go to bed."

Hector scores an early knockdown versus Cornelius Boza-Edwards during their fight in Miami Beach on September 26, 1986. *The Ring/Getty Images*

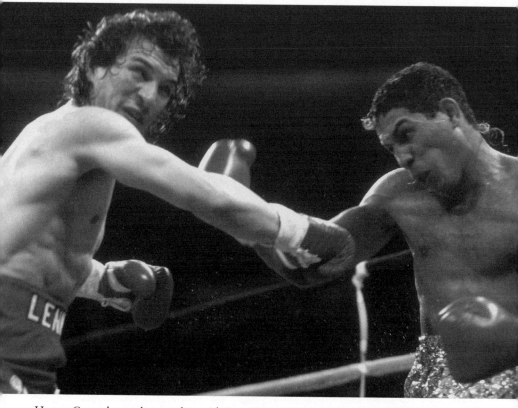

Hector Camacho trades punches with Ray "Boom Boom" Mancini during their WBO light welterweight world title fight at the Lawlor Events Center in Reno, Nevada, on March 6, 1989. Camacho won via split decision. *Getty Images*

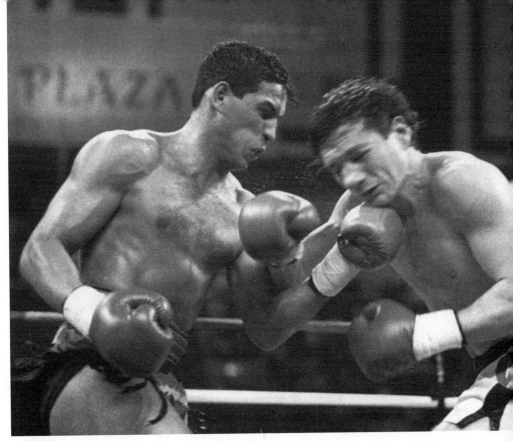

During a heated exchange, Hector stuns Vinny Pazienza with an uppercut en route to a unanimous-decision victory in which he retained his WBO light welterweight world title. *The Ring/Getty Images*

Hector Camacho shares a lighthearted moment with Pernell Whitaker before Camacho's fight with Tony Baltazar at Caesars Tahoe in Stateline, Nevada. *Courtesy of Hector Camacho Jr.*

Hector Camacho faces an attacking Tony Baltazar at the Caesars Tahoe Outdoor Arena in his second and final defense of the WBO light welterweight world title on August 11, 1990. Camacho won by unanimous decision. *The Ring/Getty Images*

Hector shows off his dance moves while promoting his upcoming fight against Oscar De La Hoya. *New York Daily News/Getty Images*

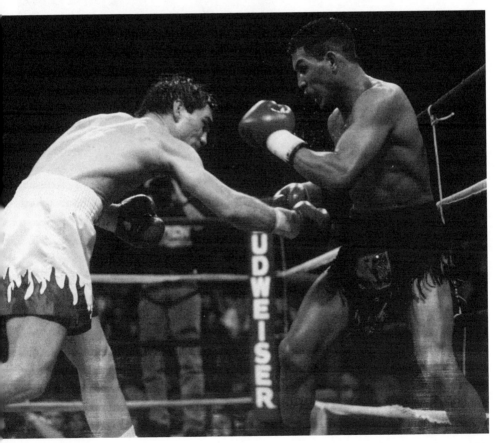

With his back against the ropes, Hector fends off a determined Greg Haugen in what would be his first professional loss. Haugen won the fight by split decision. *Getty Images*

Hector shows he's all business as he stares down Julio Cesar Chavez before their fight at the Thomas & Mack Center in Las Vegas on September 12, 1992. *Allsport/Getty Images*

In a fight in which he was dominated, Hector tries valiantly to mount an attack against the relentless Mexican legend, Julio Cesar Chavez. Chavez won a twelve-round unanimous decision. *The Ring/Getty Images*

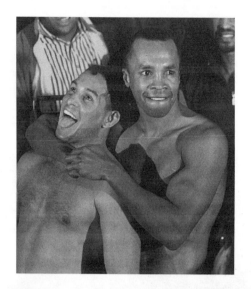

Macho and Sugar take a break and clown for the camera before their fight in Atlantic City on March 1, 1997. *Getty Images*

An animated Hector Camacho stands over Sugar Ray Leonard after knocking him down in the fifth and final round of their 1997 bout. Camacho beat the aging superstar by TKO. *The Ring/Getty Images*

Haunted by Rosario

13

Hector Camacho was very clear about the complexities of his bout with Edwin Rosario, and he complained that a fight that he had with his mother in the dressing room before the fight had affected him. Details also emerged after the fight that revealed the shortcomings of his training camp.

"When we trained for Ramirez, everything went smoothly," said Jerry Villarreal Sr. "This did not go smoothly."

For one thing, based on Hector's own account, it was unclear if Pintor was acting as trainer or if Hector was training himself. The impulsive jaunts from the camp were another concern. "One day during training, Hector decides he doesn't want to train," said Jerry Sr. "So he always would tap me by my pocket to see how much money I had. He looked at me, 'Let's go to town.' I said fine. I thought maybe he needed a rest or a break from training."

But it was much more than that. They went to the airport and flew to Puerto Rico to hang out with friends. When they returned, Maria was enraged. "When we got back his mother was waiting for us," said Jerry Sr. "She was upset at Hector for taking off and not leaving any money. They needed money for allergy medicine for [Felix, his younger brother].

In addition, for the first time, Hector had faced an opponent who challenged him stylistically by not allowing him to dominate the space between them. Holding his guard up and away from his body, Rosario refused to let Hector push the jab consistently. Surely, the way Rosario held his guard up did not change the tenor of the fight, but every little thing mattered in a fight of this magnitude.

Speaking to a reporter, Camacho added, "Jimmy [Montoya] made me mad when he was in Rosario's corner. What did Rosario pay him—a hundred or two hundred? I know it wasn't more than that. I'm by myself now. Right now I want a trainer, but who's a trainer who will train me right now without looking at the dollar signs?"

Years after the fight, when people would harp on the notion that fighting Rosario changed Hector's approach to the sport he loved so deeply, he admitted to experiencing a deeper hurt. "The turning point was the Rosario fight," Hector said. "I started losing interest in boxing, in the fans and all the antics. I was doing just enough to get over. You try to fight to have some fun, and all you get is criticism. The fans get on you. You hear it on the street, you hear it in the mall, you read it in the papers. It starts to get to you. It stops being fun."

Unlike other boxers, Hector's performances were based on energy, enthusiasm, and showing the fans how much he enjoyed entertaining them. Debates raged after the fight, but one thing rang true: Hector no longer performed like the star he was. Fans and experts alike felt that Rosario, the aggressor, had forced Hector into unknown territory. Some fighters thrive when opponents force them out of their comfort zones. Marvelous Marvin Hagler, Thomas Hearns, and Roberto Duran all delivered in the clutch, but Sugar Ray Leonard set the standard for finding the opportune times to shine. When one fighter provides a blueprint of greatness (as Hector had), it is discouraging when that fighter doesn't fulfill those expectations. Is it a fair litmus test? Maybe not. Every fighter is allotted their share of mediocre performances. Hector was not a great fighter but an elite one with otherworldly skills. Rosario exposed how Hector's lifestyle outside the ring influenced the discipline he appeared to be adhering to inside of it.

Hector tried to frame the performance with his own perceptions of his shortcomings: "I fought in the Rosario fight like a Macho, not a Hector," he told Jeff Ryan of *KO Magazine*. "In the fight, I never moved my head. I was never cocky. In the Ramirez fight, I was movin,' I was shakin,' up, down, body, head. In the Rosario fight, I was more straight. I was backin' up straight. I had sting to my punches . . . but the guy really got off the most crisp punches."

During the same interview, Hector addressed his biggest mistakes: no head movement and slow footwork. Against a fighter as active and destructive as Rosario, he needed head movement and feints and different looks and angles to deny Rosario a stationary target. The inability to move swiftly may have started off as a minor problem but quickly became a defining issue.

Hector's honest assessment of his own shortcomings and his opponent's strengths was refreshing. Fighters rarely speak so candidly. Hector did not attempt to fabricate a narrative about why the fight played out the way it did. Although the tenor of his responses changed over time, initially, he was honest about what he lacked in the face of such a powerful puncher. Sure, he was still undefeated, but he no longer maintained that aura of invincibility, and that would have bothered any fighter. Loyal fans wondered if he would rebound and be great again. The experts weighed in.

"When it came to Rosario, Camacho completely changed his style," said Puerto Rican journalist Rafael Bracero. "Even the people that didn't like Rosario said Camacho lost the fight. When he took that left hook in the fifth round, it turned around his career. If early he was Ali, then he became like a fly that swarmed around his opponent avoiding any damage."

"I can't think of one fighter where one fight marked so clearly a turning point in his career," said boxing journalist Steve Farhood. "And he won the fight. Most people might not ever remember that he won. At that point after the Rosario fight, the joy he showed for the sport was not apparent anymore." Farhood continued: "The thinking in that fight was that Rosario was the big puncher going in, but he would never hit Hector, and that Hector would outbox him, which he did in large chunks. Hector dominated great fighters, but he didn't come through as a great fighter would."

★ ★ ★

For Hector, it only mattered how he responded in the next fight, because, as he had proven in the past, one fight could change everything. He needed time to reassess his career, but he also needed to spend time with his son.

So he took his family to Disney World. Soon he would have to get back into the gym and figure out why he made so many mistakes in fighting Rosario, but now, it was time to sit back and relax.

During the interim between Rosario and his next scheduled bout with Cornelius Boza-Edwards on September 26, 1986, Hector also spent time in Clewiston with his family. With his new trainer Chuck Talhami by his side, Hector got to spend the summer with Junior, and Kisha would visit often. Observing Hector away from the ring was eye-opening for Talhami. Few people got to see the soft and intimate side of Hector, but that is what Talhami witnessed.

"He's really a beautiful human being," Talhami, who had worked with such fighters as Claude Noel and Muhammad Ali, told the *Sun Sentinel*. "He's very honest, very loving. This was an ideal place for Hector to come, and I'm glad to see he's taken to it so well. Spanish Harlem, that's a crazy place to grow up. He's been through so much. There was too much pressure on him. Here, he can mature. He's twenty-four years old, and with age, you mature."

Getting Hector up for early running sessions also exposed Talhami to the quieter, more subdued Macho. "I opened his door and he was sleeping with his son," Talhami said. "They were in each other's arms. It was just beautiful. He's really a very good father."

Hector wished he could bottle up the soft, happy moments with Junior and preserve them.

In the same vein, Junior cherished his time in Clewiston with his father. It was never easy for him to go back home at the end of the summer.

Of course, Junior did not always benefit from having a celebrity for a father. After the Rosario bout, he became the talk of his class. He had told everyone that he was going to be on TV, and when he did his little flurry in the ring at the Garden, his classmates watched in awe. When he came back to class, everyone wanted to know what it was like. Junior ate it up. But as much as he loved the attention, he also struggled with being Hector's son. With so much to live up to, Junior was forced to prove himself to tough kids who didn't care who his father was—and who wanted to prove they were tougher than the son of Hector Camacho.

Junior often lived in fear. His father, a good man, was around to lavish him with gifts, but it was his aunts and his mother who raised him. They loved him and doted on him, but he also received conflicting signals about toughness and standing up for himself. Maybe one day, Junior would be a good fighter and follow in his father's footsteps, but the ability to defend yourself does not emerge magically. So when Junior started to get heckled by his peers, it was difficult for him and his family.

Junior came to dread the final bell ringing at school. In his mind, he mapped out places he could hide. But there was no place to go. In a couple of minutes, his famous father would pull up outside with his fancy sports car. A couple of classmates would notice the celebrity and crowd around, and then in minutes the car would be surrounded. Junior knew the perks of having a superstar dad: summers in Puerto Rico, endless gifts, a sense of freedom, and a peek into the fast life that his friends only dreamed about.

This was not one of them.

One day, the bell sounded and Junior was off—through the hallways, down the stairs, and outside as a beam of sunlight shot through the trees. A fight, orchestrated by his father, was about to happen, and Junior would be forced to participate. What his father was doing scared Junior. It did not feel like love but rather an attempt by his father to make Junior tough—to form him in his own image.

Junior loved his father deeply, but times like these made him cringe as if to say, *Dad, I am not you, is that ok?* He knew that if he fought poorly, his father would chide him. If Junior got the best of the other kid, he knew the kid would be back for more another day. "It was always, 'Your father is this' or 'Your father is that.' It used to take a toll on me," Junior recalled. "It came to a point when I started to hate him because of all this."

Junior's younger cousin, Manuel Fragosa—Racquel's son, whom everyone knew as "Pito"—understood the fear Junior felt. Unlike Junior, who moved to Orlando to attend high school, Pito stayed and lived in their grandmother Maria's house with Hector.

"I didn't have a father. I was raised by the crazy Camachos," said Pito. "Macho was like my uncle mixed with my father. He was my Superman."

Since both boys were raised primarily by women, with the exception of occasional boyfriends who came and went, they viewed Hector as someone who could help them navigate the difficult teenage terrain. But Hector only knew one way to respond: like a macho uncle or father. Part of the problem was that Hector only visited sporadically, not because he was irresponsible or neglectful, but because his lifestyle didn't allow for frequent visits. Not one family member ever painted Hector in a negative light because of his inaccessibility. If he was detached or distant, that complaint reflected his inability to discuss *real* problems that existed about his increasing drug use.

Pito would also spend the summers with Hector in Puerto Rico or Clewiston. When Hector came home for Christmas, Pito would get the luxury of spending the holiday with him too. When Hector was around, he would shower Pito with hugs and kisses to let him know how much he cared. That is the Hector that Junior and Pito want to remember. Sure there were crazy moments and endless chaos, but the warmth of Hector's kiss and the tight squeeze only reinforced why they idolized him.

However, for Hector, "toughen up" often translated to frightening the boys. Since Pito was always crying—Pito himself admitted he was a "crybaby" back then—one day, Macho threw him into a closet and left him in there crying.

"Let me out," Pito cried. "Let me out."

Pito's screams did not register with his uncle. To Hector, it was funny—a rite of passage that Pito had to experience. Macho wanted to see more of himself in his nephew. In the HBO special before the Solis fight, Macho also jokingly left Pito in the closet but immediately picked him up to soothe him.

"My dad was always doing stupid shit like that," said Junior, who was there when Hector locked Pito in the closet. "He did that shit to me too. But I had a knack for when he would do it. I understood him and his boundaries."

Overall, the tactic didn't work, as Pito, distraught, had no one to seek out for help. But Macho didn't know any other way.

"He wanted to make us men at eleven, twelve years old," Pito recalled. "He took us to strip clubs, and we were smoking joints. You know the life of a rapper? I was living that life at eleven and twelve. He was that type of uncle."

Inevitably, as the boys got older, another more complicated aspect of Macho became more pronounced—he wanted them to be "real" men. Not just respectful, polite men who understood how to treat women and express themselves in a positive way. No, Macho wanted them to *be* with women. He would often tell them, "I don't want you to be fags."

Not yet a teenager, Junior knew he liked girls, so his father's obsession with trying to force the issue shattered him. One day when they were swimming in the pool at the Luxury Apartments ESG Towers in Mare in San Juan, Hector Sr. brought a girl over.

"You like this?" he asked Junior.

"Que Papi," she flirtatiously called Junior over to make him a man.

"I knew at the time what was about to happen," said Junior.

Crying, Junior reluctantly obliged.

And then it was over. Macho got his wish while his son sat in shambles, wondering why.

In Macho's mind, there were so many lessons that Pito and Junior needed to learn, lessons that only a former street kid could properly teach. Macho meant well, but his approach had its limitations.

"He showed us with women and money how to survive," said Pito. "[H]e would take us to Puerto Rico to stay with him and then disappear. He would just take us to places and leave us. He wanted to toughen me up. Sometimes he would karate kick me. It was really difficult at first. [My uncle] would laugh at me. It felt like bullying. As I got older, it cooled down a bit. A lot of it was teasing and verbal stuff—stupid things he said to me got to me."

As Pito began to discover himself, he, like Junior, felt the need to hide his identity as Hector's nephew. By the early 1990s, Junior had moved to Orlando, and Pito was on his own. "Hector Jr. left to go to Orlando, and I stayed in Harlem," Pito lamented. "Because of my uncle, I was getting harassed 24/7 . . . I never told people that he was my uncle, but when they found out, I was like, 'Damn!'"

Two things blinded family members to Hector's behavior: one was that he was so lighthearted and charming that he could get away with anything, and the other was that nearly everyone relied on his big purses for help, so it was hard for them to take a stand. Indeed, everyone thrived when Hector became world champion. The money poured in. The adoration. The fame. "There was mad love there between my mother and my uncle," recalled Pito. "But it was always about money. He became a cash cow. In the beginning it was all sweet. But through the years, they wanted money. My uncle had an attitude about that. He would start to come, say what he had to say, and leave. Then cut out. He would come to the house and stay after he went to the club and needed a place to stay. Then I wouldn't see him for three or four months. There was always respect there, but then he started to stay away."

But for all of the love that Pito and Junior received, the journey was fraught with complexities that they had to face without the proper resources to arm themselves against the anti-Macho element that they encountered daily. Macho existed in his own bubble where he did as he pleased. But his brand of toughness was not for everyone. He didn't consider that the brutality of his teachings may be doing more harm than good.

Waiting for Bramble

14

After the Rosario fight, Hector connected with Tim Cinnante, owner of Hi-Tide Hideaway, a popular nightclub in New York City. It became a haven for Hector, who felt comfortable with the clientele, most of whom he grew up with or knew from his neighborhood. One of his closest friends, Raymond Muhammad, a paraplegic wounded in a street fight, frequented the bar, as did a host of regulars who were deeply involved in the drug trade. Having become famous for hanging off the Brooklyn Bridge by his wheelchair, Muhammad knew Hector well from his early days in Spanish Harlem. Reluctant to part ways with old friends, Hector would often bring Muhammad to training camp and fights. Unlike some others who leaned on Hector for money, Muhammad always paid his own way.

"Raymond would come and give me chains and jewelry," Junior recalled. "My mom would hate it. He would give money to Grandma. I loved that motherfucker, but you didn't want to fuck with him."

It was hard for Hector to distance himself from his past completely. He never stopped being a street guy. Muhammad, who also never left the streets, was the strongest link to the underworld that Hector occasionally flirted with. Despite the concerns of those who visited the camp and wondered about Muhammad's role, Hector kept him around.

"Ray loved him, even though they fought a lot. Raymond bought my father the 'Macho' chain that he loved," Junior recalled. "That was his love. He always hid it. . . . You couldn't touch it or play with it."

Along with bringing an element of Spanish Harlem to training camp, Hector also immersed himself in the music industry. Emanuel Raheim, lead singer of the band GQ, introduced Hector to club owner Cinnante after the Rosario fight. Cinnante recalled Hector as sorely misunderstood in some social circles. "He was the type of guy if you don't know him you either like him right away or you hate him," said Cinnante. "In the club he was laid back, [but] if he didn't like you, he would light a cigarette right near you. He used to wear those same sequined suits in the streets. He was a loud dresser and a show-off. Coming up, you would have thought he was the mayor. The mayor of New York, Ed Koch, called him the toughest thing since the cockroach and gave him the key to the city."

Cinnante continued: "You wouldn't know it, but he had a lot of empathy. And he had a huge heart. He knew how it was to be in someone's shoes. One time when [former world champion] Davey Moore was down on his luck, Hector came in and built him up so much. He told Davey that he would bounce back and everything would be fine. He really picked him up. He made Davey feel like a million bucks. Not many people knew about that side."

Those who did not get to know Hector well may not have been able to see past the entertainer to the man. It was easy to label him arrogant if you didn't know him, but many who knew him better insist on his humility. "When there was no negative stuff around," said Kisha, "and he was in that zone, he was wonderful to be around. He would take time to work with other boxers. He would always stop to take pictures or sign autographs. And he would always get the name right, even if I had to help him with them."

Although Hector had come away from the Rosario bout with a deviated septum, breathing issues, and hand concerns, these problems were not severe enough to postpone a bout three months later with Cornelius Boza-Edwards, a tough southpaw, on September 26, 1986, at the Abel Holtz Stadium at Flamingo Park in Miami Beach. Don King Productions and Willy Martinez of Ivette Promotions co-promoted the bout. Hector, defending his WBC lightweight title for the second time, the first being his split-decision victory over Rosario, would earn $750,000 for the bout.

Loyal fans and curious journalists alike arrived at the stadium, hoping to see a revised version of Hector Camacho. They wanted confirmation that the Hector who nearly gave away the Rosario fight was nothing more than an aberration. In their mind, Hector needed to resuscitate the original fighter who stepped in with a double jab, then pounded a straight left; they needed to see him move with the same fluidity and grace that he exhibited against Jose Luis Ramirez; they needed to see him wade in and attack with precise timing. But the one thing that they most needed to see revived against Boza-Edwards was head movement.

Fortunately, Hector was not facing another Rosario, a strong fighter who maintained a blistering pace and deftly cut off the ring. A 5-1 favorite by fight time, Hector entered the bout 30-0 with sixteen knockouts, whereas Boza-Edwards was 44-5-1 with thirty-four knockouts. A native of Uganda, Boza-Edwards was on the tail end of a career that began in 1976. Having faced nearly every great super featherweight of his generation, including Alexis Arguello, Bobby Chacon, Rafael Limon, and Rocky Lockridge, Boza-Edwards was slowing down. It was not the ideal time to face a resuscitated Hector. Hector claimed to "need a knockout," whereas Boza-Edwards, managed by Mickey Duff, discussed his advantages: "He moves faster, but I hit harder," Boza-Edwards said of Hector. "He's a short fellow [five feet six to Boza-Edwards's five feet nine]. I have to get my reach in there."

Hector trained with Chuck Talhami, who was working with Rudy Mata, for the fight and sparred with another southpaw, welterweight Joe Baker, who expressed high praise for Hector's strength. Boza-Edwards trained with Bobby Neill in the Catskills.

Often proclaiming that he was moving beyond the rumors or distancing himself from the reputation that plagued him, Hector focused on his training. But how long could he maintain this new mindset? On the surface, he had everything he needed. He was looking at another payday and his family was content. Was he at peace with himself? That remained to be seen, but he was saying all the right things. "It's not easy to change suddenly," Hector said. "But I'm getting there. Hey, everybody changes."

It wasn't easy for Hector to change, but it also wasn't easy for him to make the 135-pound weight limit anymore, and rumors of poor training habits surfaced again. Hector had to lose 8 pounds in the two weeks leading up to the bout. Just a day before the fight, he weighed 138; he didn't eat anything for thirty-six hours prior to the weigh-in. His handlers got him up at 4:30 a.m. the day of the fight to shave off the remaining pounds. Eventually, with a little help from his friends, Hector made weight. "Friends lifted me by the cheeks and they called out 135 and took me off," he said.

Before the fight, Hector promised to not stand in front of Boza-Edwards as he did for Rosario, and he assured supporters that the vintage Hector who beat Ramirez would return. The press had recently taken to reminding him about the impact of his split-decision victory over Rosario. It haunted him.

A precursor to the main event was a fight between Edwin Rosario and Livingstone Bramble; the card was aptly named the "Preamble to Bramble," but it could have easily been titled "Macho on My Mind," as Rosario noted before the fight: "I'm fighting Bramble, but I see only Camacho." By staging the doubleheader, Don King attempted to breathe life into the lightweight division. And before the matchups, King was confident: "[A]fter [Hector and Bramble] beat these two guys, which I am certain they will, then they gonna meet each other in a unified bout, which is gonna be big, whooweee!"

Bramble was a 3-1 favorite entering the match and knew that he was expected to dispose of Rosario in order to uphold his part of the bargain to arrange a unification bout with Hector. "I think it's going to be a heck of a fight as long as it lasts," Bramble, a native of the British Virgin Islands, said of his bout against Puerto Rico's Rosario. "Right now, the way I feel, I'm predicting a first-round knockout. I've got good strength right now. So I've got to predict a first-round knockout."

Promoters clamored for a Camacho–Bramble showdown, and the contrasting styles would have made for an entertaining fight. But plans for a Camacho–Bramble future bout were dashed when Rosario, a 3-1 underdog, needed only two rounds to knock out Bramble and dissolve those plans. Ironically, Bramble was the same guy who squashed Hector's superfight dreams earlier in 1984 when he beat Ray Mancini. As disappointed as Hector was, Don King figured to lose the most. He had invested $400,000 with Main Events for Bramble's next three bouts. King's "tune-up" did not have the results he had been looking for. But the brash promoter quickly made a beeline for Rosario after the co-feature to raise his hand and announce, "The Preamble to Rosario!"

Although the Rosario–Bramble fight hadn't gone as he had hoped, Hector readied himself for his own opponent that night: Boza-Edwards. Heading down the aisle draped in a black-and-white robe, Boza-Edwards appeared serious and extremely focused. At 135 pounds, the fighter was 6-0-1 in his last seven bouts and had drawn with Terrance Alli in his last fight. In an unusual twist, Hector and Rosario joined each other's teams for their respective fights. Fresh off a second-round drubbing of Bramble, a shirtless Rosario led the charge as Hector, in a delay, eventually entered the ring, pissed off and frustrated at the situation. Pushing one of his handlers, Hector screamed loudly, "What time is it?" and the crowd responded accordingly.

A glitzy, light-blue sequined robe with a stylish "Macho Time" on the back provided the perfect complement to the champion who grooved in the ring prior to the introductions. Giving up three inches in height and five inches in reach did not bother Hector. A mass of people, including Trevor Berbick, Alexis Arguello, and Jimmy Paul, were in the ring at the start of the fight. Jerry Villarreal Sr., Patrick Flannery, Marty Cohen, and Talhami were running Hector's corner. Once the introductions were made, referee Carlos Padilla brought the two fighters together. Having spent nearly thirty minutes dancing and singing before the fight, Hector had not helped his cause. He looked soft compared to his sculpted appearance in previous bouts, while Boza-Edwards looked loose and well aware that he was the set-up guy. "I understand that the promoters have already painted the picture," said Boza-Edwards. "But they're going to have to make another plan."

As the two men faced off in the middle of the ring, one thing Talhami said must have echoed through Hector's mind: *You're still the same old*

Hector. He would find out if that were true over the next twelve rounds. The fight began with Hector charging out, throwing right hooks to the body, a tactic that Talhami preached in training camp and throughout the bout. Working off his internal clock, Hector felt that he had a couple rounds of good conditioning to dispose of an opponent who had been knocked out in the past. After that, Hector knew that he wouldn't be as mobile and active. That intensity worked well early on when Hector drilled Boza-Edwards with a straight left that left him wobbly and then smothered him with a jab, a left hand, and two body shots, causing him to go down.

At that point, Hector pulled away, and Padilla came in to administer the count. Stunned but not hurt, Boza-Edwards crouched down and waited until Padilla got to eight. Then, he stood up and survived the rest of the round as an overanxious Hector could not close out the show. The broadcast team, specifically Sugar Ray Leonard, suggested that Hector's early intensity was his way of trying to overshadow Rosario, but Hector was not that type of fighter. What Rosario did or did not do had little bearing on his performance. Hector and Talhami had devised a game plan in training camp not based on Rosario at all. It was all about conditioning and how much Hector could or could not do.

Over the course of the next five rounds, Hector, no longer bouncing and elusive, gave away rounds to a lunging Boza-Edwards, whose punch of choice was a winging left hand. Listening to his trainers between rounds, Hector heard a familiar theme: "You're making him look terrible" or "You're frustrating this guy like crazy," but that was not the case. Hector had lost effective use of his legs by the fourth round, although, because of talent and guile, he could still get inside and land intermittent combinations. Unable to take advantage of Hector's weaknesses, Boza-Edwards chased him, cut off the ring, and landed one or two punches, but he couldn't sustain a significant attack. Pushing the jab out there was a necessity for the exhausted Hector, mouth agape, as he moved into rounds seven through twelve.

Hector had other distractions as well. "He came back to the corner at one point. He had this long strip hanging down his legs from his jockstrap," said Jerry Villarreal Sr. "It was wet, and he turned to me and asked, 'Did I just shit myself?' I said, 'No man,' and just sent him back out."

The first six rounds in the Boza-Edwards fight made clear that Hector was not the same fighter he once was. He used to attack with speed and combinations; now he jabbed and occasionally went to the body. He used to set up vicious combinations with a sharp jab; now he threw jabs with nothing behind them. His movement used to dictate the pace of the fight; now he moved to avoid any confrontation. What truly bothered his legion of fans was his obsessive need to clinch—a tactic that may have saved him but destroyed the texture of what a fight should be. Could one blame this approach on the residual effects of Rosario? Partly. However, Hector, as good as he was, could not dominate a good fighter if he didn't train properly. Cohen stressed that Hector had such a propensity for junk food that he thought he would have to move to 140 by his next fight.

In the last forty seconds, Padilla clapped his hand, put his fist out, and pulled the fighters together as if to implore them—"Fight, fight." Unfortunately for Hector, it marked the dawn of a new era in which escaping replaced attacking and preservation replaced calculated risk taking. Seconds before the bell, Hector did something that he rarely did in previous fights: He put his arm around Padilla's waist. It was done in the middle of a clinch, and it was a subtle move to buy himself time, but it was his way of saying that he was going to use any tactic available to avoid punishment. Using the referee as a pawn would become the symbol of the new Hector, who exerted less energy, applied less pressure, and eschewed confrontation. Ringside judge Harold Lederman summarized what many were thinking when he said, "Camacho didn't give the people their money's worth."

As the last round ended, people saw Hector turning and walking away from Boza-Edwards. Critics saw a fighter unwilling to engage, and the resentment toward *this* Hector may have started right there. Still, Hector was rewarded with a unanimous decision with the scores: 115-112, 120-108, and 118-109. A hostile crowd may not have objected to the three-point difference, but the other two scores were too one-sided.

In the post-fight interview, Hector went right to the weight issue and confirmed that he would move up in weight to 140. All indications were that he did not want a rematch with Rosario, although he did claim that it might happen down the road.

"I can't make the weight," said Hector. "No excuses or nothing. All that bragging is over."

When pressed on his performance against Boza-Edwards, Hector tried to locate a silver lining in his mundane performance. If he had been honest with himself after the Rosario split-decision victory, he was less forthright after this victory. "I thought I fought a sharp fight," said Hector. "But I was not strong enough to stand there and outslug him. In the later rounds I wasn't able to stand there and push it out."

Two schools of thought emerged: one was that he ran and did not deserve such a wide decision on the scorecards; the other was that he wasn't at his best but Boza-Edwards didn't do enough offensively to earn the decision. "All he did was play," said Boza-Edwards, who lost his sixth career fight and first at 135 pounds. "How can a guy win a fight flicking? You have to take the fight to someone to win. You don't run all day long, and flick and flick and call that winning."

Meanwhile, plans for Hector to face WBC super lightweight champion Tsuyoshi Hamada never materialized, despite Hector's wishes. He had envisioned beating Hamada and then coming back to face Rosario again at a catchweight of 138 pounds, with the intent of negating Rosario's power. But there was no logic behind his actions, and some felt his erratic behavior carried over to his business decisions when three months after the Boza-Edwards fight, he cut ties with Cohen. Hector, who had set his sights on a huge payday with Bramble, had branded Cohen persona non grata, accusing him of having tricked him into signing a promotional deal with King. For monetary reasons, Cohen—and King—wanted Hector to fight Rosario again, but Hector had moved on. He felt betrayed, but King and Cohen countered Hector's charges by arguing that he had received $100,000 bonuses in each of those defenses. Reports in January 1987 noted that a $1 million rematch with Rosario was in the works for February or March to unify the lightweight title when the relationships began to dissolve.

Cohen had given Hector good financial advice, which Hector had followed, accumulating him over $2 million that would be accessible when he turned fifty. At the very least, Cohen had been a friend and confidant when Hector most needed one. He did not have to take Hector's desperate late-night call, but he did. So when Cohen suggested that Hector get a good psychiatrist, it was clear that things with the fighter had gotten out of his control.

By moving up to 140 pounds, Hector could negate the $2 million, five-fight contract he signed with King and also bypass Rosario. But with King, the lightweight champ realized he had few options. "King ain't going to let me go that easy," he lamented.

A Star
Dims

15

Eventually, Hector would bring in lawyer Jim Levien to fill
Marty Cohen's role on the Macho team. Kisha and her mother
had worked in Levien's law department for years and helped
bring them together. There was much excitement about
Hector facing Ray "Boom Boom" Mancini in a long-awaited showdown,
but the three fights leading up to that possible bout were anything but
scintillating. Several issues had arisen: Hector called all the shots in his
camp (which may not have been a new thing, ever since Giles departed)
and became harder to control; he no longer stayed away from the partying and vices that he had occasionally abstained from; and his inactivity
ruined any type of rhythm that he could muster.

Hector was rarely in the ring anymore; the bout against Howard
Davis Jr, to take place on May 2, 1987, would be only his third in two
years. The inactivity reinforced critics' and fans' consensus that the
Edwin Rosario bout had taken a physical and mental toll on Hector. Still,
Hector showed up at a press conference for the upcoming bout between
Julio Cesar Chavez and Rosario in November 1987 just to make his
presence known.

"There was no hatred in this kid's bones for other fighters," said
Hector's friend and club owner Tim Cinnante. "One time at a press

conference with Rosario and Chavez—me, him and a couple of guys went to the fight when Chavez kicked the shit out of Rosario. We were ringside. For that press conference, Hector stands on the table where the guys were sitting and just looked at them like Elvis. It was always for the cameras. He didn't even dislike Chapo."

Fans had branded Hector a malcontent or villain not because he was rude or disrespectful, but because of his defensive fighting style, his intermittent cheap shots when the referee turned his head, and the arrogance that emanated from the "Macho Time" chants and his shocking attire. They wanted Hector to lose, which made him more marketable than ever.

"Macho was very respectful to everybody. In front of the cameras, he was different because it sold papers. But he was smart like a fox," said Cinnante. "He didn't hate anyone. That was all for the press. That was all part of the show. Macho wanted to make boxing like wrestling. He wanted to make it like a show and not a sport. And he was good at it."

It had been years since Hector had sparred with Howard Davis Jr. in Jimmy Glenn's Times Square Gym; back then, Hector held Davis, a 1976 Olympic champion, in high regard. Although Hector was too fast for a host of professionals when he was emerging as an amateur star, Davis fared well in their sparring exchanges. Voted the best boxer among a brilliant group of gold medalists including Sugar Ray Leonard and Michael Spinks, Davis entered the professional ranks primed for success. However, the fighter had never lived up to the high expectations. At 29-3-1, he had lost decisions in his two bids to become a world champion at 135 pounds and had at most one final opportunity to win that elusive world title. When he and Hector sparred years back, no one would have believed that after a decade of professional fights, Davis would still be without a title. As he prepared to meet Hector, Davis still had something to prove.

Meanwhile, Hector was beginning to establish himself as an Atlantic City fixture. Fighting at the Convention Center, he enjoyed shopping— and entertaining—on the Atlantic City boardwalk, and especially loved the post-fight celebrations. He often brought a following to these fights, and the party never seemed to end.

Former manager Jimmy Montoya recalled a cold morning in Atlantic City when Hector wanted to shop. They walked around, taking in the sights. Montoya, who often carried wads of cash for his fighters, was holding a couple thousand dollars. Having created ring outfits for him in the past, Montoya was more than aware of his fighter's predilection for the flashy, stylish attire that defined him. As Hector tried on clothes, Montoya waited patiently. Hector eventually chose a tight leather outfit, but he was not done.

"C'mon, Jimmy. Now it's your turn," Hector implored. "We have to look alike."

"I'm not wearing that shit."

"Jimmy, come on, Papi."

After back-and-forth banter, Montoya gave him a *You've got to be kidding me* look and finally gave in and squeezed himself into ultra-tight leather pants. Hector and Montoya, sauntering down the boardwalk in the stylish outfits, were a sight to behold. Macho had that quality; it was hard to say no to him. Eventually Hector and Montoya split, but Hector's meticulous attention to his outfits only increased.

If there was any real concern going into the fight with Davis, Hector's camp may have been worried about losing a decision to a very good boxer who had a decided reach advantage—71 inches compared to Hector's 67 inches. The thirty-one-year-old Davis did a lot of things well and was a good fighter, but he did not excel in any one area. Conversely, twenty-four-year-old Hector, still undefeated (30-0), excelled in many areas. However, making weight was never one of them. Because of his inability to train or make weight consistently, he was always on the move. First, he and Billy Giles escaped Don King's clutches when they announced that they would abandon the 130-pound division; then, after winning the lightweight belt, Hector hung around long enough to make two defenses and escape King again.

Now promoted by Jeff Levine, who with partner Dennis Rappaport made up Ring Warriors Inc., Hector yearned to prove himself at junior welterweight. The division was not swarming with talented fighters. Fighting Davis would certainly prepare Hector to face bigger guys and look spectacular beating them. The bout, a ten-round nontitle fight, was televised on ABC *Wide World of Sports* before 3,600 spectators. Davis predicted a knockout before the bout, and ABC's Alex Wallau stated that "Hector needs to be Macho." For his part, Camacho earned $250,000, while Davis earned $65,000. Part of a nondescript fight card, Camacho wanted to distance himself from his less-than-stellar performance against Boza-Edwards. Conditioning-wise, Hector had initiated a pattern of early power surges and then late-round clinch and survival tactics because he had not trained with the same vigor as he once did.

Villarreal wanted the corner to be in sync—and in style. He bought the entire team warm-up suits with "The Incorrigible One" printed on the back that perfectly suited their fighter. Looking stylish in a spit curl with a baby tail in the back, Hector might have felt even more motivation seeing Ray Mancini ringside.

Hector took charge in the first round in the form of a straight left, and then with 1:30 remaining he countered over top Davis's jab. Prior to that punch, Hector trapped Davis against the ropes and jammed him with an uppercut. Finding a rhythm, a spirited Hector sprinted to the middle of the ring to meet Davis in the second round. As listless as Hector had been against Boza-Edwards, he was just as energized against Davis. Wracking him with a four-punch combination, Hector had already committed to body shots and on three separate occasions in the second round he doubled up on those hooks. Impressive and bold, Hector landed the best punch of the fight in that same round as he unleashed a huge right hook to the body and a follow-up left hook. Fans sometimes reflect on stereotypical boxing "chess matches," but a real one was emerging in Atlantic City. Whether he was playing possum or just relying on slick strategies, Davis covered up in the middle of round two only to come out of his shell to place a nicely timed right cross. Davis, who claimed to be sick throughout the fight, demanded that Hector maintain a fast pace.

Being more aggressive left Hector vulnerable to Davis's right crosses. Countering with a straight left, Hector showed grit and the will to engage. Offensively, Davis tried desperately to cut off the ring on Hector, but no one, with the exception of Rosario, had capably pulled off that maneuver. By the start of the fourth round, commentators Alex Wallau and Jim Lampley started to speak of a landslide victory for Hector. Keeping to a promise he had made before the fight, Hector did not run but instead attacked. He also tried a tactic that would reappear later in his career: attempting to steal the first twenty seconds of every round. That approach backfired in the fifth, when Davis weathered the early storm and then cornered Hector and slammed home another straight right. It was a difficult round to score, but Davis appeared the more assertive fighter and earned the round.

Leading up to the fight, Hector, trained by Rudy Mata and acting as his own manager, stressed that he not only had to win, he had to look impressive in doing so. He probably had not planned for conceding rounds to Davis, who discovered that Hector was open to the uppercut on the inside (landing twice) and that using his left hook to stabilize Hector against the ropes was perfect for setting up his straight right.

With only four rounds to go in the nontitle bout, Hector, who appeared vulnerable at the end of the sixth, returned at the start of the seventh with a torrent of activity. Still, it was a clean right hand and an offensive surge at the end of the round that left a lasting impression in favor of Davis. With the fight potentially slipping away, Hector turned to the straight left and two hooks to the body as his most damaging combination. Instead of biding his time against the ropes, Hector stalked his opponent. Closing out the fight in the final rounds, Hector proved that he could outslug and outshine Davis, a skilled boxer. He won a unanimous decision, by at least four points on all three scorecards, with the closest score being 97-93 on two judges' scorecards. Thus, Hector managed to keep his undefeated record intact, whereas a disappointed Davis fell to 29-4-1.

By beating Davis with a workmanlike performance, Hector did not look overwhelming or unbeatable. Hardly able to catch his breath in a physically demanding performance, Hector told Alex Wallau in a post-fight ABC interview, "[At this weight], I feel good, I feel strong. C'mon everybody . . . Mancini don't hold me up because I ain't going to go away. I'm back. I plan to stay busy. I'm mentally clear. Mancini, two weeks, sign the contract or Terry Marsh I'm coming after you."

On a calmer note, Hector talked about how much he respected Davis as an Olympic champion and what a great fighter he was. But he was not done. Genuinely concerned about how he was perceived, Hector pushed back against what he considered unfair and unjustified stereotypes. Hector told Wallau: "People write about me like I'm some kind of freak, like a hoodlum off the streets. I'm happy to say I'm the classiest young man I know." But his inability to adhere to and live by certain boundaries that society accepted as appropriate left him feeling targeted. Exposure of his chosen lifestyle and his refusal to mature were also part of the Macho mystique.

Hector waded in obscurity for the next year, deflating any momentum he had culled from the Davis bout. There is no doubt these gaps of inactivity severely detracted from his best years. Still, no matter what was happening, Hector always tried to attract attention.

"I went to a signing in Las Vegas with Hector," said Puerto Rican journalist Rafael Bracero. "Famous people like tennis star Andre Agassi wanted to meet him. But O. J. Simpson and Pete Rose were doing a signing, and they knew that Camacho was like the new kid on the block, and he started to make a lot of noise there in the lobby with all these people surrounding him. He talked loudly and always wanted to be the star."

Hector never missed an opportunity to change the mood of a situation by acting bizarre or taking a risk. As in the ring, he often ended up successful in those situations because everyone else had already determined (without hesitation) that they were not going to put themselves out like that. In many cases, his act was refreshing.

"He just liked to be the center of attention," said club owner Cinnante. "He would come to the club to hang out. Some idiots tried to challenge him, but he was pretty smart. He would just walk away. People had this idea that he was a troublemaker, but he was really a gentleman. He just had a flamboyant way about him that people took the wrong way."

Hector's next match was set for June 25, 1988, against Reyes Antonio Cruz. Six months earlier, however, on February 2, 1988, an incident changed the landscape of the fight. While showing a popular boy band around a local Clewiston high school, Hector allegedly pulled a gun on a high school student he thought had given him the finger. Hector was arrested and questioned on February 4 after the boy reported the incident.

During the interrogation held at the Hendry County Jail, Hector was caught on camera trying to stash a bag of cocaine and brought up on charges of assault and possession.

"You have to file this thing under Believe It or Not," Hector told the press. "It all started when I sent my girlfriend to Miami to pick up these Puerto Rican kids at the airport who were coming here as part of the Charisma program. Since we had the kids with us, I decided to show them around Clewiston. I stopped by the high school, and you have to remember that I am a superstar. Everybody knows me, so I started signing autographs at the high school. All of a sudden, this one kid starts talking and saying things like (lightweight) Julio Cesar Chavez could take care of me. I asked him why he was being so disrespectful and why he couldn't be nice to me. Then he gave me the finger. It turns out that the kid had a friend who was a police officer. He told the policeman that I had pulled a gun on him. What did I need with a gun against a kid? I've got two guns right here in my fists."

Hector continued: "They arrested me and put me in handcuffs. Just before the police came, I was looking at postcards with my trainer, Rudy Mata. Rudy handed me a small envelope he found. He doesn't speak English and made some joke in Spanish to me. Anyway, we were checking out, and I put the envelope in with my change, into my wallet. When I was arrested and brought to jail, all of a sudden I thought of the envelope. I tried to hide it, but a policeman saw me on the monitor. They came in, took the envelope, and it turns out it contained traces of cocaine. I told you this whole thing goes under *Believe It or Not*."

Later the same year, Camacho was pulled over on the highway while, according to the police officer, "doing the wild thing" with a woman on his lap. The stories were getting harder to spin as Hector's descent continued. People were asking how Hector, a fighter who had been on top of the sport several years earlier, could let this happen.

Hector tried to deflect the negative attention by getting back into the ring against Cruz. It had been thirteen months since he had last fought, in his decision over Howard Davis Jr. What precipitated that lengthy gap between fights? Hector claimed he had been waiting for a Ray Mancini fight to surface, but it never did.

Being away from the ring left Hector detached and struggling to find an identity. He would often appear moody and give bizarre, rambling interview responses: "I'm practically in the beginning of what's going to be a successful career. I want to be like Michael Jackson, he doesn't come out. People have to pay a lot of money for him to come out, and every time he comes out he's explosive." He needed the ring more than anything in his life—at the very least, he needed it to protect him from himself.

"After this I want to immediately come back," Hector told a journalist a week before the Cruz fight from his new $300,000 home outside Clewiston, Florida. "I want to be impressive, then fight four weeks later. I have a promoter now, Jeff Levine, who all I have to do is whisper and he comes running. It was never like that with Don King, he always had other things to do." Initially, Levine had facilitated the contract in which Hector signed options with King when he won the title, but now he had agreed to come back on as a promoter.

On paper, Cruz, 37-2-2 with twenty-four knockouts, did not appear threatening in any way, but he had knocked Saoul Mamby down twice in a decision loss representing the first two knockdowns in Mamby's career. The promotion team of Gerry Cooney and Dennis Rappaport of Superfights Unlimited worked with matchmaker Mike Acri on the USA-televised card at the Tropicana Hotel and Casino in Atlantic City. Not too concerned about Cruz, Hector told a reporter before the fight, "I'm scared of the guys I don't know. It's hard to get up for the easy fights." In front of a sold-out crowd of nearly two thousand spectators, Hector needed to come back and shine in order to earn a title shot at 140.

Leading up to the bout, Cruz had to take off three pounds the morning of the weigh-in. Hector also had to shed almost a pound to make 142. Both fighters weighed in at 142 pounds, and Hector, undefeated in thirty-one fights, pranced, juked, and jived around before the fight in the ring in his new leopard-skin outfit asking, "What time is it?"

Confident and aggressive when the fight started, Hector fired a beautiful right hook early on only to be caught by one later in the round, which left him sprawled out on the canvas. His handlers screamed for him to get up. Seconds prior to getting knocked down, he appeared to try and use his left glove to deflect or block a right hand, but he was too late. Instead, he started to fall to his left and ended up halfway out of the ring—face first. Immediately, he pushed himself up, and then used his left hand to balance himself on the middle rope. Off balance, he bounced off the rope and ended up face to face with referee Steve Smoger, who stepped in to give him an eight-count.

Bleary eyed and clearing his head, Hector tried to process what had just happened. Never before had he been knocked down. His brother, Felix "Boo Boo" Camacho, who was victorious in his professional debut earlier that evening, and his mother, Maria, were shocked at what they had just witnessed. As deadly as the punch appeared, Hector, at that stage, should have never put himself in position to get hit by it. He had carelessly stayed on the inside of Cruz's lead foot and had gotten nailed. Was it a flash knockdown? Yes. Was it a sordid reminder that Hector's life outside the ring had begun to interfere with his ring identity? Absolutely. For some who had pegged Hector as an untouchable early on in his career, seeing him on the canvas was sad and perplexing. Gingerly, he moved backward and out of harm's way. After weathering one final combination, he clinched and survived. Maria prayed in the stands.

"He looked over at us, and we were like, 'Get the fuck up,'" Jerry Villarreal Sr. recalled.

Stunned and hurt, Hector was breathing hard. Having to go into that second round must have been one of the most distressing moments in his career. Not only had he been knocked down by a lesser fighter, he also hadn't participated in the sport for over a year. The fight was supposed to feel more like a reunion than a wake-up call. Some boxers use knockdowns as motivation, but Hector was broken spiritually, coming down from an ambitious dance rendition to start the fight, and exhausted physically from not being in shape.

Being away from the ring felt like a prison sentence for Hector. Turning within proved damaging, as he explained: "I haven't been around people in a long time, I don't know how I'm going to react," he said. "The last time I was out was at the Edwin Rosario–Chavez fight (the previous November) and 10,000 Mexicans tried to kill me."

Instead of shedding the ring rust early and then feeling refreshed later on, Hector got knocked down and then attempted to win points back in the middle rounds, but if the judges were looking for positive signs in the last two rounds, they were not evident. In fact, Hector's body language reflected pure exhaustion. Bear-hugging Cruz, walking away with his back turned, and boldly grabbing on to Smoger to buy time and avoid further punishment were all acts of a fighter hanging on. And that is what Hector did, resulting in a unanimous decision: Al Devito, 96-95, Lynne Carter, 97-95, and Henry Eugene Grant, 96-95, all favored Hector in the unanimous-decision victory that drew the ire of some fans.

Over the next couple of days, the coverage reflected the narrative of Hector's survival tactics and homed in on the first-round knockdown. After the fight, he masked the disappointment well when he said, "I feel proud. I took a punch and fought one of the best guys in my division [Cruz was not in the top ten]. We want to stay busy, so I can be sharper." He added: "I showed the heart of a guy who wants to come back," as if he had to convince himself. When a reporter mentioned how the majority of journalists had him losing, Hector spat back, "You people aren't the judges. I don't feel like answering no negative questions."

Away from the ring, Hector was at a point financially where he and his family had security. Hector, who was not frugal, could not get enough of his beloved cars, clothes, and other toys. "I would do the contracts and then Hector would want to buy this and that. I asked him once, 'Why do you have so many cars? Why do you need more? You can only drive one at a time,'" said Hector's lawyer, Jim Levien. "He loved cars and they were always black."

In a new role, Levien was getting more acclimated to Hector's moods and behavior. "He was the first guy to bring those costumes into the ring," said Levien. "He was in that mode when I met him. I had to get the material for them in New York. He wanted to do this and that with the costumes. If they needed material, I had to find it. I knew very little about this at the time."

Along with the near slip-up against Cruz, Hector was trying to settle into a life without Kisha. Having gotten into law school, Kisha could no longer deal with the excessive string of parties that grew more intense during every layoff. Hector continued to do drugs and could not let go of a corrosive lifestyle that alarmed those close to him. It was hard for Kisha to imagine that this was the man whom she loved so deeply.

Deep down, Kisha knew that starting a family with Hector was not an option. Before their breakup, she saw red flags. When Hector hit her during a physical confrontation in Clewiston, her fears were confirmed.

"I had had enough," she said. "He ended it by harassing me at school for a couple months. He would want to come over all the time. I was trying to focus on school. I had to get this guy away from me. He didn't take it well. I ended it. I was worried that something would happen to me [living that lifestyle]."

As Hector's behavior became more outlandish, Junior became more accustomed to each new wrinkle. Whether Hector was facilitating his first sexual encounter or bringing him to a nightclub, Junior knew that his father lived in a world where other people set limits that he repeatedly crossed. By the age of ten, Junior was used to going to nightclubs with his father or being forced to hold his drugs. At times, during the summer, Junior would try to hide in the hotel.

"When he said, 'Papi, let's go,' I didn't know if I was coming back," said Junior. "I knew that I would be missing going to the pool. I wanted to play ball, but I did not want to hang out with the old guy. Sometimes we would go on a mission for two days."

It was unusual, but driving for days was not all bad for Junior. He got to know his dad and spend time with him without fans calling his name. It was *their* time, even if it meant sacrificing time with his friends. Driving was a way of de-stressing for his father, but also a way of telling Junior, 'I just want to be with you.'"

"It meant a lot," said Junior. "We had some one-on-one time. Everyone wanted a piece of him back then. I got sick of all the attention, 'Macho, Macho.'"

With no one around to impress, Hector gave Junior his undivided attention. A softer side emerged during the long car rides. No friends from the neighborhood. No girls hanging around. No leeches. Just Dad. But Hector's unpredictability never faded. One second, Macho would be loving, and the next, he would demonstrate his darker side.

Back home, Junior lived a quiet, more reserved lifestyle focused on school and sports; instead of nightclubs, he went to museums and Coney Island; instead of late-night drives to a bar, he went fishing early in the morning; instead of drugs and liquor, he went to Yankees or Mets games. But sometimes Junior missed Hector's world. When time in la-la land with his famous father ended, Junior raged.

"I was upset," Junior recalled. "I wanted to know why I lived in the projects with the pissy hallways. I'd go to Disney and then come back to the ghetto like it was a dream. [Then] realization kicked in."

And while his aunts and mother stressed schoolwork and education, his father disregarded them completely. "He didn't give a shit about school," said Junior. "He would pick me up from school, but that's it."

As devastating as it was to cope with bullying and the widening gap between his parents' lifestyles, Junior did not complain. Working in a furniture store on 138th and 3rd Avenue, his mother was his "ace." "I didn't need [a father figure]," he said.

Still trying to navigate the diverging worlds of fatherhood and his boxing career, Hector started to feel more comfortable with his current team. Levien had developed a bond with Hector and was beginning to get more deeply involved in negotiations for one of the biggest moments in the fighter's career.

"I didn't know boxing intricately, so Hector came to my office after I was recommended by Kisha's mother [who at the time was Levien's secretary]," Levien recalled. "He felt me out for a while, and we got along and I became his lawyer."

Hector also started working with Ismael Leandry, a man who never took any money with him but became his surrogate father. The president of Pavilion Sports, Leandry lived in Puerto Rico, where he had made a fortune in the housing market. Leandry was a beloved figure in the boxing world. He advised Puerto Rican world champion Wilfredo Gomez and promoted his bout with Azumah Nelson. No one in the Puerto Rican boxing community had a bad thing to say about Leandry, and when he was introduced to Hector, a longtime friendship ensued.

Joining Leandry and Patrick Flannery, Levien felt confident about the direction of the Macho team, whose members were all good-hearted and always prioritized Hector. Even after they parted ways later on, Levien considered Flannery a friend.

"Pat and Hector shared a common bond. He was a terrific asset," Levien recalled. "He came down to camp to keep Hector in line, which was not easy. Hector was a wild guy who needed supervision, but they respected each other. Hector never had to turn his back when Pat was watching it for him."

The fight between Ray "Boom Boom" Mancini and Hector was finally coming to fruition, but it would play out much differently than it might have if it had occurred in the early 1980s, when both fighters were in their prime. Nearly six years earlier, as 1983 closed out, Hector and Mancini had been close to facing each other. Had it not been for Livingstone Bramble, who doused the flames of the huge showdown by beating Mancini on two occasions in 1984 and 1985, Macho and Boom Boom may have been facing off in a rematch rather than an initial encounter.

Back in the early 1980s, Hector was still a ring magician, flitting in and out of danger at will, while capitalizing on his opponent's every mistake. Meanwhile, Mancini was still thriving on a level of intensity and exacting pressure that sustained a brief lightweight championship reign. Both fighters' styles were intoxicating for different reasons. Because Mancini was so relentless in a blue-collar attacking style, it was impossible to stop watching him. Yet quick but talented opponents who were able to seamlessly shift their weight to the left and right without ever staying still were difficult for Mancini to handle. Hector, Mancini's antithesis, moved with the fluidity and rhythm expressed in a Carmen McRae jazz tune—a style that reached the elixir of "pure" boxing for the educated fight fan. Occasionally, the gritty, streetwise Hector would emerge and attempt to hold and hit or hide behind the referee to bide time. These little things often helped his cause. Of course, they were also the types of tactics that Mancini resented and avoided.

But so much had changed over those six years. Inactivity and immaturity defined the middle to late 1980s for Hector as he had completely
transformed from a stylistic dynamo to a flamboyant, petulant bad boy
more concerned with cultivating an image than improving his craft.

Mancini had never liked Hector, and the resentment did not appear
fabricated. On several occasions, Mancini stressed, "This is the one fight
I wanted," whereas the sarcastic Hector urged Mancini to either retire
or not, but to not keep coming back. "What do you have to do for your
father that you have not done yet?" wondered Hector. "Regardless of
what anyone can say, I am going to get my three titles, and that is something that they can never take from me."

Having fought Bramble, Mancini had heard it all before, but something
irritated him about how Hector shaped this fight as the All-American
Mancini vs. the street kid, because in Mancini's mind, this was so terribly wrong. "Looking back, I could never take Camacho seriously," said
Mancini. "I got a kick out of him. He would say those things to everybody. . . . I got a kick out of Camacho. He didn't bother me."

One of the Macho team's demands was to dictate the ring size. During
negotiations, Hector's lawyer, Jim Levien, and promoter, Jeff Levine, who
were working with co-promoters Lou Falcigno and Joe Gagliardi, agreed
to the stipulation that Hector would not take any tune-ups prior to the
fight in order to satiate Mancini's camp, which was interested in giving
their fighter any edge possible.

Making that compromise was not easy for Levien, or anyone else in
the camp, who knew of Hector's predilection for the nightlife. Levien had
become skilled at putting out his fires. In early 1988 when talks of a
Mancini bout were beginning to gain traction, Levien had had to deal
with the high school incident in Clewiston. The arrest, for allegedly pulling a gun on a Clewiston high school student, continued to haunt Hector.
Unlike previous encounters with law enforcement, Hector hadn't been
able to use his celebrity status to avoid arrest. Whether or not Hector
pulled the gun on the student, the incident represented another in a laundry
list of regrettable decisions. What was missing from the embarrassment
surrounding the case was Hector's attempt to resuscitate his career and
public image. But the "I'm not that guy you think I am" schtick had begun
to wear thin. Several times throughout his career, Hector had expressed
resentment at reporters' constant harping back to his stint at Rikers

Island as a teenager. Regrettably, he kept giving them more material to work with.

Initially, Hector had moved to Clewiston to get away from the allure of the city and its inhabitants, some of whom reflected the worst elements of himself. Paradoxically, Hector's flaws overlapped with his wonderful strengths. He was charming, but his sociability also got him into trouble. He knew that immersing himself in extremes could be toxic as he dabbled in the corners of the drug trade. It didn't matter where he was—Hendry County or New York City—Hector, the restless rascal, found trouble through fame.

Hector also sought to nurture his reclusive side, building the training camp amid the idyllic landscape outside of Clewiston, for example—and making sure that he was surrounded by cornfields to block the view of any cops heading that way. He also built a fireman's pole in the garage to go nicely with his getaway jeep. Always ready for anything, he was prepared to leave everything behind in a second.

So when news of his arrest at the high school and the subsequent drug revelations surfaced, those closest to him were not shocked. But these charges were not just going to disappear. This was not a small shoplifting case that could be pushed aside with a mere fine. Eventually released on $20,000 bond, Hector returned home to sort out the mess. Negotiations were being made for his showdown with Mancini, but nothing could be confirmed until the ordeal at the high school was settled.

Being loyal was one of Hector's strong suits, but now he was looking for a scapegoat. No one could figure out why Hector, who was demanding million-dollar paydays, still lived so recklessly. And no one could predict what he would do next. That unpredictability put his closest confidants in harm's way.

In a separate incident during the late 1980s, Jerry Villarreal Sr. and his wife went to visit Hector in Clewiston and were treated to an afternoon on his boat—and an unpleasant surprise. "Hector thought he was captain of his boat," said Villarreal Sr. "He had the hat and the jacket, but I go check the boat out and it had no oil, no tools, and the fan belt was loose. I go to a store and get $250 worth of stuff, including ammunition because Camacho had Uzis and shotguns. As we were leaving, Hector sneaks some hair products and other little things in there. We head out."

They went to put all of the merchandise in the car, but Rudy "Tio" Mata had locked his keys inside it. As they waited for Villarreal's wife to bring the extra set of keys, the manager of the store came out and questioned the men. Villarreal showed him the receipt and reassured the man that he had just bought over $200 worth of merchandise, but the man noticed that there were items in the cart that were not paid for. Hector went back in with the man to soothe the situation and pay for any stolen items but was arrested for shoplifting and brought to a local jail. Eventually, Villarreal and Mata located him at one of the two possible jails and paid his bail. Aware that he was on probation, Hector took off. When Villarreal Sr. called to find out his whereabouts, like a fugitive, Hector discreetly whispered, "I'm on the run."

Apart from his legal troubles, Hector was dissipating as a fighter. The adage that "styles make fights" carried weight going into the showdown with Mancini. Implicit within that adage is that tactics reflect that style. This version of Hector lacked the speed and dominance of the past. His decline could not be attributed solely to what happened with Edwin Rosario. Much more factored into it. Even though he altered his style and persona to stay more relevant over a longer period of time, he could no longer fight with the same fluidity and pace. His refusal to stop using drugs was the determining factor that contributed to this decline, while his inactivity between fights also accelerated his downfall.

"The trouble with Hector was that everyone got in his ear," said Levien. "He was easy to sway. He was not easy to relate to if you were an outsider. Still, he took care of his sisters. There was pressure on him to provide for his family, especially living day to day."

By 1989, fighters had to prepare for a skilled but defensive-minded opponent in Hector. Regarding Hector's style, Mancini recalled, "We knew he [would be in clinch mode]. We prepared. As soon as he clinched, we would pull his hands down, but we wouldn't struggle. No. We wanted to walk him backward so the referee could see it. That way the judges could also see who was holding."

When the fight finally arrived, the matchup, first announced publicly in 1983, had been considerably diluted. Mancini said he wanted to feel the thrill of victory again, but it would have to be a much different kind of victory than he was used to in his previous twenty-nine wins. Back in the early 1980s, Hector and Mancini were hovering near the top-ten pound-for-pound list. Both were TV darlings who became stars on network TV: Mancini was easy to love, and so was Hector, although for different reasons. When it came to fostering a wholesome image, Mancini embodied the perfect loving son and ideal action fighter who never took a step backward. To Mancini's delight, Hollywood beckoned. Meanwhile, Hector's charisma was both infectious and fun-loving: he was a fighter who had not yet made the complete transition to style and little substance. With their matchup finally looming, fans wondered what the future would hold for the two fighters.

The All-American versus the Street Punk

16

Hector got the news he was looking for when, on October 29, 1988, he got three years' probation and a $1,500 fine handed down from the Hendry County Sheriff's Office for the incident at the high school. He also had to attend a drug rehabilitation center in Fort Myers, Florida. That news cleared his mind to focus on Ray Mancini, as the fight was close to being confirmed.

Campaigning at 140 pounds, Hector had struggled to match his energized dance-offs in the ring prior to fights, but he was now being given the opportunity to redeem himself in the eyes of his fans. He wanted a third title so badly. A third title—whether it was WBO, IBF, WBC, or WBA—would vindicate him. Promoter Dennis Rappaport reneged on the initial deal the previous May after agreeing to contracts that would have paid Mancini $2.25 million and Camacho $1.5 million. Rappaport had too many concerns, so he backed away, leaving space for co-promoters Lou Falcigno and Joe Gagliardi (with Rappaport and Superfights as the co-promoters) to save the fledgling fight. By the following November, Falcigno had letters of intent from both fighters, who were looking to benefit from pay-per-view and closed-circuit percentages to supplement their $1 million purses.

On November 18, Falcigno confirmed the Camacho–Mancini showdown for March 6, 1989. Falcigno was not as convincing when he billed the fight as "not Tyson–Spinks, but . . . still a multimillion-dollar fight." He planned to charge $19.95 for the pay-per-view and $300 for a ringside ticket. Whether or not it would be a title fight was unclear, although that fall Falcigno had approached the newly formed World Boxing Organization (WBO) about making it one.

At the Manhattan press conference on December 20, 1988, both fighters got in early jabs.

"Camacho runs like a dog and holds like a woman," said Mancini, to which Camacho meekly countered, "I'd rather run than get beat up." Resentment toward Mancini felt a bit contrived, but the "All-American" was in Macho's way now.

Without a blemish, Hector, 140 pounds, walked in the ring with a 33-0 record, and although he was not goal-oriented, he desperately wanted that elusive third title, even a less prominent WBO one. Hector wanted the third title to find closure, as if to confirm to himself that a kid who came from nowhere could achieve. Unfortunately for Hector, having Mills Lane referee the bout only created more stress, as the two men had bickered in previous bouts.

After a four-year retirement, Mancini entered with a 29-3 record. The clear narrative for Mancini was that Hector had irked him enough for him to believe that a resurgence was possible. Not one to fool himself about his strengths and weaknesses, Mancini saw Hector as defined by limitations rather than strengths. It was very black and white for Mancini: Hector did not have—and never had had—what it took to beat him. The one thing Hector did for Mancini was motivate him. "He is the only guy who could have brought me back to boxing," Mancini said.

Public sentiment also refueled Mancini's inner fire. Deep down, Mancini knew that he could not live with himself, or be fully content, without silencing Hector. So he stepped away from acting and devoted himself to a furious training regimen.

"All these people kept saying to me, 'Ray, you've got to beat Camacho. You've got to shut his mouth.' So I thought, if the people want to see it, why not?" reflected Mancini.

With the crowd behind him, Mancini, dressed in a white silk robe, heard the fans at the Lawlor Events Center in Reno call his name. It had been so long since he had heard the cheers. Hector felt that same sense of pride as he was hoisted up by his followers from Spanish Harlem. But this was Mancini territory, and as Hector, replete in his suit of lights and red cap, went down the aisle, he heard the chorus of boos calling for his demise. Dressed in a matador outfit, Hector, also sporting a bleach-blond rattail, disrespectfully tossed his red matador hat at Mancini.

As they prepared for introductions, Mancini felt like he was home again, and although he had been candid about his concerns about getting back in the ring, he knew that after shaking off the rust, he would feel good. Reports before the bout had some concerned about Mancini during sparring sessions. He did not look like the old version that so many fans had grown to love. But the criticism did not faze Mancini. He was just happy to be back, performing again. The rush of adrenaline took him to a place that acting could not.

"I never looked great in the gym," said Mancini. "I was working on things. I was prepared. Pressure fighters never look great in the gym. I just wasn't a gym fighter."

One regret that Mancini had was not taking a more assertive stance on the size of the ring. Although he settled for a 20-by-20 ring, Mancini wanted 18 feet, to which Hector quickly replied, "I'll fight him in a phone booth."

Hector also got the nod on negotiating a 2:30 a.m. weigh-in the morning of the fight. Mancini wanted it for 8 a.m. so that Hector could not comfortably regain his strength by 7:40 p.m. start time, but to no avail. Reports had Hector coming down from 162 pounds before the fight; subsequently, Flannery had Hector on a "grapefruit diet." Days before the fight, Hector's weight was still randomly fluctuating, giving his team reason for concern. When he did show up for the weigh-in, Hector brought a birthday cake for Mancini and ate it all by himself in front of him.

Hector also penned the poem "Beans and Rice vs. Italian Ice" and eloquently performed it open-mic style:

My name is Hector and I'm the real director,
I have the fastest hands in any sector,
The other guy's called Boom Boom,
If I play him cheap, it will be my doom doom.

Cheap jokes aside, the men finally met in the center of the ring. Making a beeline for Hector, Mancini threw a right hand to start the bout.

Executing his game plan early in the first round, Hector landed a nice jab, stepped back, and shot a straight left—the ideal plan to offset Mancini's ambushes. It wasn't until the end of the round that Mancini landed his first punch—a right hand. Matching each other in intensity, both fighters missed as the round closed out. Still persevering, Mancini did land a telling left hook as he stared at Hector. Once macho gunslingers who instilled fear in their opponents, Mancini and Hector now merely forged ahead, trying to salvage what was left.

There was a real concern that Mancini needed several rounds to establish a groove after his time off. By the second round, Hector had developed more of a rhythm. Not only was the Macho Man landing counter rights, he was also tripling up on his jabs—and landing two of them. Movement was vital as Hector, ever the matador, moved gracefully to his left, stopped briefly, and deposited an uppercut. Going to the body became a major theme for Mancini as he returned fire with a strong right and left hook. Having relied on buzz-saw-like pressure, Mancini recognized the frustration of coming back after four years, and as he chased Hector, that level of futility reared its ugly head. Even the greatest athletes in the world can't make up lost time. Ring rust is debilitating, but there is nothing that saps a fighter's confidence more than the realization that his legs are gone. Closing out the final ten seconds of the second round, Hector held and landed two more uppercuts.

Between rounds, Hector confidently shook his head; conversely, Mancini knew he would have to intensify the pace and become more physical. But could he put himself in position to accomplish that feat? Any fighter facing Hector knew that he would have to keep evolving in the bout, or it could quickly become a whitewash of jabs and angles.

At the outset of the third, Hector almost hit referee Lane, and the interaction between the two men indicated a growing dislike. A more physical and determined Mancini, now with his feet securely under him, missed a left, but connected on a short, straight right hand. He was not finished. Back at it, Mancini sprinted after Hector and landed another straight right. That punch boosted Mancini's spirits, which before that punch looked deflated.

A different narrative emerged in the third round—one to Mancini's benefit. As Hector moved to his left and stuck occasional jabs, Mancini timed him nicely with his right hand. Those confrontations aggravated

Hector. As Mancini jammed one final right hand and left hook, he ended the round exactly how he envisioned it. Hector, a 3-1 favorite, turned to his uppercut over the next couple rounds. On the inside, he jammed an incoming Mancini. When Mancini blindly waded in, Hector was more effective and found an easy target amid the chaos. Effectively applying his aggression to counter Hector, Mancini did not back off.

Combinations were few and far between heading into the middle rounds for Mancini, who was forced to adopt a style that belied his bull-like intensity from his prime. Now more herky-jerky and less fluid, Mancini was not moving well, which hindered him from positioning himself to do more damage. That inability was never more evident than when Mancini landed a left hook, jumped up, and attempted to capitalize on the punch but could not follow up. As often was the case, Mancini also started to bleed from his right eye.

Both men punched valiantly as the sixth round got underway, but neither felt the effects. What had not changed since the first round was the approach: Mancini came forward with occasional head movement, and Hector tried to time him with the right jab and slip away. As crafty as Hector was, his performance revealed a somewhat basic mentality that at times did not serve him well. No longer relying on precise angles, Hector was not setting up Mancini or throwing winning combinations. It was quite ordinary, and the fans bore the brunt of the mundane showdown.

Like other pressure punchers, Mancini knew that even if he did not land clean punches, the unencumbered pressure got him closer to his opponent. Mancini, going headfirst, started to make things very uncomfortable for Hector. Mancini pushed him to the ropes again to land body shots as he leaned against the Macho Man, agitating him as his rapid pace dissipated. Mancini capitalized with a left to the body and one to the head. Yet, as Hector had done so beautifully throughout his career, he bought time—even if it was only seconds—by retreating after Lane stepped in, which allowed him to reset. Hector then landed a straight left and right jab. After getting nailed by Mancini's right hand, Hector landed a jab and then spun away with his fist raised as the sixth round ended.

No one had great expectations for a bout that came six years too late. Even casual fans looking for an entertaining chess match chock full of strategy, high-energy exchanges, and savvy veteran moves were disappointed. Mancini relied on his right hand and body punching; Hector had his most success off of his straight left. Whenever a fight of this magnitude occurs years after the due date, there is always resentment and little fulfillment. Surely there was a contingent of fans who asked themselves, *I waited six years, for this?* Whatever the crowd in Reno expected that evening, the two fighters had at least engaged in an intriguing cat-and-mouse game full of peaks and valleys.

Past the midway point in the fight, Mancini understood the urgency. Although Hector was a shell of his former self, he was also limited in the sense that he could no longer keep up a grueling pace for twelve rounds. There was now a clear strategy to beat him, whereas he had been virtually unbeatable in his youth. And in the seventh round, Mancini got closer. First, he landed the best punch of the night, a sharp right hand—and then walked into a left by Hector. Mancini landed one more of those right hands at the end of the round. Looking at the bigger picture, Mancini could only land one shot, either because of Hector's lateral movement or because of his own limitations to trap his opponent. Nevertheless, as the round ended, Mancini shot a look at Hector to remind him, even as the underdog, that he was still right in front of him, refusing to back down.

"I didn't find him difficult to fight," Mancini recalled. "I had the ability to watch a guy and draw a bead on him. I remember he had certain, what I call 'tells.' He would walk to his left, throw a left, an uppercut, and a hook. He would throw that combination even if he missed you. Then he would walk to the left and come back to the right and throw those two jabs. What I did was try to break him up with my jab. For most guys, the speed and movement made Camacho really difficult to fight, but not for me."

In the eighth round, Hector started surviving rather than fighting. He moved directly into clinch mode, something that Mancini had strategized for. In some fights, Hector manipulated the referee to assist in his delaying tactics, but clearly, Lane was neither his friend nor a fan of his style, nor very subtle about his disdain as he slapped down Hector's clinching hands in the eighth, allowing Mancini to rake the Macho Man with a left hook and a short right on the inside.

Hector never stopped thinking; every movement, every jab, every counter was a by-product of his mind working in confluence with his capabilities. Thus, at twenty-seven, Hector tried to measure exactly what he could do within a twelve-round fight, which was much different than what he could have accomplished earlier. As Macho landed a scintillating seven-punch combination within the final ten seconds of the eighth round, he resurged, triggering the combination with an uppercut, then a short left on the inside, followed by a blend of a left uppercut and a hook, and then closing it out with a right hook. During their late-round exchange in the eighth round, Mancini must have—at the very least—felt some admiration when the old Hector emerged during that brief onslaught.

"I felt comfortable (in the middle rounds)," said Mancini. "From the beginning [my trainer Murphy Griffith] told me, 'Walk this guy down.' I remember I tried to pick up the pace."

Exhaustion set in by the ninth round, and both men fought carelessly. At one juncture, a Mancini punch sent Hector reeling, but he was not hurt. As much as Lane infuriated him by slapping his hands down during clinches, Hector still took advantage of the referee's positioning and used him as a pawn to hide behind to buy time and regain his legs. After screaming at Hector at the end of the ninth, Mancini intensified his actions to catch him with a nice right hand over his jab in the corner of the ring in the tenth. In the same round, Hector appeared overly concerned about a possible cut on his eye that may have resulted from a clash of heads.

During the pre-fight hype, Mancini had exclaimed, "He always has been and always will be in my shadow." Neither fighter, though, separated himself with his performance over those first ten rounds. As the fight unfolded, Mancini revealed some flashes of that youthful authenticity reflective of his smile and outward demeanor. But Mancini felt as if the path he was charting was more arduous than he had expected. And, in the tenth round, although Mancini was getting closer to beating Hector, he failed to attain his goal.

Mancini's biggest fears emerged in the eleventh round: Hector turned the fight into a clinch-fest. He landed a big straight left in the middle of the ring—one of the few significant punches of the round. In the midst of the banter between Hector and Lane, Mancini must have wondered how the judges viewed such an uneven round. Would they reward Hector even though he was the aggressor? Or would they detract points for these shenanigans that had nothing to do with boxing? What the judges did see was Hector insert two major uppercuts within a minute—one on the inside—and then close out the round with a jab and left hand to secure it. For Hector, the jab was quite valuable and, unlike many fighters, he never strayed from it. He used it not only to stabilize his opponent, but also to give himself space and time.

If Mancini was discouraged, he did not show it as he rushed out in the final round. "I felt in control at that point," Mancini recalled. "I was landing the harder punches, and he couldn't hurt me."

Unable to contain his anger, Mancini got in Hector's face and provoked him at the start of the final round. In return, Hector pushed him away. Still rushing, Mancini missed with a wild hook at the beginning of the twelfth. If Mancini fans prayed for one knockout punch to silence Macho, the obscene loudmouth, it was not a possibility. Amid the delays, exhaustion, and holding, the final round reflected an extension of the previous one. In the last thirty seconds, Mancini waded in, Hector briefly halted him, and then they clinched. Only a few substantial punches landed—two Camacho uppercuts while Hector held Mancini's head, and later a final jab and right hand. With seconds remaining, Hector ran behind Lane one last time, went to the corner, and used enough movement and tactics to not get hit again. The bell sounded as Mancini was about to release a right hand—a microcosm of the fight as Mancini was always a half step behind. The men stood in front of each other, not sure whether to hug or throw another punch. They opted for shaking hands and briefly embracing. It was not the way Mancini envisioned closing the fight or shutting up the fighter who once called him the "All-American White Boy." Neither fighter could deny the fact that the fans deserved more.

Griffith hoisted Mancini, who waved his fist to the crowd, certain he was the winner. Lacking enthusiasm, Hector gave one final "It's Macho Time" as his wraps were being taken off. When the split-decision win for Hector was read, Mancini could not hide his shock. Judge Keith Macdonald scored the fight for Mancini (116-112), while Chuck Giampa and Doug Tucker had Camacho ahead, 115-113.

Visibly disappointed by what he considered an unjustified score by Giampa, Mancini acted like a fighter who had achieved some of the closure he was seeking. "I accomplished everything I wanted."

Post-fight, journalist Michael Marley asked Mancini if he thought he won the fight: "Absolutely. I thought I pressed the fight, and got the job done."

Hector, on the other hand, stressed, "I thought he would get cut up. . . . It wasn't as close as I thought it was going to be, but he fought a great fight and he [Mancini] knows it."

From the start of his career, Hector was vocal about winning three titles. It was the one accomplishment that truly gave him a sense of self, allowing him to escape the media label "Kid from Rikers," replacing it with "Three-Time Champ." He was one of the few guys who escaped the neighborhood to be something more. Though he was not a sentimental guy, Hector definitely cherished this victory.

Although the fight would have been a fascinating war of pressure versus grace if they had each been in their prime, no one foresaw how much this battle would anger so many fans. It produced nothing of note: Hector ran, Mancini followed; Mancini punched, Hector clinched. Both men immediately called for a rematch that few felt was warranted.

"After the fight, we made amends," Mancini recalled. "It was cool. By then, we understood each other."

In private moments, Hector may have scolded himself for not being the best fighter he could be. But the more entrenched he got in the Macho image, the more he began to implode as an elite fighter. To those who remembered when he had startled the boxing world with his charm and charisma, the fighter they witnessed against Mancini left them feeling betrayed.

And a little sad.

Against
Pazienza

17

Hector Jr., now in middle school, never embraced being a fighter merely to impress or defend his father. He wondered why his father used harsh methods to "make" him tough. He was a kid trying to figure out how to maneuver in a world where everything revolved around his celebrity dad. That pressure alone was enough to crack any twelve-year-old.

"I never wanted to fight," Hector Jr. recalled, "but I didn't want to be a pussy. It was hard to hold that Macho image, but I wanted to show my father that I ain't no sucker. I wanted to be Macho too."

In order to be Macho, Junior also had to show his father that he was a man in other ways. When it came to drugs, Hector Sr. grew up around drugs in his house and everywhere in the neighborhood. It was part of the culture and difficult to avoid. During training in his prime, Hector Sr. rarely dabbled in drugs. Unlike any athlete in any sport, Hector was able to shift back to his competitive mode without a hitch. For many on his inside circle, it was an amazing transformation.

But Junior was not his father. Facial features? Yes. Boyish smile? Yes. Attitude? Not even close. Still, Camacho wanted his son to smoke, so he got Junior high behind Lady Queen of Angels Church in a small basement area and, in his mind, satisfied his thirst to make a man out of him.

Coughing uncontrollably, with his head spinning, Junior wondered if this was the type of man he wanted to be, but he never told his father how he really felt.

"The only thing I cared about was getting a He-Man action figure," Junior recalled. "He told me if I took a puff, we would go to Morris Toyland on 108th and 3rd Avenue and I would get it. That was all I thought about. I was so high"

Junior continued to follow right alongside his father, his hero.

Dennis Rappaport and Superfights promoted Hector's next fight against Tommy Hanks. Although he did not develop a close relationship with Hector, Rappaport saw the fighter's redeeming qualities and believed that he would shake off his own ring rust to beat Mancini easily. It did not happen. Rappaport felt that the fighter was in good company with Patrick Flannery leading the camp, but he also liked what Hector stood for.

"With Hector you have a lot of variables and question marks," said Rappaport. "He was a paradox. He had a lust for life and would dance to the beat of his own drum. He could be, at times, good-hearted, volatile, a man child, and someone who lacked discipline. By all accounts, a 'lovable rogue.'"

Doing his best to monitor Hector's whereabouts, Rappaport had to often take matters into his own hands. "We rented a car for Hector, and there is a bar in the hotel where he's staying," said Rappaport. "We get a call from the guy who leased him the car who tells us that he saw Hector jumping from the hotel window onto the car. We immediately call Hector."

"What the hell are you doing? You have a fight coming up and you're jumping on cars?"

"Wait a second, you've got it all wrong. That wasn't me. That was Bruce Lee," Hector replied.

"Hector, Bruce Lee has been dead for years!"

"Well, I guess it was me then."

These moments left Rappaport and his team at a loss, but they had rationalized the unpredictability factor as "Hector being Hector." Other times, Rappaport watched helplessly as Camacho got on the highway going in the wrong direction.

"He was very likable," said Rappaport, who promoted him on a handful of bouts. "He was hard to control and Patrick [Flannery], who was very straightforward and honest, did the best he could. But it was hard to maintain any discipline. Hector brought his own set of challenges. He did not have a filter, was all emotion, and would react without processing."

Hector's next opponent, Tommy Hanks, his sparring partner from the Mancini fight, was a surefire victory. Out of loyalty, Hector gave many of his former sparring partners opportunities to fight him; there was little risk involved. It was a win-win situation. The Friday before the Hanks bout (which was staged on a Monday evening), Hector met with Don King, whom he had been estranged from—along with Marty Cohen—since they parted ways in 1986 over money issues regarding an Edwin Rosario rematch. According to the report, King approached Hector and said, "We got to get married again," to which Hector replied, "Not so fast, Don." The underlying theme was that Hector wanted $1 million for a showdown with Julio Cesar Chavez, who often shifted between King and Bob Arum depending on his mood at the time.

On July 17, 1989, Hector traveled to the Trump Plaza Hotel in Atlantic City to face Hanks in a ten-round nontitle affair. Hanks, 18-3, could not keep up with Hector, who came in at 145 pounds, three pounds over the contracted weight of 142, his heaviest as a professional.

Hector's laissez-faire attitude after the fight reflected the performance. "I was able to do everything I wanted," he said. "I could have pushed the issue more but figured why not go ten rounds, what the heck? We were looking for a safe opponent before a million-dollar fight against Pazienza or Chavez." "Safe" was the key word; a UPI report had Hector looking "pudgy." Having been paid $600 per week as a sparring partner, Hanks earned $10,000 against Hector.

"I looked terrible against Mancini, but I could do everything I wanted tonight," said Hector.

Hector was well aware that despite the obvious lack of competitive edge between the two fighters, he needed Hanks, and similar opponents, to keep his body and mind fresh. So $50,000 and an easy victory over Hanks made sense from that perspective. Would that type of fight prepare him for a guy like Vinny Pazienza? Probably not, but in his mind, Hector had the skill to beat pressure guys. It was just a matter of maintaining an acceptable level of intensity during the training camp.

A short time after the Hanks decision, on August 1, 1989, Hector, then twenty-seven, flipped his jeep over three times while exiting a highway in Fort Lauderdale, Florida. Alongside him in the jeep was his brother, Felix. While Felix escaped without injury, Hector suffered a head wound and had to cancel his next fight scheduled for August 27 against Bobby Nunez in Sacramento, California. Hector was set to earn $50,000 against Nunez, but the crash, his ninth, sidelined him indefinitely.

What was less acceptable for fans in Atlantic City was Hector's unmotivated performance in a unanimous-decision victory over Raul Torres (10-3-2) on November 4, 1989. Yet it was his reaction to the booing of the crowd that got the most attention. "I'm going to go down as one of the most hateable fighters in history," Hector said. "The more they know me, the more they hate me because I'm so perfect. I get mad when they don't boo me. My girlfriend boos me when we make love because she knows it turns me on."

Clearly, Hector had calculated that being hated meant he was still relevant in a boxing world that was moving on to new idols. Not only was Chavez taking over, but other young Latin prospects were preparing to make their presence known. By showing up ringside at Chavez's and other future opponents' fights, Hector felt that he could maintain his star status.

A month after the victory over Torres, Hector joined King in the Mayfair Hotel Ballroom in Miami for a press conference. Outrageously demanding $4 million for a fight with Chavez, Hector continued to irk the flamboyant promoter.

"First, I am going to fight Meldrick Taylor because I have a contract with him," said Chavez. "Then, if everything comes out all right, then I'd like to fight Camacho, if for no other reason than to shut him up."

After only fighting once in 1987 and twice in 1988, Hector had made three appearances in 1989. He had renewed purpose, possibly because he saw how much he had slipped as a fighter. He turned to another showman, Vinny Pazienza, to prove that he was not the same lethargic fighter content to go through the motions as he had against Hanks and Torres.

After losing to Roger Mayweather by a unanimous decision in November 1988 for the WBC super lightweight title, Pazienza won his next three bouts and then positioned himself for another title shot. Still the WBO 140-pound champion, Hector had fought less-than-impressive nontitle tilts against Torres and former sparring partner Hanks. Pazienza represented his first defense. Main Events coordinated with Hector's adviser, Jim Levien, to bring the fight to the Convention Hall in Atlantic City. Although some observers noted that Mancini and Pazienza adhered to the same come-forward mentality, Pazienza did so with reckless abandon, as if engulfing an opponent in a torrent of activity. With a tendency to get out of control and thrive off of that approach, Pazienza saw his intensity as a necessity to unravel whoever was in front of him.

Assessing Macho's last real performance, the split-decision against Mancini, Pazienza may have been encouraged, since Mancini imperiled Hector, even after a four-year layoff. Who would have thought that Boom Boom, years removed from his prime, would have come so close to defeating a high-profile, elusive opponent like Hector? Likewise, few would have bet that Hector, the scintillating fighter on the rise to superstardom after he won the 130-pound title, would have to *pull out* a fight against Mancini. It did not equate. Though it was impossible to factor in the impact of Hector's lifestyle on his performances, critics could not ignore the obvious—he was no longer an elite performer, meaning he could no longer walk through lesser fighters he would have toyed with in his prime.

More important, Hector now had to extend himself against the good but not great fighters, a stinging rebuke of who he had become—or better yet—let himself become. The more Hector embraced his Macho image, the less he appeared a topflight fighter. To many, the entertaining sideshow blinded fans to his downfall, but those who were honest, observant, and realistic understood the repercussions. When Hector had worn an Alaskan fur coat into the ring and pranced around against John Montes years earlier, the act was entertaining, but the performance that came next overshadowed the dancing and pre-fight histrionics. Now there was no guarantee that Hector's talents would be the headlining act. That imbalance infuriated longtime fans. At times even Hector acknowledged the evident weaknesses even as he tried to mask them.

A Hector proponent might argue that he was still great because he still possessed an abundance of skills. But although he was as fast as and moved better than the majority of fighters in any weight class, speed and movement do not make one a great fighter. Hector occasionally did some things a little slower or less accurately than he had in the past, as when he let himself get trapped against the ropes toward the end of the Mancini fight. Macho weathered the storm in most cases, but if he had stayed more dedicated and devoted to his craft, he would have stepped aside, countered with a jab and an uppercut, and then drifted out of trouble. Instead, Macho got hit with a right hand and had to clinch.

Pazienza had his own interpretation of Hector's title fight with Mancini. "Boom Boom did as good as he could have done," said Pazienza. "He couldn't have done anymore. He fought balls to the wall, but Camacho was unhittable. Left-handed and fast as lightning. But Camacho was just too fast and too elusive. Too many tools, and too hard to beat. And he was still almost in his prime."

The offensive theatrics between Pazienza and Hector were so contrived that anyone on the promotional tour could see it had turned part Ringling Bros., part WWE. Hector expressed frustration when the script was not followed, but fans didn't seem too concerned. When asked if there was an agreement between the camps to intensify the antagonistic stuff, Pazienza did not waver.

"No, it was real. I didn't like him," said Pazienza. "It was all off the cuff. But it was wild. Hector was such an entertainer. I needed to hate my opponent. The more I hated them, the harder I would train."

The hype tour began when both fighters agreed wholeheartedly to sell a fight that was an attraction, but not a superfight on paper. Main Events and Trump Sports and Entertainment collaborated to promote the fight in Atlantic City at Convention Hall. It was Trump's first promotion under this banner. Initial reports had Hector earning $1 million and Pazienza getting $600,000, his biggest payday to date. The bout was set for February 3, 1990.

Pazienza's efforts to coax Hector to fight at 143 or 147 pounds were frustrated, as the Camacho camp wouldn't budge. Losing weight became a chore for Pazienza. Hector was putting his WBO super lightweight title on the line. Dan Duva of Main Events weighed in: "He's not a Ray Mancini who lost a decision to Camacho last year after chasing him fruitlessly for twelve rounds," said Duva. "Vinny is very coordinated, with good leg speed. He has more speed than anyone Camacho has fought. Camacho can't run from him for twelve rounds. . . . Vinny doesn't have great punching power, but he's got enough power to bother Camacho. I think this will be one of the most entertaining fights of the year."

The Camacho defense would be part of a pay-per-view tripleheader, which included a WBC lightweight title bout between Freddie Pendleton and Pernell Whitaker as well as Michael Moorer defending his WBO light heavyweight title against Marcellus Allen. The PPV cost was $19.95 for the card billed "Put Up or Shut Up."

In order to reassert himself for bigger paydays, Hector needed to prove that his subpar performances leading up to the bout were mere aberrations, and Pazienza, who had won his last three fights, needed a big-name victory on his resume after splitting with Greg Haugen and losing by unanimous decision to Roger Mayweather. To prepare for Pazienza, Camacho went to war with Pendleton in vicious all-out, no-holds-barred sparring sessions. The fights got so heated that Pendleton threatened to leave.

Few, however, were concerned about the actual fight itself; pay-per-view had ushered in a new era of entertainment and created new opportunities to make money. The stage was set and both guys were briefed on the proceedings.

In order to sell "Put Up or Shut Up," Pazienza would provoke Hector by calling him a "sissy," buying him a tutu, and hitting him during a press conference in his hometown, Cranston, Rhode Island. In one of the more notorious exchanges, Pazienza chided Hector for wearing a "skirt with Reeboks." Skilled at setting the tone for the pre-fight histrionics, Hector relied on Fred Flintstone and Barney Rubble salvos to illustrate his disdain for trainers Lou Duva and Kevin Rooney, gleefully yelling, "Yabba Dabba Do" whenever they were in the vicinity. At every press conference, Hector threw at least one punch or set off a riot, turning the gathering into a farce. Whenever Hector felt slighted or could not muster a comeback, he urged Pazienza to "Sit down, Mr. Class!"

Everyone involved understood why Hector and Pazienza were trying so hard: a vicious cycle had begun. Hector slapped Rooney, then Mancini (an analyst); Pazienza punched Hector. The cumulative effect of the verbal sparring overshadowed the fight itself. "You have two glitter boys, but people are buying it," trainer Emanuel Steward said. "When you think of these guys, you think of them saying, 'I have a better dance than you,' or 'I have better sunglasses,' or 'I have more rhinestones on my robe.' It just goes to show anything promoted properly will sell."

Hector tried to convince reporters that he understood and justified the crass direction he was taking the promotions by stating, "I created me." Yet with each fight, Hector was distancing himself from the charismatic and creative fighter he had once been, even labeling the conflict a "phony grudge." Because Hector had set a standard for being so ebullient and spirited, the promotions seemed that much more pathetic.

"When we were on tour, he used to say, 'Vinny, you look soft. I am going to get ready for you Vinny, I am gonna get ready for you.' He said that like fifty times," Pazienza recalled. "But he was a fun guy. He was a nice dude. He was a cool guy. He was wild. He was different. He was not your average fighter."

When Pazienza and his girlfriend were riding in one of the rickshaws on the Atlantic City boardwalk, Hector went into vintage Macho mode, pulling up alongside Pazienza's girlfriend to get in some final personal shots.

"What are you doing with this guy? Look at that nose. Look at me, 'I'm pretty,'" Hector told her. "And after I get done with him, he'll be even uglier."

As heated as Pazienza was, all he could do was smile.

"You could tell Pazienza was getting upset, but he was cool about it," said Jerry Villarreal Sr.

Despite his frustration, Pazienza could not bring himself to hate Hector, even when Hector channeled his inner Gloria Estefan and sang "Macho Man's Going to Get You" at a press conference.

Hector continued his bizarre behavior away from the pre-fight hype and almost ended up in jail. "We were headed back to the hotel, and we stopped at a store to grab some food," Jerry Villarreal Sr. recalled. "Mach just started opening up ice cream cones, taking bites, saying, 'I don't like that one,' and then putting them back. And the cops came looking for him in his room, and I put him out the back door into my room. We were trying to give them Boo Boo [Hector's brother] instead since they looked alike. Donald Trump sent over some of his suits to handle it, and we went back to the store and the guy gave the owner some comped tickets, a couple hundred dollars to pay the slots, and a hotel suite. . . . [Hector] did things like that because he thought it was innocent and cute, but he never thought it would hurt anybody."

Pazienza had difficulty regulating his emotion and troubled his opponents with a turbulent style that, at times, included precise punching and effective combinations. He and his team practiced how to attack the clinching version of Hector. Likewise, Hector still possessed speed—though not blinding—and better-than-average foot movement. When he was in shape, he could sit and rip opponents with that jab—or double jab—and then step inside to land the straight left.

Undefeated, Hector (36-0, fifteen KOs) had already fulfilled his quota of three titles, although critics questioned the validity of his most recent WBO version. At 28-3, with twenty-three KOs, Pazienza salivated at what a win over Hector could do for his career, setting his sights on million-dollar paydays and a prospective showdown with WBC champion Marlon Starling

Hector's team, headed by Flannery, claimed to have a verbal agreement to face fallen Aaron Pryor for $1.75 million. For some reason, Hector was fixated on a bout with Pryor, a no-win situation on any level. Since Hector liked to help his friends get a payday, he may have been trying to help the down-and-out Pryor. Flannery outlined Hector's next three bouts as Pryor, a rematch with Mancini, and then a showdown with Chavez.

Pazienza, if privy to Hector's previous three performances, may have felt that he was meeting him at the ideal moment in his roller-coaster career. Just a year earlier, in March 1989, Hector had eked out his disputed split-decision victory over Mancini. After the victory, Hector had looked average in his next two bouts. These were not Hector's best moments.

On a grand stage again, Hector had the opportunity to show the boxing world that, despite his continuous party lifestyle, he could still summon up and call upon his extraordinary boxing skills for one final bout. The impromptu moves and blinding speed that captured audiences when he was in the amateurs and during his first fifteen or twenty bouts had become nearly nonexistent. Some fans still sang his praises, but they did not take into account how easy a twenty-year-old Hector would have beaten Pazienza.

Likewise, if Hector had seen Pazienza get manhandled by Haugen, he, too, would have been only slightly concerned about this version of the Pazmanian Devil.

After the pre-fight hype campaign with theatrics from both camps, Hector amped up the flamboyance as he donned a Native American headdress straight out of the Village People as he came down the aisle at Convention Hall in Atlantic City on February 3, 1990, promoted by Main

Events. Boos rained down on him. Tony Perez, familiar with Hector's ring demeanor from working previous fights, was referee. Pazienza came in at a trim 138 pounds, two pounds under the 140-pound limit. Standing in the middle of the ring, Pazienza glared at Hector, at 140 pounds, who looked down and refused to engage.

As the fighters waited for the opening bell, one thing was clear: Pazienza would not stray from his herky-jerky style and would nettle Hector at every juncture, and Hector would pump that jab, move laterally, insert an uppercut, and time his moves to offset Pazienza's relentless charges. Early in that first round, Pazienza moved in hot pursuit. The stylistic contrasts created several awkward clinches as the round progressed. In the midst of Pazienza's fiery antics, Hector stayed cool and composed. By switching up the distance in the round, Hector befuddled Pazienza with a sharp jab and a straight left hand.

Then came the tactics: Holding Pazienza's head with his left hand, Hector darted in with a right uppercut. Perez was determined to minimize any of Hector's dirty stratagems. Ironically, Hector, a fast starter, reverted back to that straight left as he doubled up on it to jam Pazienza. With no plan to get inside, Pazienza forged ahead and walked directly into a Hector jab. As the round ended, Hector, all business, stared in Pazienza's direction. For an inactive fighter like Hector, earning that first round proved vital. Fighters working off adrenaline like Pazienza tend to crumple when a technical boxer stands back and allows him to wade in.

A Camacho pattern continued in the second round: Let Pazienza ambush him, stay back or sidestep him, and then plant an uppercut from the side of Pazienza's body or a three-punch combination. Every time Pazienza missed in the second round, Hector made him pay for his transgressions. Pazienza used more head movement as he tried to get inside, but he did not succeed. With twenty-seven seconds remaining, Hector sliced Pazienza with a straight left and followed the punch with a three-punch combination, which clearly bothered Pazienza, standing directly in front of him.

During the final moments of the round, Hector nailed and spun Pazienza, who had been fueled by his frenetic pace and a maelstrom of movements. At his best, Hector relied on speed and his own brand of intensity that, unlike Pazienza's, did not cede control. Pazienza did land significant punches, but Hector integrated a startling array of moves, tactics, and mind games to lure Pazienza into his fight plan. This version of Hector orchestrated his movements perfectly, in comparison with his lackluster performance against Mancini, which lacked any discernible cohesion and felt fragmented.

"Vinny exposed himself. For Vinny it worked, but for that fight it played into Camacho's strengths. Vinny was always an action fighter who was looking for a fight," said former boxer turned boxing commentator John Scully.

But Pazienza recalled a different version of events: "I knew—in my heart of hearts—that after that first fucking round that I wasn't going to win that fight. I pressed my heart out, but I just couldn't get over the weight [issue)]."

Throughout the fight, Hector summoned up brief glimpses of himself in the prime of his career—the masterful boxer who took risks and delivered as much as he clinched. In the third round, Pazienza, now antsy, started to sprint at Hector on occasion where frustration ensued. Pushed back by a short uppercut, Pazienza went back to establishing the jab. With Hector already in clinch mode, the fight slowed down for Pazienza. And although Hector flurried off the ropes on one occasion, the shots were mostly arm punches. Fueled and salivating, Pazienza, having trapped Camacho on the ropes, landed the best punch of the round—a straight right that landed cleanly. As the round ended, Pazienza scolded Hector: "That's what you're gonna get."

Typically, the high-energy Hector began to slow down in the middle of the fight. Pazienza and every other opponent were aware of this flaw. So Pazienza made the fight even more physical and pushed Hector against the ropes with nowhere to escape. "[Rooney] didn't even mention that I needed to make the fight physical," said Pazienza. "We knew that from the beginning. When you fight Camacho, you have to deal with a motherfucker who was fast as lightning. In that fight, I felt like half of me was there. There were five fights like that. I felt like I was in the middle of a bad dream where you can't hit somebody."

Ten years earlier, Hector would have easily jabbed, spun, and then turned the tables, but this Hector did not have access to those skills. Instead, he absorbed numerous punches to his arms, chest, guard, and occasionally clean shots to his head. Agitated, Hector didn't want to accept that he would have to forge through Pazienza's frenetic exchanges against the ropes, but he also understood it was part of who he was now as a fighter, and the Pazienzas of the world, although light punchers, now had at least a fighting chance to land one solid punch.

Toward the end of the sixth round, the revitalized Pazienza placed a hook to Hector's body and a straight right that landed cleanly in the trenches. The tenor of the fight had not completely changed, but Pazienza was closing the gap against a fighter who controlled early rounds. Animated and pissed in the seventh, Pazienza boldly raised his fist into the air to ignite the crowd as he accidentally drifted to Hector's corner. Referee Perez had become an unwilling pawn in the fight as Hector started to use him as a shield to buy time. More important, Perez allowed Pazienza to fight out of Camacho's clinching fiesta, which had become as much a staple of his repertoire as his double jab, step-back, and straight left had.

Just as Pazienza the cheerleader started to bring the crowd back into the fight, Hector used jabs and movement to establish his version of normalcy. The more Pazienza charged and yelled, the more composed Hector became as he started to put multiple shots together. "Yeah, I was banking on him a little bit to get tired late in the fight," said Pazienza. "But I was worse than him . . . and I had no power."

Dipping into his reserves in the ninth round, Hector spun, hit illegally, tripled up on his jab, sent Pazienza off balance with a straight left, and forced the judges to notice his resurgence. Perez, passive, only warned Hector, even though the combination of holding and hitting warranted at least one penalty. The crowd reacted as Pazienza landed a powerful right hand and then battered Camacho with a right uppercut. Despite Pazienza's energized performance, Hector emerged victorious in the round by landing four to six vicious uppercuts that derailed the incoming challenger.

"You couldn't hit that motherfucker with a bag of rice," said Pazienza. "He was very defensive minded. He did not want to be hit."

Heading into the championship rounds, a content Hector offset an exhausted and flailing Pazienza. Having employed all of his strategies, Pazienza's controlled aggression morphed into agitation and recklessness. By the tenth round—one in which Hector controlled the last ten seconds—Pazienza, bleeding from both eyes, stormed in. But his desperate attempts were too little too late, for Camacho had secured too many rounds and driven him back with cleaner punches. Although Pazienza scored on hooks to the body, Hector used his jab to fend him off.

"He was so cagey . . . because he was a left-hander with speed, which made it worse," Pazienza recalled.

Things got worse in the last two rounds, mirroring the chaos of the pre-fight fiasco. Perez deducted a point from Pazienza for butting. Pazienza also shoved his left elbow into Hector's face and then screamed at him. Pazienza could not contain his emotions, and Hector, exhausted, had little left to give. To his credit, Pazienza won the last round, punctuating it with a crowd-igniting right hand and a rare uppercut, which had been Hector's staple punch. But Hector nevertheless earned a unanimous decision with scores of 117-116, 119-109, and 115-112 in his favor.

"I was weak, weak, weak," Pazienza recalled. "And he was great. He really got up for me. No drugs, no nothing. My fight against Camacho was the last great Hector Camacho you have ever seen. After the win over me, he went crazy. He was never the same again."

Pazienza added: "Fighters know whether they won or lost. Some fighters bullshit themselves, but they know if they won the fight. Deep down inside they know it. If you hit me three times, and I hit you once, ok, you won the fight. It was close, but he won the fight."

After every fight, Hector felt the need to release his pent-up anger and hostility. He grabbed a microphone and addressed the crowd. First, he told them he fought well, then burped. Then he made an obscene gesture at those who verbally questioned his performance, noted that he was a "good father," and asked for a female to accompany him. All in one night's work. Later, he dashed off on to the Atlantic City boardwalk in a black robe and boots after exclaiming to a reporter, "I think I am the only Mr. Excitement out there today."

Meanwhile, a fight erupted in Pazienza's camp when a process server attempted to serve a summons to trainer Kevin Rooney. In the fracas, Dino Duva was arrested and then released; Duva later berated the sportswriters covering the bout for being too critical of the matchup. Amid the turbulence, Hector called out none other than Aaron Pryor, who was all but finished as a fighter.

After the hard-fought victory, Hector wanted to go back to New York to party, so he and Jerry Villarreal Sr. got in a black Ferrari and went back to Spanish Harlem. Still buzzed from the victory, he was looking forward to the ensuing celebration. As he drove near his mother's apartment in Spanish Harlem, everyone knew that the Macho Man was back.

"The cops see him with all this gold and they think he's some kind of drug dealer," Villarreal Sr. recalled. "Instead of Hector driving around the block, he backs up a block and a half. The lights go on and a cop pulls up, 'Who the fuck do you think you are driving like this?'

"I called Jeff Levine and told him: 'We're here at the precinct.'

"'For what?' asked Levine.

"'Hector backed up the car like a block and half.'

"'Oh my God.'

After learning who Hector was, the cops let him go, reminding him to be careful. Instead of slowing down, Hector started to race his Ferrari up and down the streets of Spanish Harlem, clearly disregarding the warning. The lights came on again; this time it was a group of four undercover cops in a taxicab.

"They pull up beside us and yell, 'Pull over that fucking car!' All I am thinking is, 'We're going to Rikers tonight.' When the guys come to my side, Hector gets out and leans against the car like James Dean. He's got a black eye from the [Pazienza] fight. I look at the officer and tell him, 'Excuse me officer, but that's Hector Camacho.' He looked at me and said, 'I thought I recognized him.' 'They gave us this car I tell him, and I'm trying to get him to park it. It's too much vehicle for him, officer.'"

At this point, the police officer said to Hector, "You got one black eye, do you want another one?"

"But officer, why would you want to do that? Do you know this is a million-dollar head you're looking at?" Camacho responded.

Another officer intervened, "Kick his ass and then you can tell people you kicked the shit out of Hector Camacho."

Unbeknownst to him at the time that it was the actual champ they had pulled over, the officer, once full of bravado, relented and let them go. Exhausted, Villarreal Sr. wanted to head home; Hector, despite being still full of energy, succumbed and headed back to his condo. Just to get one final jab in, Hector ran a red light as he pulled into the parking garage. The lights came on again. Jerry Sr. jumped out of the car and started running toward the elevator. "If he was going to jail, he was going alone," he said.

The cop came over, "Camacho, is that you again?"

"Yes."

"You've been on the fucking radio all night long. Are you in for tonight?"

"Yes, officer."

The cop told the parking attendant: "Take his keys and don't you dare give them back to him until the morning."

In the end, the antics of both Pazienza and Hector paid off as the fight made millions on the pay-per-view platform and both men reaped the benefits. Duva announced to the press that Main Events and Trump Plaza collaborated to put out a promotion that exceeded a $1 million price tag. Instead of a typical promotional campaign, the Main Events/Trump affiliation targeted homes digitally with the conventional wisdom that the newspapers would only dilute the competitiveness of what looked like an average showdown on paper. The risk worked brilliantly.

As belligerent as Hector could be, he was equally adept at transitioning back away from the glitz and flair after the fight ended. Before the Pazienza fight, Hector was driving his Lamborghini back from California when the alternator went out in a small town. Hector and Villarreal Sr. met a kid at a gas station who would go on to repair the car so they could return to New York. Later at the dealership, they were given the black Ferrari as a temporary replacement for the Lamborghini. Hector never forgot what the kid did for him.

"I remember seeing some kid at the fight and asking Hector, 'Who the fuck is this kid?' He told me it was the kid who helped them with the car. Hector sat him ringside and paid for everything. The kid must have told that story a million times. [Hector] had such a good heart," said Villarreal Sr.

Being Macho Again   18

Junior, now twelve, grasped the impact—and intent—of his father's idiosyncratic behavior in and out of the ring. He began to see how the events unfolded and what his father's reactions meant in the bigger picture.

When Junior was in Puerto Rico for the summer, he often stayed at the Dupont Plaza Hotel with his father. One night his father put him to bed, and, as usual, promised he would be back. At 7 a.m., the initial alarming ring of the phone did not wake Junior. Eventually, Junior, bleary eyed, did get to the phone, which had continued to ring.

"Papi, you okay?" his father asked. "I've been calling you."

"I'm okay, Pop."

"I need you to do me a favor. Look under the pillow on the other bed. There is $600 for you."

"Pop, where are you?"

"That money is for you to get some food and clothes. Write my number down. I'm in Miami. I'll be back tomorrow."

Alone in the hotel, Junior went downstairs and saw yellow tape blocking everyone off from a fire that had taken place in the hotel. Luckily, family friends would come pick him up.

"My grandmother was scared shitless," said Junior. "But I was used to that stuff. I knew he would never do me no harm. He had his limits, and he wouldn't pass them."

Macho did what he wanted, when he wanted. He did not worry about how leaving his twelve-year-old son alone in a hotel would scar him. While the rest of the family was up in arms and panicked about Junior's whereabouts, Macho calmly went about his business. In his mind, his son was fine.

Junior was now old enough to be Macho's lookout. He would stay in the car while his father would barhop. "My dad would be shaking hands with people, and he would look back at me and I would nod my head," said Junior. "I would watch the drinks. I would be able to tell him, 'That guy was fake' from what I saw."

After a couple more hours of driving, Macho would just stop the car and start dancing in the street. Depending on the time of the drive, Macho might be taking drugs. "The guy was nuts," said Junior.

But Junior rarely was shocked by his father's behavior; it was part of the culture and family lifestyle. "With all the drugs, and everybody doing everything—it was big for a ten- or twelve-year-old to see all that," said Junior. "They tried to hide it, but I knew what they were doing. I didn't care. I loved my dad immensely. I just wanted to be around him. I knew that it wasn't right what was going on, but it felt good."

When the possibility of a bout with Tony Baltazar emerged, Jimmy Montoya, who hadn't worked with Hector for years, reached out to old friend Dan Duva at Main Events—which was now promoting Hector, Meldrick Taylor, and Pernell Whitaker. Hector and Montoya came to an understanding that they would stick to business and agreed that Baltazar, Montoya's fighter and a former Camacho sparring partner, would be a worthwhile opponent. Montoya knew that his decision to work with Edwin Rosario had hurt Hector deeply.

"I regretted it," said Montoya. "I was hurt. He was hurt. It was a stupid thing to do."

But in boxing, some fighters are willing to give second chances. Whether or not Hector felt that he deserved blame for the breakup or not, he didn't show it.

"I had a good talk with Hector," said Montoya, "and he said, 'This is a business, let's get it on.'"

Not one to hold grudges or badmouth someone through the press (unless he initiated it), Hector learned a lot from Montoya. When they separated, Hector told a boxing reporter that he was open to working with Montoya again. Four years had passed, and Hector felt comfortable enough to open up the dialogue.

Statistics proved that after they split, Hector was still a great fighter, but not close to a brilliant one. How much credit did Montoya deserve for corralling Hector enough to exhibit that level of mastery is unclear, but before the split, Hector told journalist Michael Katz, "[There was] always one guy I could always talk to, Jimmy Montoya."

"My father was a good listener," said Junior. "He liked to work more with someone he respected. Jimmy is a good trainer and they worked well together for the [Jose Luis] Ramirez fight. He looked great, and he loved LA. But Jimmy wasn't for the bullshit. You know, getting high and the bad people. His mindset was, 'You come to the gym by yourself and not with twenty people.' It was his way or the highway."

The Baltazar bout would be held at Caesars Tahoe Outdoor Arena, Stateline on August 11, 1990. Before the fight, Hector signed a four-fight, $10 million deal with HBO that would end in 1991. All roads led to Julio Cesar Chavez. At the time, Hector was still undefeated (37-0, fifteen KOs) and coming off his strong victory over Pazienza six months earlier. Baltazar, 35-3-1, had three respectable losses on his resume, including a stoppage loss to Robin Blake and decision losses to Buddy McGirt and Howard Davis Jr. To Baltazar's credit, he was 11-1 in his previous twelve fights and was familiar enough with Hector from watching his training sessions at the Olympic Gym to understand, at the very least, what his weak points were. Exposing them would be difficult. Back when he was watching Hector, Baltazar was coming up the ranks and being trained by his father, Frankie. Hector was already established and had formed a nice bond with Montoya. The Baltazars, Montoya, and Hector all became friends.

"We had a good relationship," said Baltazar. "We hung out with Sylvester Stallone and Tony Danza at Carlos and Charlie's. [Even after we fought] we stayed friends. He was doing drugs since the beginning. And after a while I lost track of him. But he was such a nice guy and we got along so well. We were like brothers."

Sparring with him, as Baltazar did, was never easy. "In the ring, when we sparred, he was so quick and sharp. He was quick, but he threw combinations. He didn't hit hard. His punches felt like getting hit with pillows. But he was so fast . . . but he could never really punch," said Baltazar. "When we fought, I wanted to try and cut off the ring. Defensively, I didn't want to get hit. I wanted to cut off the ring, and dig to the body and legs. You hit him where you can, to slow him down."

Having had so much experience with Hector, Baltazar knew all his little tendencies in the ring. He continued his analysis: "Hector was a hit-and-run guy, whether it was in sparring or in the ring. I never saw him slow down or go toe-to-toe."

"After years of sparring and hanging out, Hector said, 'One day I will give you a shot at the title.' Montoya told me and, at first, I thought I would hit him and knock him out," said Baltazar.

The fight itself reflected a much different reality: two old chums, who, at times, showed a competitive edge, collecting a payday. Making his first defense of his WBO super lightweight title on August 11, 1990, Hector had managed to stay undefeated despite some questionable decisions. Sugar Ray Leonard and Larry Merchant called the fight, which was televised by HBO. Ranked fifth at 140, Baltazar had a puncher's chance against Hector. Referee Richard Steele officiated the bout. Before the fight, Hector and Baltazar shared a laugh in the middle of the ring, making some ringsiders question the validity of the contest.

"At the beginning of the fight, I laughed like we were buddies," Baltazar recalled. "They wondered, 'Why is he laughing? Why are they acting like buddies?' But we were friends for years. It was hard for me to try and hurt him."

No one would have a problem with a fighter challenging a former sparring partner, as long as the fight had an authentic feel to it. However, as Hector easily worked his way inside, pulled back, and then landed a straight left, there was an odd feeling that he had no real concerns about the man in front of him. Returning fire in the second round, Baltazar had success with his left hook and went to the body in the third round with right and left hooks. Analyst John Scully summarized Hector perfectly when he said, "He hits you when you're not ready for it." At twenty-eight, trained by Rudy Mata, Hector was also more vulnerable to absorbing punches than ever before. He was just crafty enough to deflect the harder punches when necessary.

An 8-1 favorite, Hector fought beautifully in the fourth round as he broke out and unleashed a torrent of jabs and left hands early. Within that sequence, Hector landed eight jabs, a counter jab, and a left uppercut to Baltazar's ear, and also whipped a right hook off the jab. Loyal fans looked on nostalgically as Hector proved that he could still unveil a vintage Macho round. Not all great fighters had that ability to summon past skills and remind fans why they were once so iconic. But Hector sustained that magic over the course of the entire round; of course, in pure Macho style, he had to pull Baltazar's head down and ravage him with a left uppercut. But, as was the case over the next eight rounds, Steele turned a blind eye to the antics. By the end of the fourth, an arm-weary Hector slapped hands with Baltazar and headed back to the corner.

Feigning exhaustion at the start of the fifth round, Hector put his hands on his knees but quickly got into his stance and missed three punches. In hot pursuit, Baltazar, now moving to his left, just missed with two hard body shots and a counter that whizzed past Hector. On two occasions, Steele warned Baltazar, "Let him go, Tony," and watched with little concern as Hector deftly placed his right glove squarely on Baltazar's head to stabilize him for another uppercut, to which he received a harmless rebuke. It was hard to imagine that Hector had only been deducted a handful of points throughout his professional career. Some referees may have reasoned that taking points away meant that they were detracting from Hector's game plan, because he was so adept at integrating the moves into his strategy.

A careless Baltazar walked into an uppercut in the sixth, but, refreshed, started to dig body shots. With ten seconds remaining, Baltazar attacked with a right hook but could not get into a rhythm as Steele inexplicably broke them up, saving Hector from any punishment.

Looking at his fighter between rounds, Montoya told Baltazar, "Now, you're working man. Keep it up." In the other corner, Hector, who constantly looked into the crowd and even asked Leonard, "Is Larry behaving himself?" was singing to the audience. Having fun again in the ring in the seventh round, Hector ripped off an eight-punch combination and landed a strong right hand that shook Baltazar, whose counter missed its mark.

Seemingly always a half step behind Hector, Baltazar could not cope with the speed factor. Unable to avoid that right uppercut, Baltazar still landed two right hands at the end of the eighth round. Steele inserted himself again in the ninth by deducting a point from Baltazar for low blows. He stayed silent regarding Hector. Still, Baltazar was holding himself back by letting Hector tie him up and by staying passive when Hector appeared vulnerable. Those two components also quieted a once-spirited crowd.

Covering up and hurt in the tenth round, Baltazar retreated. For the first time, the fight, which initially felt like a sparring session, now had Hector surging ahead and dominating, whether he was spinning Baltazar and frustrating him or starting a vicious combination with a straight left hand and then blistering him with a barrage of uppercuts and hooks. A masterful Hector then slipped to the left to create more angles. At his zenith in this round and earlier in the fourth, Hector had begun to convince critics that he could still fight. What worked best for him, as he showed in the eleventh round, was a right uppercut. Hector then stepped to the right to avoid any counters. Psychologically, Baltazar had stopped aggressively seeking Hector, and even though he landed a nice shot in the final round, his fate had been decided. Hector retained his title, with scores by judges Doug Tucker, 118-109; Cindy Bartin, 117-110; and Keith MacDonald, 118-109.

Montoya approached Hector after the fight: "You sonofabitch. You're too damn intelligent."

Not only did this fight improve Hector's mindset, it also opened doors to big fights, since he had shown more talent, stamina, and fighting spirit than he had in years. "My confidence is coming back," Hector said. "The desire is comin' back. Did you hear the people? They loved me. I still got my own show. I'm cute. I'm smart. I'm undefeated."

The performance also soothed concerns at Main Events. Hector had put to rest any questions raised by his uneven performances in the past. Duva and Main Events looked ahead to a revitalized career. "I thought it was his best fight in five or six years," said Duva, "He really put on a show. He showed me that he and Julio Cesar Chavez would be a hell of a fight." HBO's Seth Abraham, less than complimentary in the past, also felt that Hector seemed rejuvenated.

Then the old impulsive Hector was back. "I wish Sugar Ray would make 147 pounds," said Hector. "I'd beat his ass too."

As Oscar De La Hoya looks on, Hector embraces promoter Bob Arum after a press conference before a fight for De La Hoya's WBC welterweight world title in Las Vegas on September 10, 1997. The "Golden Boy" easily outpointed Macho, winning a twelve-round unanimous decision. *Getty Images*

Hector often sketched out his flamboyant outfits. He loved the process of creating them.
Courtesy of Shelly Salemassi

The Macho Man shows off the finished product. *Courtesy of Shelly Salemassi*

Shelly Salemassi with Hector at the height of their love affair. *Courtesy of Shelly Salemassi*

Hector shows off his "MACHO" chain. *Courtesy of Shelly Salemassi*

Hector poses with his brother Felix, Shelly, Hector Jr., and boxer Kevin Kelley. *Courtesy of Shelly Salemassi*

Always the life of the party, Hector sings with the band at his favorite bar in Detroit. *Courtesy of Shelly Salemassi*

Hector poses with his family. *Courtesy of Shelly Salemassi*

Hector Jr. stands
in front of a mural
in Spanish Harlem
honoring his
father. *Courtesy of
Christian Giudice*

The residents of Spanish Harlem haven't forgotten Hector (and his iconic chain).
Courtesy of Christian Giudice

Hector's mother Maria reminds us that "It's still Macho Time!"
Courtesy of Christian Giudice

Macho and Junior. *Getty Images*

Haggling with Haugen

19

Inactivity had sapped Hector of his will to fight in the past, so his team looked to sign him up for another fight quickly after his defeat of Tony Baltazar. Dan Duva speculated that Hector would ideally stage one more fight and then be ready for a $4 million payday against Mexican idol Julio Cesar Chavez. Despite facing some opposition, Duva opted for Greg Haugen to be the setup guy for Hector.

Going into the bout with Haugen, Hector was coming off his wins over Vinny Pazienza and Tony Baltazar. In each of those victories, the once great fighter displayed glimpses of what he had been in the early 1980s. Shifting his weight to sit on his punches, deftly fighting while moving backward, creating distance, craftily buying time, shooting multiple jabs and uppercuts, Hector, at his best, worked like an artist. But he was not that same fighter anymore. He was more predictable now, as Haugen would later affirm: "We knew Camacho only boxed for one third of each round." If once Hector's performances were fluid and dictated by moments where his power funneled through his speed, now his performances were fragmented displays of occasional attacks shielded by extreme caution.

With a historic fight with Chavez on the horizon, there was good reason why members of Hector's camp were not calling out Haugen. "We had a wonderful contract with Chavez's people already," said Hector's lawyer, Jim Levien. "It was with the Duvas for $3 to $5 million. It was a great contract, and some contracts were really difficult. But it stipulated that we couldn't lose the fight. I wanted him to wait, but he didn't want to."

"Hector did not see it as a big fight," Levien recalled. "And he was a much better boxer than Haugen. He thought it would be easy. He wanted that fight."

Haugen had been waiting patiently for this bout. In the Pazienza and Baltazar bouts, Hector had stayed disciplined and had followed a clear strategy. Pazienza recklessly attacked him from the start, whereas Baltazar, oozing respect, allowed Hector to set the tone for most of the fight. Neither of those fights had prepared Hector for Haugen, even though Haugen was inextricably linked to Pazienza from three previous wars.

The lead-up to the Pazienza and Baltazar bouts could not have been more different: Pazienza appeared to have colluded with Hector to stage their own B-movie extravaganza. Meanwhile, there were no expectations for Baltazar, as he and Hector were good friends and former sparring partners. Unlike Pazienza, Haugen was not in on the charade; he just did not give a shit. That agitated Hector, who needed to dictate the direction of the show. With Haugen, he could not. In Haugen, Hector was facing an opponent potentially as belligerent and obscene as he could be.

Fully aware that he had a gem with the Chavez contract, Levien tried to understand Hector's decision to move forward with this bout. If the press conference (which included Haugen and Bob Arum in Las Vegas, and a telephone hookup with Main Events with Hector and two other fighters in New York) leading up to the fight foreshadowed what was about to occur, Hector and his team needed to be prepared for psychological warfare. Haugen excoriated opponents, whereas Pazienza displayed a playful side but did not transgress boundaries.

"[Camacho] is not one of my favorite fighters," said Bob Arum, Haugen's promoter, at the press conference at Caesars Palace in Las Vegas. "Deep down, Camacho is nothing more than a punk. I give [Greg Haugen] a good shot at finally ridding the world of Camacho."

On the same call, Haugen added, "I don't think that Camacho does the sport a lot of good. I think he is a disgrace to boxing—the things he says, the stupid things he wears."

Taken aback, Hector noted that both men were "disrespectful" and pointed out that Haugen was "just a tune-up, don't forget that. I also remember you said I put candy in my nose."

Hector's perspective had changed the minute Haugen had mentioned his drug use publicly. Haugen immediately transformed, in Hector's eyes, from a decent boxer to his enemy. Hector made clear things had just become personal for him.

Hector then let a litany of pejoratives fly regarding Arum and Haugen's sexuality, and the promotions took off from there.

"Hector didn't get along with Arum," said Levien. "In the buildup to the fight, they had words—'Fuck you,' that sort of thing. Hector was at fault too."

Although Hector loved to mix things up to help sell a fight, he wanted to sell it on his terms. So when Arum and Haugen ganged up on him before he had even said a word, he could not let it go. They also had the advantage of offending him over the phone where Hector, defenseless to fight back, had no recourse to come at them physically. First round went to Haugen.

"Hector was not a hateful guy," said Levien. "He lost his temper quickly, but he could not keep hating someone or hold a grudge. Haugen was very nasty with him and maybe that was his technique to get himself in a certain mindset."

For Hector's camp, things got worse from there, as he experienced weight problems, and the pattern of partying for weeks at a time after a fight had taken a nasty toll on him. Levien knew that Hector would come in overweight to camp and Patrick Flannery would have to whip him into shape. Flannery did a nice job, but, at twenty-nine years old, Hector's body no longer responded the same way, and taking weight off was now more arduous.

"I knew he had to cut weight, and it killed him," said Haugen, "especially if you are dehydrated. There's no way to recover in twelve hours. That's why I always wanted the weigh-in the morning of the fight, so there was less time to recover. If I'm in good shape, I'm hard to beat."

As astute as Haugen was regarding Hector's mental state, he was also vicious when it came to matching Macho's hysterics. But Hector had millions waiting for him against Chavez, and Haugen, an early 7-1 underdog, recognized how blatantly he was being overlooked. Hector felt he could still stir fans up. "I guess that's what makes me colorful," Hector said. "Some people just don't like me."

Before the weigh-in, Haugen attempted to render Hector irrelevant by giving him his own stage. Knowing that he did not stand to gain anything by showing up at a Wednesday night press conference, four nights before the fight, Haugen stayed home and told Dan Duva of Main Events to let Hector be the star of the show. His absence prompted Pernell Whitaker, who was fighting Anthony Jones on the February 23 card, to pull out his best Arsenio Hall impression, when he looked at Hector and said, "That only leaves me and my friend. HMMMM."

What happened at the weigh-in, according to Haugen, gave him cause for optimism. The morning of the fight, Hector, who was pounds over the weight limit three weeks before the fight, had to sit in steam baths for seven hours in order to sweat off 4 pounds. Flannery had to pull out all the stops.

"He was walking around like he was dying," said Flannery. "In fact, I had to tell him, on the way to the weigh-in, 'Act like nothing happened or you will give Haugen confidence.'"

But it was too late. Haugen was too savvy to miss the signs of Hector's suffering. "He didn't make weight the first time," Haugen recalled. "He had to sweat it off. I went to eat and then I came back to watch him weigh in again. As soon as he got off the scale [the second time around], he sucked down some Gatorade concoction. I told him, 'Suck it up.' I knew right away. When you're as dehydrated as he was, you never show that to an opponent. It gives him an edge. A fighter can use that to his benefit. There's no way to get rid of dehydration that fast. It's a killer."

On the day of the fight, Hector brimmed with confidence: "I'll beat Haugen. After that I'm looking at nothing but Chavez." Friends with Chavez, Hector believed that the showdown would occur over the next three months.

It was one thing to look ahead to a megafight, but another to completely disregard Haugen. Hector saw Haugen as a fighter defined more by his limitations than by his strengths. But Hector was not the only fighter to make that mistake. Because Haugen did everything well but nothing spectacular, it was easy to overlook him. Even Haugen's nemesis Pazienza was more pleasing to watch. Looking to the future, Hector didn't even mention Haugen in his plans. Occupying the same card as Meldrick Taylor and Pernell Whitaker, Hector recognized the irony as he, now the veteran of the group, tried like a pampered child to steal the spotlight.

"I'm more valuable than Whitaker or Taylor," he said. "I've been around for ten years, and I'm undefeated. I'm a little more exciting than the others. The bottom line is Chavez and Camacho."

Analysts waiting for Hector's greatness to spill out over an extended period of time were not soothed by the second phase of his career, which ended with the Haugen rematch. Thus, some were not willing to categorize him as an elite fighter.

"You had Floyd Mayweather, De La Hoya, Shane Mosley, and Roy Jones Jr.," said Larry Merchant. "In hindsight, it was a rich time. This is part of the landscape, for me, in which you see Camacho. He was a flamboyant showman, and that was a talent in itself. Not many people could pull it off. A small percentage of guys are provocative and flamboyant, but that's what he was largely known for after the first phase of his career."

Taylor took umbrage with Hector's petulance because he viewed himself as the superior fighter. Likewise, Whitaker wondered what the hype was about; in his mind, Macho Time had ended years ago. Both he and Hector understood that Whitaker was doing things in the ring that Hector used to do with ease in the early 1980s, although shockingly, Hector had done it with more speed. The two had a history: a sparring session in 1984 at Emanuel Steward's private gym in Detroit.

At the time, Hector was preparing to make his first—and only—defense of his 130-pound crown against a southpaw, Rafael Solis, so he would have benefited from getting looks from another left-handed fighter. Whitaker, a recent Olympic gold medalist, obliged and got in the ring. What happened once the two fighters started the session is still up for debate. Steward went public to say that Whitaker "beat the hell out of [Hector]." Mark Breland, Whitaker's Olympic teammate, who had stuck around to witness the chaos, corroborated Steward's story that Hector was successful at first, but then Whitaker started to gain momentum.

Jerry Villarreal Jr. refused to accept those perspectives. He saw his friend Hector dominate the younger fighter. "Whitaker started quick and then began to slow down. He wanted to take a break, and Camacho said, 'No, no, no.' He beat the shit out of him. At one point, when Hector was going to throw a left hand, Steward went up and grabbed his arm. Billy yelled, 'That's my fighter,'" said Jerry Jr.

Whitaker took a more diplomatic approach. "Hector was the best pro and I was the best amateur," Whitaker recalled. "We put on a show. It was classic Macho Man and you know how I get down. Hector brought out the best in me. You had to have a special gift—a special talent—to be in the ring, let alone the presence to be around him. You just had to have great experience. Hector was a special fighter who brought out the very best of myself."

Iran Barkley, a friend of Hector's who was keen to all of the little nuances of Hector's style, understood that both fighters had their own unique way about them. "They had a good sparring session," Barkley recalled. "Macho was getting to Pernell. But you couldn't compare the two because one had been around longer. Hector was the man and had the experience, while Pernell was coming up and was faster and stuff like that."

As a heavy favorite, Hector wanted to preserve his undefeated record with a victory over Haugen, who was managed by George Chemeres. Conversely, Haugen (27-3-1, thirteen KOs) was 4-2 in his last six bouts, with unanimous decision losses to Pazienza and Whitaker. Contracts for the HBO-televised championship bout stipulated that Hector would earn $500,000, whereas Haugen settled for $150,000. Haugen had only made $10,000 for each of his two previous fights. Few expected Haugen to pull off the upset; no one wanted him to disrupt what some considered an instant classic between Hector and Chavez, a virtual guarantee with a Hector victory.

When Hector—and his mother—entered the ring in Caesars Palace with army fatigues in support of the U.S. troops in Iraq, he may have won some fans over. But he was not the Macho Man that so many had once loved. He displayed none of the charisma or flair of previous entrances. He had once thrived off of being energetic and spirited. Macho Time meant hugs, flurries, dancing, and all-out fun. His present lack of energy was not because he was dispirited, but because he was deadly serious. During one telling interaction, Hector screamed at his handler, Rudy Mata, for taking too much time with his army uniform, a preview of the frustration that would extend all evening. Hector was frustrated that he had had to go through hell earlier that day to make weight, and he was frustrated that he wasn't in ideal shape. He clearly needed either to end the fight early with an unlikely knockout or preserve his energy and outbox Haugen, a more realistic scenario.

The referee, Carlos Padilla, recognized the complex task ahead of him in navigating a ring where the fighters harbored such ill will for each other. In the first round, appearing tight, Hector was content to show-case his speed and sharp jab, whereas Haugen landed a nice upper-cut. Both men exhibited supreme confidence in the second round, with Hector using jabs, movement, and a three-punch combination culminating in a straight left to Haugen's neck. Clearly, Haugen felt the upper-cut would land and hurt Hector, but the undefeated fighter was more effective.

Neither fighter had a clear edge moving into the third round, but that quickly changed. First, Hector landed a jab to Haugen's chest and followed it up with a stinging three-punch combination, the last punch targeting Haugen's head. Resilient, Haugen rarely took a step back and returned fire with his own three-punch combination that caught Hector's attention. Unfortunately for Haugen, the rest of the round confirmed his biggest fears that Hector would time him perfectly.

It started with two jabs.

In the final thirty seconds, Hector landed the two jabs, then missed a left hook but did not get discouraged and came back to land a perfectly placed right hook. Few fighters were tougher than Haugen, but even the best chins could not withstand the placement and timing of this special punch. Down he went. It was not a flash knockdown or even a lucky shot. Hector uncoiled as he landed the shot, and Haugen caught the brunt of it. Padilla administered an eight-count. It was clearly not over for Haugen, but he felt the punch and quickly went back to his corner for guidance.

His cornermen, as well as everyone else in the venue, wanted answers. *Are you hurt?*

"It was more of a slip," Haugen recalled. "He hit me when I was off balance and I went down. I was not hurt. The punch looked better than it was. If Camacho put three or four punches together then he had a chance to knock a guy out, but he didn't have one-punch power."

How would Haugen recover? Would he still be able to best and beat Hector at his own game? That remained to be seen, but Haugen had hit the canvas before and knew the consequences.

"I wanted to prove to the judges and the crowd that I was not hurt," Haugen said. "I needed to press and press and make sure that I did not get too crazy. I needed to continue to fight my fight."

Which is exactly what he did. Three major things occurred as a by-product of the knockdown. Not only did the punch serve as a wake-up call for Haugen; it also forced him to go on the offensive and be more physical. Haugen could take Hector's biggest punch and emerge unscathed. More important, Hector's plan to come out early and try to get rid of Haugen did not work.

When the fourth round started, Haugen made it a point to strike first and land a three-punch combination, and then evade Hector's counter. He then started to push Hector around and apply rough tactics to upset his game plan. Not far removed from the 10-8 round, Haugen, for the first time, started to influence the pace of the fight—and also move to the body. Intent on taking the life out of the champ, Haugen specifically targeted him with hooks. A round later, Haugen caught Hector sliding against ropes, another one of his stalling tactics that had worked against lesser fighters on better nights.

"When he fought Haugen, Hector was still very, very good, but I got the impression that he didn't push himself all out. He had such great skills and reflexes," said John Scully, former boxer and analyst. "He didn't push himself to use all of his skills. Against Haugen, I felt that he pushed a button and turned it on, but, by the same token, he was never able to show everybody just how great he was. . . . On his best day, he has no trouble with Haugen. The timing of the fight was in Haugen's favor."

Tired in the fifth round, Hector went to the ropes, and Haugen, so intuitive, knew that his opponent needed a reprieve. Needless to say, the challenger refused to give him one and slashed him with uppercuts and right hands. A Haugen right hand was his reminder to Hector that he would do everything in his power to hinder him from establishing a rhythm. Applying mental and physical pressure, Haugen started strong, but on occasion throughout the round, Hector reacted favorably.

"I wanted to push him hard through the first six rounds, so that [for Camacho] it would feel like the equivalent of a twelve-round fight," said Haugen. "That was the plan, and in those fifth and sixth rounds, I would hit him in the belly and he would grunt. I knew that the body shot would take away his speed and legs."

Feeling the pull each second of each round, Hector needed a lot of things to go in his favor, including at least thirty seconds of downtime in each round. The champ flashed early jabs to buy time early in the eighth, but Haugen was more structured and composed than Pazienza and Mancini. Refusing Hector a breather, Haugen smothered him at the end of the round with jabs, after he landed a couple strong rights earlier in the round.

Committing to the jab, Hector was still engaged in the fight but no longer landing multiple punches. He knew he could no longer take those types of risks. Displaying his toughness, Haugen punched through a clinch, stabilized, and slowed Hector with a left hook to the body, then closed out with two uppercuts—one looking more like a hook—and followed it up with an elbow to Hector's face. The tempo was neither relentless nor debilitating for Hector, but there were enough stops and starts and difficult moments that it put the champion in more peril in the ninth than he had been in since Rosario. Picking up steam, Haugen didn't let up in a crucial tenth round that he closed out with a right hand. The judges could plainly see Haugen's confidence, aggression, and tactical excellence as he neutralized a worn-out Hector struggling to find a second wind.

When Hector pissed fighters off, he held them, tackled them, pulled down their heads, stiff-armed them, and just disrupted their rhythm. Often, a passive referee followed in lockstep. While Hector worked over his opponent, he also talked to the ref as if he were both shocked and dismayed that he, the Macho Man, was guilty of such transgressions. Some referees did not have the mental makeup to disagree, so they just kept issuing empty warnings that never amounted to anything. Meanwhile, an opponent was getting slaughtered with illegal uppercuts and overwhelmed with excessive holding. The act was part of Hector's repertoire.

Every fighter knew that coming in, but Haugen was one of the few who could neutralize it, partly because Hector was not in great shape.

"[Hector] was not always in tip-top shape, and that allowed guys like me to wear him down and follow my fight plan and tire him out," said Haugen.

Shifting into high gear, Hector moved and jabbed incessantly during the eleventh round. They traded shots, but Haugen excited the crowd when he tripled up on short left hooks and then jolted Hector with a right hand and a left to the head at the end of the round. There was no time to dwell on the past, as Hector needed to produce, at the very least, a winning twelfth round. He knew that. His trainer, Rudy Mata, knew that. More important, Haugen knew that. So many people had bet against Haugen and figured that he just did not possess the tools to beat Hector.

Haugen knew that Hector was not in condition to fight ten, let alone twelve, good rounds. Haugen screamed to the crowd at the end of the round. The corners conveyed disparate messages: In Hector's corner, they tried to create some enthusiasm within a listless fighter—*It's Macho Time*—whereas in Haugen's corner the message was clear and direct—*Three minutes to be the champion.*

So when Padilla began to plead with Haugen at the start of the twelfth round to touch gloves, Haugen responded "No." Hector had seen enough, and, frustrated, walked toward Haugen with his right hand to initiate contact. He gestured to Haugen to do the same. But after Padilla looked at him to do it one final time, Hector attacked and missed a lunging left hand before Padilla caught him in the act. Sensing that he was losing control, Padilla swiftly deducted a point, easily the biggest point deduction of Hector's career. Staunch Macho backers bristled at Haugen's power to toy with a man who had made a career of integrating illegal tactics into his game plan. Haugen smiled, laughed to himself at Hector's impulsive reaction, and jumped as if he had won the fight. In his mind, he had.

"It wasn't an act," Haugen recalled. "I just didn't want to touch gloves. I didn't respect him. It was a rule that you had to touch gloves before the first round, but not after that. I just said I didn't want to, and he jumped in and sucker-punched me. I looked at him and said, 'You missed again.' But I saw it coming. I goaded him into it."

There was nothing Hector could do to him at this stage in the fight. Dejected but not angry, Hector forged ahead. Despite showing no interest in closing the round aggressively, he managed a left uppercut against the emboldened and more active Haugen. After an uneventful last thirty seconds, both men walked back to their corners. Ridding Hector of his precious undefeated label, Haugen earned a split-decision victory as Bill McConkey and Dalby Shirley scored the fight 114-112 for Haugen, while Art Lurie called it 114-113 for Hector. The controversial point deduction kept Camacho from earning a draw and keeping his title.

Padilla didn't appear at the post-fight news conference, but reached by phone hours after the match, he said: "I was talking to Haugen and all of a sudden Camacho throws a punch. So he committed a foul. He should not throw a punch. I'm in the middle of them. I do not know what comes over Camacho."

More impactful than the loss itself were the financial implications. "That loss really hurt us," said Levien. "We had a wonderful contract with Chavez for around $3 to $5 million, but we couldn't lose or we would lose the contract."

The controversy following the fight didn't bother Haugen. He had won the fight fair and square, and he disproved the doubters who overlooked his skills and branded him a huge underdog. Looking back, Haugen knew he was always "two or three steps ahead of Camacho."

"That was huge," said Scully. "He got Hector out of his character. If you catch a guy on the wrong day, he might do something he wouldn't normally do. Hector was able to control himself in most of his fights. That was an off moment."

Boxing analyst Al Bernstein supported that theory: "Haugen really got under Hector's skin. He was a master at that."

Along with losing that undefeated label, someone stole $15,000 from Hector after the fight in an apparent inside job. The Macho Man had not experienced a loss since the Olympic semifinals in 1980. Since then, Hector had dominated lesser fighters, bombarded excellent fighters, left good fighters damaged goods, or won razor-thin decisions, but losing a close fight to Haugen was a significant blow to his ego.

After the fight, Haugen got his revenge: "I just wanted to thank Hector Camacho for giving me the chance for a tune-up fight."

★ ★ ★

After Hector experienced his first loss, he left the venue with Tim Cinnante, Mike Tyson, and a host of other friends and acquaintances. Tyson was extremely fond of Hector, and was always looking for him. Nothing stopped Hector from going out and partying after the bout, but a guy as competitive as he was recognized the repercussions.

"Mike was in the audience," Tim Cinnante recalled. "After that fight we were walking out . . . and we had to walk there from the hotel. We were walking back to the hotel. I was emotional. I fucking kicked a garbage can and said, 'That's bullshit.' [Hector] looked at me and said, 'What are you, crazy? It's no big deal. Relax. Don't worry about it.' Tyson and his guys looked at him and said, 'Your boy's right.' Camacho said, 'No, that's it. It's over.' He said he won and he won. They said the guy won. He would never dwell on a situation."

Hector eventually earned a rematch with Haugen, but not without a series of tumultuous events that created negativity on both sides. Along with the controversy that emerged from Padilla's decision to deduct a point from Hector in the final round, on March 2, the Associated Press reported that Haugen's post-fight urine analysis showed traces of marijuana. Haugen received a $25,000 fine, was ordered to attend drug counseling, and serve 200 hours of community service. More important, the World Boxing Organization stripped him of his title, called the fight a no-contest, and ordered an immediate rematch, placating both fighters. After a brief threat to protest the deducted point, Hector decided to give up on moving forward with any legal action, and, instead, focus on the rematch.

A lot can happen between an initial matchup and a rematch. Fighters can stop training and celebrate too much. But Hector immediately went to train in Atlantic Beach, North Carolina, and then finished up his training in Reno, Nevada. After his first loss, Hector didn't hide away or fall back on his vices. Instead, he picked himself back up. "I thought he would be suicidal," said Flannery. "[H]e calls me up and says, 'We'll kick this guy's butt.'"

When Hector lost to Haugen on February 23, he had never imagined losing to a fighter that he did not consider in his league; in fact, he thought he would walk right through him. Despite the controversial drug incident involving Haugen, Hector's loss stayed a loss in the record books; that would not be overturned.

Three weeks before the rematch, Hector re-signed with Duva and Main Events for three additional fights. When Hector and Haugen met again in the Reno-Sparks Convention Center for their May 18, 1991, rematch for the now-vacant WBO 140-pound title, Haugen, who traveled to Reno three weeks before the showdown, was well aware that this version of Camacho would be more complicated to figure out.

Coming into the fight, Haugen weighed 138.5 pounds, while Hector entered at 139 pounds. This time, Hector did not come into the ring with a scowl, nor was he berating his cornermen. Instead he sprinted to the ring in a brown-and-black outfit flocked with tassels and MACHO and an ax embroidered on the back. Hector got to the ring in record time rather than spending time on his standard posturing, dancing, or getting into a "Macho Time" chant, as if to tell Haugen, "I let you fuck with me the first time. Not again."

In his gray-and-purple robe, the hometown favorite Haugen entered to loud cheers from his fans, and he flexed for them for approval. Despite all of the controversy surrounding both fighters in the interim, the narrative of Hector's loss had never changed.

Hector got to Reno nine days before the fight to ready himself, whereas Haugen had arrived three weeks before the fight. For the first time, Hector had to deal with a controversy that did not directly involve him. At a press conference on the Thursday before the fight, *New York Post* reporter Michael Marley and Camacho camp coordinator Flannery got into a verbal altercation regarding an article in which Marley blamed him for the Haugen loss. At 2:45 a.m. on the morning of the fight, Marley called Flannery from the lobby of the Clarion Hotel Casino and told him to meet him in the casino. That morning, Flannery ended up in the hospital with a fractured left leg and bruised ribs.

"Things got really nasty at the press conference," Levien recalled, "and someone called Pat that night. When Pat went downstairs, someone came up and whacked Pat from behind with a club. He ended up missing the fight."

"I remember Pat didn't like something Marley wrote or said, and went up to him at the press conference, and I got between them," said Cinnante. "'Pat, this is not the place. Don't stoop to this guy's level.' But I didn't think anything of it. Pat would have kicked his ass in a fair fight."

Directly involved in the dispute, Cinnante vividly recalled taking Flannery to the emergency room. "I was hanging in the lounge, and Macho was in his room," he recalled. "The next thing I knew they jumped Pat in the elevators. Actually, they jumped him from behind while he was waiting for the elevators. . . . It all happened very fast. Pat was a gentleman, but he was a tough son of a bitch when he wanted to be. We didn't tell Macho right away because we didn't want to take his concentration away from the fight." Macho's camp knew firsthand how shaken its fighter could get before big fights.

Marley, to this day, refuses to back down from his behavior. "I wrote an article that said if Flannery was a boxing manager, then I was an astronaut," said Marley, who covered Hector for years. "He took exception to that. [That night] I was attacked by a group of them."

The team protected Hector, but all was not well. Flanked by Ismael Leandry and Rudy "Tio" Mata, Hector barely looked at Haugen during the pre-fight instructions. This time around, the roles had switched, as Haugen garnered a payday of $1.2 million and Hector settled for $500,000. As Haugen leered at him, Hector threw his glove out as he walked away. The last thing he wanted to do was engage Haugen before the fight. Clearly, Haugen had beaten Hector psychologically as well as physically in the first fight.

In the first round, Hector bounced in and out of range while attacking early and often. He was no longer distracted, and Haugen noticed the difference. At one point, Haugen covered up and got nailed by a right uppercut. Mixing in counter lefts and rights, Hector was sending a message to Haugen. By fighting assertively, Hector provided glimpses of his old self, reverting to holding Haugen's head and inserting another uppercut. It was rare that Hector committed to the uppercut so early, and Haugen struggled. Since Hector was so quick to get inside and then retreat, strategically, throwing the uppercut proved a natural fit. Those first three minutes were not all one-sided, as Haugen perfectly timed Hector with a stinging right hand to close out the round, just to remind him *I'm still here.*

Neither fighter was particularly effective in round two. Referee Bobby Ferrara warned Hector about holding. Hearing the warning, it would have been impossible for Hector not to expect the worst after referee · Padilla's controversial deduction of a point in the first fight. Between the second and third rounds, Hector turned to Ferrara and stressed, "I'm cool. I'm cool. Easy." Yet there was an arrogance to the reassurance. As the men jockeyed for position in round three, Hector could not reenact the perfect series of punches that knocked Haugen down in the first fight. Still, he stayed true to form with the jab, and with 1:09 remaining, he landed a four-punch combination and then pushed Haugen back into the ropes. Thirty seconds later, one more Camacho left hand sent the upright Haugen into a crouch but could not send him down. To close out the round, Haugen landed a right hand. The crowd chanted "Haugen, Haugen" as the men went back to their corners.

Between rounds three and four, Haugen pleaded his case that the cut over his left eye was the result of a Camacho headbutt. The replay disproved his claim, and the fight continued with an energized Haugen in the fourth. One man would take control in one round, and then the other would come back with his own attack in the next. Haugen, the crafty counterpuncher, landed a left counter and a running right hand to start the fourth round and later forced Hector to retreat. Focused, Haugen paid no attention to Hector as he raised his hand and moved back to his corner. Haugen *knew* it was his round.

"I was in good shape for that second fight," said Haugen. "I trained with good fighters like David Sample. I was peaking by fight time, not four or five weeks before."

Fighting Haugen was similar to fighting a mix of Jose Luis Ramirez and Edwin Rosario in the sense that Haugen did not move particularly well (like Ramirez) but he was always in position for a tricky right cross (like Rosario). Hector hated that right cross that came across his face, rather than as a straight right or even a more looping hook. But he negated any right cross in the fifth as he moved to Haugen's body. After tolerating a shoeshine of six punches, Haugen deposited his own uppercut, patiently waited during a short delay, and walked directly into a big left hand. The break served Hector well as he nailed Haugen with one more straight left that sent him off balance. Still energized, he nailed Haugen again, this time with short left hooks, and then hustled back to his corner with the momentum

"He was a lot more ready for the rematch," recalled Haugen.

In comparison with the first fight, Hector seemed calm and composed. Never rushing or breathing heavily from a torturous bout with the weight, he glided on the canvas and picked from his assortment of punches. Still, in the sixth round, Haugen found him with a left hook to the body that opened him up along the ropes. Stalking Hector as the round ended, Haugen just stared at his opponent in the middle of the ring. All business, Hector paid him no attention.

"He was not standing in front of me," said Haugen. "In that second fight, he was more confident and, although I was still able to get to him psychologically, I was not able to rattle him."

The real test came in the eighth round. Where Hector had begun to tire in the past, he came out with a renewed energy. Haugen wasn't ready for the straight left, and then was clearly not prepared when Hector shifted to land another straight left. Tapping into his reserves, Haugen, now more physical, fought out of clinches, which rattled Hector and caused him to look to Ferrara for some explanation. A nice one-two combination by Haugen forced Hector to clinch and grab. Haugen, bouncing and not plodding, felt justified in raising his hand victoriously at the end of the round. Ringside scorer Harold Lederman had it 78-74 at the start of the ninth round.

If the rematch itself did not mirror the first showdown, the approaches and patterns did. Haugen came forward; Hector either redirected, jabbed, or escaped. And with twenty-seven seconds left in the ninth, Haugen punctuated his round with a jab, a hook to the body, and a right hand. Pissed off, Hector pushed Haugen's head down. Not faring much better in the tenth, Hector tried to flick Haugen away with uppercuts and short, swift combinations, but undeterred, Haugen nailed Hector with a right hand and muscled him throughout the round.

Tensions flared in the corner as both men understood how important the last two rounds were. Hector's corner pleaded for him to move; Haugen's corner wanted him to continue pressuring. So much had happened between these men over twenty-two rounds that the twenty-third and twenty-fourth meant the world to their careers. A point here or there would affect their legacies. Tired and defensive, Hector could not avoid a Haugen straight right at 2:08 of the eleventh round. With an assortment of punches, Haugen brutalized Hector at intervals in the round and absorbed a crafty little uppercut by Hector on the inside.

Then, as in the first fight when Padilla intervened at the start of the twelfth round, Ferrara deducted a point from Hector for punching after the bell as Haugen jawed at him. Despite the error, Hector emerged with intensity in the final round. Before coming out of the corner, he listened intently to two conflicting voices: Mata assured him of victory; promoter Dan Duva exhorted him to win. After three rounds of fighting defensively, Hector came out of his shell.

Grabbing at opportune times, Hector thwarted some of Haugen's attacks in the second half of the round, but he was defenseless in the last minute as Haugen forced him to the ropes with a straight right hand. Nevertheless, Hector landed enough uppercuts and left hands to hinder Haugen from moving into attack mode. It was impossible for Haugen, who was also exhausted, to throw multiple punches. The fight ended with Haugen standing in front of Hector, ready to wade in. Hector threw one last harmless shot as both raised their hands in victory at the sound of the bell. Haugen followed Hector and tapped him on the back three times to embrace, but Hector was done with him.

Too much had happened between them for Hector to even acknowledge him; he let Haugen go to places with him that no other fighter—with the exception of Rosario—had. Leandry carried him around the ring. But seconds later and minutes before the scores were read, the petulant Hector ran down the aisle and back to his dressing room—a huge personal blunder. Hector's impulsive nature thwarted him again and gave Haugen reason to spin a loss any way he pleased. Leandry hurried Hector back to the ring, where Duva chewed him out.

After splitting 115-112 scores, Hector eked out the victory with a 114-113 score from judge Dave Moretti. Winning the twelfth round on two of three scorecards made the difference. Not managing even a smile, Hector stayed near family and friends. Overall, in another tactical fight, Hector had out-landed Haugen, 305-223, and was able to do so because of his excellent conditioning.

"I felt strong, but not as accurate as I was in the gym," said Hector in the post-fight press conference. "Age is getting to me. It's getting hard. He's a slick fighter. I couldn't reach him with my jab, even when I tried."

After all of those rounds, and so much shared between them, Hector let go of the animosity. "I don't hate him, but I should," he said. "Because he gave me two terrific fights. I walked out of the ring because of the point taken away. I just thought I'd cry in my dressing room." Later, when asked about the cruel irony, Hector added, "I thought, 'Here we go again.'"

Haugen was clearly disappointed with the verdict. "Did you see him leave the ring before the decision?" Haugen asked. "He thought he lost, Hell, I know he lost." Managing to draw the ire of a man who rarely felt or showed animosity, Haugen exposed Hector over those two fights as a very good but flawed fighter who could no longer adapt completely. In the second fight, Hector fought well—and improved—but Haugen still confounded him in moments of pressure. As for the ridicule, Hector let it go.

And later, so did Haugen. "I always respected the hell out of [Camacho] as a fighter," he said.

Entering the Danger Zone 20

There were no lingering effects after Hector ditched his team and ran back to the dressing room immediately after the Greg Haugen rematch. Winning the fight and regaining his WBO title softened the blow to his ego, but Hector knew he had problems. "I can't be abusing my body and living the night life," he said, adding, "It's going to kill me down the road."

And kill him it nearly did. A week after the March 6, 1989, Ray Mancini fight he had ended up in a palm tree after crashing his Lotus. He had squeezed out of the car and down the tree, but then had realized his championship belt was still in his car. Instead of checking for injuries, he had retrieved the belt and walked back home.

He was high and drunk at the time of the crash.

Patrick Flannery could help stem the flow of recklessness, but he couldn't stop it entirely. Years earlier, Flannery had helped mold him into a man, and to Flannery's credit, he never backed down from the challenge. But Macho was soon turning twenty-nine, and he was nowhere near the man that Flannery had hoped he would be.

"It wasn't easy trying to defend Macho," said Hector's friend and club owner Tim Cinnante. "Patrick [Flannery] was a conservative Irish American educator. He was not flamboyant or loud or a show-off. Now we know that in public, that was Macho. So Pat had to withstand a lot of grief . . . but he defended him through thick and thin. As did I. But I was more 'street,' if you will. Pat was the polar opposite of Macho, so it was ten times harder."

Looking back, Cinnante expressed without hesitation what no other confidant was willing to say: "Maybe without Patrick Flannery, there is no Macho Camacho."

Hector's split-decision victory over Haugen in the rematch put him back in the running for the Julio Cesar Chavez fight and a multimillion-dollar payday. Moments after the Haugen decision, Dan Duva suggested that Hector had four options for a big payday: Meldrick Taylor, Pernell Whitaker, Loreto Garza, or Chavez. They opted for Chavez. The fight with Chavez was already set for September 12, 1992, which allowed Hector time for a tune-up. But the public perception of Hector had changed. No one was gushing over his skill set, and the decline in public confidence was magnified because of his demand for excellence.

"I can recollect, for example, when he fought Greg Haugen," said boxing analyst Larry Merchant. "I gave him credit when credit was due, but what he was against Haugen was no longer near what he had been back during days when he was young and ambitious and still trying to make a statement." He continued: "Over time, you build up expectations and have a level of what we think you bring to the dance. You are then viewed through that prism. He was young and ambitious, and then he was not the same fighter as he was trying to maintain his commercial image. But you get judged by the standard you create. If you don't live up to those standards, whether it's professionalism or an erosion of skills, the way you're looked at will be different."

To make the Chavez fight happen, Hector would have to fight a tune-up fight with Eddie VanKirk on August 1, 1992. VanKirk (26-7-2) was a good fighter, but not in Hector's class. The fight would be held at the Hilton Hotel in Las Vegas on the same evening when Chavez defended his WBC super lightweight title fight against Frankie Mitchell. For many, Hector had seemed reinvigorated during his victory over Haugen. Now 38-1, Hector still had the ability to offset the attack of good fighters. No one expected that he would struggle with VanKirk, who had a slate of less-than-heralded competition lined up before the showdown with Hector. With Chavez ringside, Hector needed to find a way to steal the show. At 80-0 with sixty-six knockouts, Chavez had set a new precedent in the sport.

With VanKirk already a sidebar to the superfight, Hector likely had to consider two alternatives: *Do I attempt my wild, offensive antics to get Chavez in a foul mood and off his game plan? Or do I stay calm and throw in an occasional barb, fearing the worst repercussions?* With a clear vantage point to the punishment Chavez dealt Edwin Rosario five years earlier, a tamer Hector may have made a more prudent decision; however, he could have also focused on the boxing lesson that Philly stylist Meldrick Taylor gave Chavez over eleven rounds in March 1990 as indication that the Mexican king had faded. Being a stylist was not enough to dethrone Chavez; one also had to be perfectly conditioned, a defensive juggernaut, and throw and land combinations that disrupted his rhythm. Either way, Hector, clearly on the back end of a Hall of Fame career, understood that with a huge payday came major risks. If Rosario had disfigured him, what was Chavez capable of?

Leading up to the bout, Chavez spoke to boxing journalist Steve Farhood about the showdown. "I will pray for Camacho to win tonight," Chavez said through an interpreter. "And Hector better pray that I win."

Before the fight with VanKirk, Hector, dressed as a fireman with radio in hand, gestured as if signaling to people in a burning building. Then he looked at journalist Steve Farhood and began to perform his own personal comedy show: "This is supposed to be a tune-up. It's not a tune-up. The guy is hot. The guy he's fighting is hot. Chavez is hot. You know what happens when things get hot. There's a fire. I'm a fireman. I turn off the fire. (Looks up) don't jump yet. You missed him. . . . You—I said don't jump yet. It's Macho Time."

"It was all impromptu on [Hector's] part," said Farhood. "I had no idea what he was doing or where he was heading. It was kind of refreshing in retrospect. It was the funniest moment in my forty years. It was a taped interview, a rookie experience. I remember I benefited because I knew Hector well. He had this fireman's hat on and he's pointing to the top of the building. 'There's a fire!' he said. 'Do you know what to do?' It was good TV at my expense. His silliness was appealing. You never knew where he was going."

A few fighters over the years may have been able to pull a Macho stunt. What Hector did so skillfully was to infuse an absurdity into an aseptic situation and take it to an extreme. Sometimes he was innocent and other times he was hostile or crude, but he was always entertaining. Occasionally, his act misfired completely and became offensive, but more often than not the split-second decisions to make light of a situation endeared him to his fans—or riled them up. Years earlier he and Billy Giles had pondered whether Hector could be a punk and be Macho at the same time. Even when chaos reigned in his world outside the ring, he managed to balance both parts simultaneously—and it worked. All the while, younger boxers were taking notes.

"You can put a fight on and put on a costume," said Junior. "But it doesn't work. You're born with that. You just don't develop it. You can't just put on a costume and become the Macho Man."

After scoring a quick knockdown, Hector lurked over an injured VanKirk in the first round. It all happened too fast as VanKirk feinted, threw a right hand, and then got nailed by a Camacho left counter. After an eight-count, VanKirk got off the canvas and had already regained his senses. By the third round, Hector had opened a cut over the top of VanKirk's right eye, but that didn't stop VanKirk from coming forward.

Sensing the end, Hector attacked VanKirk at the beginning of the fourth round, and landed a strong left hook before a clinch halted any further damage. Seconds later, VanKirk, crouching at the time, crumpled to the canvas from a Camacho left hand. Bloodied, VanKirk listened intently as referee Joe Cortez counted to four, but there was no reason to keep counting as the bloodbath was over.

Bloodstains marked the place where VanKirk fell. Showing no concern, Hector, victorious, walked away. Wanting to ensure that VanKirk was okay, Rudy Mata walked over and tried to help him. The "Chavez" chant started as soon as the fight ended. After inciting the crowd, Hector turned his back to the ropes, stuck his ass between them, and pretended to moon the Chavez fans.

Hector, in a post-fight interview with Farhood, railed on the Duva family for abandoning him and keeping him "sterile." Then, in typical Camacho style, he moved into a tangential diatribe: "Free Mike Tyson! Forget about the nonsense, we all see what happened. The fight is on. The Chavez fight is on." At the end of the interview, Hector talked about the harsh reaction of the fans: "They boo me because they love me because they all know who's the man. They see me at the hotels, and they drive me crazy. The promoter has got to be in front of the door to keep people away."

Following the script, that same night, Chavez defeated Mitchell by a fourth-round TKO and immediately told a reporter: "I was fighting Frankie Mitchell in the ring, but my thoughts were on Camacho." By that time, Hector had already stolen a Mexican flag from one of Chavez's handlers and was parading around the ring.

Ultimately, as Hector perfected his act over the years with new, improved ring attire and increasingly bizarre behavior, he still managed to charm people with his playfulness. The more mischievously he behaved, the less people pried into his personal problems. It was easy for him to become Macho Man and head to the nightclub to score drugs later that evening.

"He was happy," said Sugar Ray Leonard. "He never showed any signs of concern. He exuded that confidence that 'I'm ok, and I can control this.' And I think we all do this at some point in our lives. The way he walked around that ring like a king, like 'this is my domain.'"

The Camacho–Chavez fight had been talked about since 1984 when Chavez won the WBC super featherweight belt title with a stoppage of Mario Martinez at the famed Olympic Auditorium. But Hector, then guided by a cautious Jimmy Montoya, was already looking toward the lightweight division as he dethroned Chavez's countryman Jose Luis Ramirez. Hector was used to waiting on superfights, especially after his initial showdown with Ray "Boom Boom" Mancini was put on hold for five years. When Hector came back against Mancini, his skills had dissipated, but he was good enough to beat him on the comeback trail.

This time it was different. Chavez was still a great fighter—an active fighter for that matter—and his search-and-destroy mindset had led him to eighty-one straight victories. Frightening in so many ways, Chavez was not a plodder or a one-dimensional power puncher, but a talented and vicious predator who exposed and exploited an opponent's flaws. Confronting the great fighters of the era, Chavez cut off the ring beautifully and trapped them by banging vicious shots off of their body and head. For the first time in years, Hector had to look at himself in the mirror and face the daunting reality that he could not hurt Chavez, nor was he quick enough on his feet to evade his attack. Nearly every single Chavez opponent felt the brunt of his punches, which broke their will. After Chavez stopped Angel Hernandez of Puerto Rico on April 10, 1992, he wasted no time to announce his fight with Hector.

"I hope Macho stops running from me now," he said.

By the time the Chavez fight came around, Hector had gotten married. Leading up to the bout with Chavez, Hector seemed relaxed. He lived and trained in Clewiston with Mata and Flannery for the fight. Conflicted by the ease of his day-to-day life for the last five years, Hector admitted to becoming spoiled: "It's easy being me. It's easy to dress good every day," he said. "It's easy to have money in your pocket. It's easy to have girls hanging on you all the time. It's easy. There's no challenge. I was getting fat, lazy, and ugly."

On September 12, 1992, Hector fought Chavez at the Thomas & Mack Center in Las Vegas for Chavez's WBC super lightweight title that he had held since 1989. Fighting again for Don King, Hector would earn $3 million for the fight. Both fighters weighed in at 140 pounds, and Hector entered with a 40-1 record, with Greg Haugen as his lone blemish. Conversely, Chavez, a 6-1 favorite, at 81-0, was widely considered one of the world's best fighters, and boxing experts salivated at a pound-for-pound showdown with IBF champion Pernell Whitaker in the future. Doing nothing offensive to incite Chavez, Hector maintained his composure during press conferences. Chavez took Hector's behavior as a sign of subservience and that he was frightened of the repercussions. "I finally get my chance to shut his mouth," Chavez said. "Camacho is the fight I have wanted for years and it's the fight Mexico wants. They will lynch me. I could never go back to Mexico if I lose to Camacho." Doing his best David Banner impression, Chavez added, "When my opponents make me angry, they are very foolish."

Whether to motivate or promote himself, Hector always exposed his opponent's shortcomings. In this situation, however, he retreated from any confrontation. Instead of dipping into his virtuoso comedy routines, he stayed relatively quiet. He and Chavez had agreed years earlier that when the "money was right" they would make the fight. A tame Hector said, "Julio is a great human being. He is not a hard person to relate to. He is not complicated. Outside of the ring, we get along. But as a fighter, I don't think he is as much as (the media) have painted him."

WBC president Jose Sulaiman angered Hector's camp by appointing referee Richard Steele to work the fight. Back in March 1990, Steele had made a legendary blunder by prematurely stopping a Chavez fight in the waning seconds of the twelfth round, which Meldrick Taylor had decisively won on all scorecards. Another controversy surrounded Hector's record, which promoters billed as 40-0-1, even though the Nevada State Athletic Commission refused to overturn his loss to Greg Haugen because of a failed drug test.

Ten days before the fight, Hector had a spat with his adviser, Ismael Leandry. They were traveling by plane with Don King and his people. Instead of having Hector sit with Leandry, King brought him to the back of the plane to party with him and trainer Aaron Snowell. Stunned, Leandry looked back and saw Hector with a bottle of champagne. He could not believe that Hector so easily acquiesced to King. Everything was in place, and Leandry felt that his fighter was ruining it all in one fell swoop. By the end of the trip, Hector was drunk; Leandry, furious, could not properly emphasize how damaging the decision was for his fighter's performance. Up to that point, Leandry was happy with the progress they had made.

"Leandry heard a voice in the back: 'It's Macho Time.' My dad was drinking champagne," said Junior. "He looked back and was like, 'What the hell are you doing?' They were leaving Ohio and going to Las Vegas. Don King didn't want my dad to win because Chavez was easier to work with."

Could Hector stave off the legendary Chavez? That was the question that needed to be answered. If critics wanted to use Rosario as a measuring stick, Hector had barely beaten him, and Chavez had annihilated Rosario in his finest performance to date. Each fighter's rate of activity and power were major factors; Chavez, at thirty, had stopped eighteen of his last nineteen opponents, since he won the title in May 1989. Comparatively, Hector had fought eight times during the same time period. Two of those victories were controversial split decisions.

To beat Chavez, Hector had to fight a perfect fight; Chavez just had to be himself. Having won five titles in three different weight classes, Chavez only planned for two more title defenses after the showdown with Hector. Then, he would try the welterweight division.

Shimmying out to "Ain't No Stopping Us Now," in full superhero gear, Hector showed off his sharp moves and attire. A sparkling performance did not follow. If the first round was any indication of the direction of the bout, Hector was in an untenable situation, as Chavez bounced right hands off his face. Early in the second round, Chavez backed Hector against the ropes and landed a right hook to the body and a left hook to the head. Such lethal combinations instilled fear in Hector, who did not have the same fluidity to his movement. A pall fell over him as his defensive maneuvering symbolized the regression of his skill set. Sure he was brave and tough and fighting a skilled warrior, but as the rounds passed, there was no way around the fact that he could not compete with Chavez.

A blistering right by Chavez at the start of the third round sent Hector reeling—the pace eclipsed anything Hector could have prepared for. He was forced into survival mode early, reflecting Chavez's fighting spirit and his own inability to pose any threat. When Chavez feinted to his left, he quickly whipped a straight right that Hector could not avoid. In a way it was 1986 against Rosario all over again. Hector, going straight back, put himself in danger. Ironically, Chavez's superior head movement and extraordinary ability to cut off the ring closed out any escape routes. Nearing the end of the third round, Hector, in desperate need of a reprieve, turned his back to Chavez and skirted away from him. After trying to get a breather, Hector began to grab, clinch, and tackle Chavez in that third round. The fight seemed fragmented.

In his best round of the fight, Hector stopped Chavez's forward progress with a powerful left uppercut and closed out the fourth with a short right hook and a straight left. Hector reminded Chavez that a fighter still existed beneath the flair. Only able to piece together a left counter in the fifth, Hector shifted back into defensive mode as the Mexicans continued to marvel at Chavez's precision and surprising quickness. Little nuances defined Chavez's performance as he ambushed Hector, who had only been knocked down once in his career, and dashed any hopes of a Camacho victory.

As Chavez lashed Hector with two right hands toward the end of the sixth, the narrative of the one-sided systematic breakdown was taking hold. Serious fight fans, and likely Hector himself, knew that it did not have to be this type of fight. If Hector had decided to adhere to a disciplined career devoted to good conditioning and a healthy lifestyle, he might not have been disfigured and clinging to dear life heading into the second half of the fight. Instead of moving and grabbing, he could have stymied Chavez with his speed and doused him with expert counterpunching.

But Chavez never slowed down, railing a right through Hector's guard to end the eighth. His bodywork in the ninth nearly led to a stoppage. Few would have protested the decision to end the fight as Chavez intensified the combinations and only stopped forward momentum on the rare occasion that Hector landed a telling blow. Referee Steele showed patience midway through the ninth as he allowed Chavez to continue battering a defenseless fighter.

Dismayed by Steele's refusal to act, analyst Ferdie Pacheco expressed his concern. But Hector kept fighting back, often flailing with arm punches that barely nicked Chavez, who forged ahead without regard. As brilliant as Chavez was throughout the fight, Hector was just as brave. His left eye a mere slit going into the tenth, Hector wanted to finish on his feet, but Chavez was somehow throwing the same power punches with the same speed as he had in the early rounds. One could not help but sympathize with Hector. With three minutes remaining, he showed his pride and will in the face of the inexorable Chavez. Before sending Hector out for the final round, Snowell implored him: "Wake up, Mach. Wake up."

Chavez hit Hector with a right hand that sent him stumbling along the ropes at the start of the twelfth, but the punch was not landed with the force necessary to end the fight. With eighteen seconds remaining in the twelfth round, Hector, with one good eye, fiercely fought back. He refused to succumb to Chavez's relentlessness and stayed upright for all twelve rounds. Chavez showed everything, Hector showed heart, and the fans showed their appreciation as the men embraced. Leading into the bout, Hector had admitted, "If I go toe-to-toe with him, I'm dead," and still stood in and traded with Chavez at the end of rounds. In the twelfth, Hector earned Chavez's respect; he did not retreat despite the beating he had taken.

Before the fight, Chavez had announced, "[he] is far from being Macho. I am the Macho Man." The fight reflected just that. The great Mexican had battered Hector enough to cause concern for fans and friends. The wide margins of the judges' scores only reflected part of the story line—120-107, 119-110, and 117-111, all for Chavez. Hector's swollen eye reflected another narrative that floored those who loved him. Seeing the handsome Hector beaten almost unrecognizable was difficult.

"I left in the sixth round," said Junior. "It was too much for my nerves."

Maria could not control herself as she witnessed the pounding that her son received.

"He was fine after the Chavez fight," said friend Tim Cinnante. "He just made a couple million. His eye was shut. His mother looked at his face. She took it so hard. She freaked out. The doctor came over to check him out, and his mother threw herself on the floor. . . . His mother had a nervous breakdown. He had a blown-up eye, but he lasted the whole fight. She was uncontrollable. She looked at his face, and it looked bad. But he was okay."

Nevertheless, Hector had earned his biggest purse on the back end of his career. Ironically, he may have gained more fans in the loss than in any of his previous wins. For the first time in years, fans saw Hector engage, not run, but get brutalized in the process.

The loss did not dampen Hector's spirits; he put on a pair of sunglasses and went to party the night away. At the post-fight press conference, Chavez claimed that he injured his right hand. He also said that Hector deserved a rematch, but the previous twelve rounds suggested otherwise.

Somehow Hector stayed active and relevant enough to garner million-dollar paydays against younger attacking fighters. But he did not make a conscious effort to stop abusing drugs. Having claimed to be the kid of the 1980s, he hobbled into the mid-1990s. As the world turned its collective gaze to the new grunge scene, Hector the fashionable showman appeared out of place. He was still the Macho Man and could deliver a vintage "Yeah Buddy," but he was now perceived by his peers as an opponent. Although he could still muster up serviceable performances, seeing him as fodder for a new generation of superstars forced some loyalists to distance themselves. For Hector himself, the show had to go on, even in diluted form.

"With Hector, there was a feeling that fighting wasn't his main priority, and that what happened before the fight and between rounds became a priority," said Merchant. "He used the medium to his advantage, but sometimes you must be careful what you wish for. I don't know how people saw him. I think fans had the intuition that Hector was more interested in the razzle dazzle than the heart and soul of the fight. He was never unlikeable. It just seemed that there was something sad about the way he was exposed in public for being someone he was not."

Meanwhile, Junior, living in a house in Orlando that Hector had put a down payment on after his fight with Chavez, continued to chart his own path. When he started his amateur boxing career, Junior did not consult his father, who found out through word of mouth. Macho felt slighted, but in Junior's mind that was how it had to be. When he had first started to consider making boxing a part of his life, it was his mother, Maida, who had bought him a book on Olympic boxing and it was Maida who had given her son the space he needed to do some preliminary training in his room.

Unlike his father, Junior had a multitude of hobbies, and boxing fit nicely within that mix. Junior had witnessed the pros and cons of his father's celebrity, and he desperately wanted to create his own identity. He wanted to be himself, not another manufactured child prodigy of a once-great champion. The task that lay ahead was rife with complexities as Junior was growing into a good fighter while Hector was declining.

Wanting to keep Junior in check, Hector explained to him, "I'm a superstar, and you're a shooting star. I'm the Macho Man, and you're Macho Mano."

Over the next year, Hector fought three times and set himself up for a showdown with countryman Felix "Tito" Trinidad, who had begun to carry the mantle as the next Puerto Rican legend. After knocking out

Maurice Blocker on June 19, 1993, to win the IBF world welterweight title, Trinidad made two defenses of his title before signing to face Hector on January 29, 1994, but he had looked pedestrian at times in his last defense against lightly regarded Anthony Stephens in October. Reserved but supremely confident of his abilities, Trinidad, getting 3-1 odds, bet $40,000 on himself. If Ramirez plodded and Chavez stalked, then Trinidad glided. Tall and thin, Trinidad had established himself as a knockout artist capable of one-punch power; conversely, Chavez destroyed foes through a war of attrition.

On the downside of his career, Hector (43-2, nineteen KOs) looked at Trinidad (22-0, nineteen KOs) and saw him make amateur mistakes that he could easily expose. Despite still being viewed as the main attraction, Hector surprisingly earned a paltry $100,000, whereas Trinidad, the champion, doubled that amount. Never lacking confidence, Hector felt his experience and superb boxing skills made him the favorite. He steered clear of angering Chavez in the pre-fight hype, but he was not as reticent when it came to Trinidad.

"The kid is green," Camacho emphasized, "he's the worst of all of them. He's not as good as Pazienza. He's not better than Chavez. He's not better than Haugen."

"I remember Camacho saying that he wasn't going to just beat Trinidad, he would knock him out," said Jose Sanchez Fournier, sports journalist from *El Nuevo Día*. "He said, 'The skinny kid cannot take my punches.'"

At the time, Trinidad was promoted by Don King and managed by Yamil Chade, of Lebanese-Cuban descent, who reached his peak as a boxing manager with a handful of Puerto Rican fighters, including Wilfredo Gomez, later voted best Puerto Rican boxer of all time. "Don King insisted that I matched Tito to [the] popular Hector 'Macho' Camacho who still had a great deal of respect and boxing savvy," said Chade.

Hector had to pull an upset of epic proportions. This was not Roberto Duran vs. Davey Moore in 1983; Hector was facing Trinidad, who was blossoming into one of the best fighters in the world. On January 29, 1994, Hector, ranked eighth by the IBF, entered the fight flanked by a team led by Ismael Leandry. Hector was a 5-2 underdog desperately trying to prove that time and the erosion of his skills had not completely diminished his significance in a sport where Roy Jones Jr. and Pernell Whitaker now represented the sport's gold standard.

Both Hector and Trinidad entered the fight at 147 pounds. In front of 12,500 people at the MGM Grand in Las Vegas, Hector pranced in, decked out in Viking regalia, including a horned helmet, breastplates, and shin guards.

"Don't be surprised if it ends in a knockout," warned Trinidad.

In defensive mode, Hector opened an early cut but never managed to seriously threaten Trinidad, who won handily by establishing a vicious body attack and overwhelming the veteran fighter by scores of 116-110, 117-109, and 118-106. Relegated to excuses, Camacho cashed in, but his days as a competitive fighter were over.

"He never needed to be consoled or anything like that. It was party time after any fight, win or lose," said friend Tim Cinnante. "But after the Trinidad fight, I remember him looking over at Don King. And I was there watching this unfold, and King gave him this look, a subtle one, and shook his head like, 'Not this time.' And Mach gave him this look of despair. It was the only time I remember that happening."

"I thought I could pull it off," said a dejected Hector. "The ref thumbed me."

Retirement was not an option he would even address. So Flannery weighed in on the performance. "[Hector's] been in serious boxing, smokers in Harlem since he was ten years old," Flannery said. "I think it's time for him to get out. I'm afraid of a serious injury for him. . . . [H]is skills have eroded. He can't see the punches to the head anymore."

With brutal honesty, Flannery used the media as a tool to reach Hector. It must have been demoralizing for Hector to hear Flannery's call for him to retire. But instead of looking back, Hector saddled up for the next boxing journey.

Meanwhile, during the mid-1990s, fear set in for Junior as he saw his father begin to struggle in ways he was not accustomed to. "Things weren't going well for us, and I will never forget this," Junior recalled. "I was doing homework and he comes over to me and says, 'Papi, everything will be ok. We have no money but we will be ok. I will get fights with

Roberto Duran, Oscar De La Hoya, and Sugar Ray Leonard and we will be okay.' And that's what he did. He went and resurrected his career off [mostly] old men. I never forgot that," Junior said.

Junior masked his concerns but watched as similar scenarios played out over the next couple of years. Engineered by promoter and manager Mike Acri, Hector, in full showman mode, made himself the ultimate Vegas lounge act, still able to pull off the occasional magic trick, challenging a new generation of young fighters who looked at him nostalgically, as a relic of the past. He continued working with Jim Levien, Rudy Mata, and Patrick Flannery.

"Even among those fights where he took a beating, they didn't knock him out, and that was amazing," said boxing analyst Al Bernstein. "One of the things that probably is overlooked with Camacho was his toughness."

Junior reconnected with Macho's former trainer, Robert Lee, and took advantage of adviser Ismael Leandry's vision for his career. "Hector called me, and I promised him I would take care of his son," said Lee. The two did not rehash the past.

Generous and caring, Leandry was always there for Macho and Junior, never asking for a cent, telling Junior how to invest his money, and showing him the same love he showed his father. As Junior recalled, "He took care of my father, beyond just [his career as] a boxer."

Junior, a slick, confident southpaw, became an amateur star, but he wanted to stress that he was *not* his father, and he felt motivated to show Lee that "I'm me, and no one else." Still, his father cast a burdensome shadow. After passing initial tests, Junior started to hear the echoes from Lee: *Your father did it like this. Your father moved like that.* But eventually, Lee pulled back on the comparisons, looked at Junior, and addressed him: "Your father was great, but you can be great, too."

Junior grew with Lee and appreciated his unorthodox methods, but he could not reunite Lee and his father the way he had hoped. Despite staying in his father's shadow in some regards, Junior recognized that as a professional fighter, he had to view his father through a much different lens. "I loved him despite his craziness," said Junior. "So I dealt with the distractions. But it was tough to work with him because of his lifestyle."

If ever there was a time when Junior needed his father to be responsible and more invested in him, it was as he climbed the professional ranks. But it was too late for Hector Sr. to change.

As Junior, looking to establish himself in the prime of his career, began feeling more detached from his father, Hector Sr. began mapping out the final phase of his own illustrious career. Father and son stayed close and maintained a level of respect. Even in his mid-thirties, when he would use Hector Sr. as a sparring partner, Junior viewed his father's movements and adherence to the craft as an art form.

Sometimes, jealousy set in.

"Shit, motherfucker, you don't think you're better than me?" said Macho.

"No, pops, you're a legend," responded Junior.

On July 7, 2001, Junior faced Jesse James Leija, his own Edwin Rosario in many ways. A perfect 32-0, Junior expected a difficult fight against a very good and experienced fighter in Leija, but the fight had a debilitating effect on him and soured him on the sport. Not only did Leija hurt him, but the fifth-round no-contest quickly turned into a nightmare for the young fighter as a swarm of naysayers claimed he "quit."

To make matter worse, Hector Sr. demanded "real money" before the fight for the minimal assistance he provided during training. Junior, kind and forgiving, gave him $50,000 and shrugged it off in a nonconfrontational manner, but it was not a feel-good moment. Worse, Hector stayed hidden in the background as his son was being thrashed by the media for his performance against Leija later in 2001.

"That was his way of having me learn on my own," said Junior.

As he began to understand the sport's intangibles, it was hard for Junior to accept his father's physical deterioration. For years, Junior had watched his father navigate the perils of drug use and fame with the rigor of competition. Once Hector's physical attributes diminished, the reality was discomforting.

What was unsettling in the ring was Hector's harmless straight left and refusal to engage. Often with great fighters, there is at least the possibility of one great round or one glimpse of their mastery on display, but Hector had to *ward off* Chavez and Trinidad, rather than trigger their disdain, by showcasing his superior boxing skills. It was a sad predicament for many, as Hector finally exhibited his toughness and utter resilience by staving off knockouts instead of igniting them as he did during his best years, 1983 through 1985.

After losing to Trinidad on January 29, 1994, Hector won nineteen of his next twenty bouts to justify another big payday. One of the victories was a forgettable showdown with the forty-five-year-old Roberto Duran on June 22, 1996. Realistically, no one expected much from the affair, but the emotion before the fight at the very least sparked a fire under the combatants and entertained spectators. After arriving late for a press conference in New York, Hector interrupted Duran in mid-sentence with a Macho jingle and dance number. Scolded by Duran for showing such disrespect, Hector began to cry. "I've always respected you as a great fighter," said Hector. "And you come here and disrespect me."

Then, the fighters attacked each other.

The fight itself was not Hector's finest moment. Despite being eleven years younger than Duran, he only managed to come away with an unconvincing unanimous decision. All three judges had Hector winning by at least two points.

During the Duran fight, Hector sought out Sugar Ray Leonard, who was working as an analyst, and began to whittle away at him. When Hector saw a future payday, he became voracious. He wanted that Leonard name on his record to enhance his legacy. Comfortable finding his niche in a host of different spectrums, Leonard had no intention of coming out of retirement until Hector started to provoke him.

"I watched that fight and that sort of got things going," said Leonard. Angered by the provocations, Leonard took the bait and called for the bout. "I just saw a smaller man, much smaller than I was physically," Leonard recalled. "And I know how to fight southpaws. Just walk him down. Things happen differently. When you're in the gym, it's one thing, but when you get in the ring, it's a whole different story. As you get older, those punches hurt. When you're in your twenties and thirties . . . it's part of the game. I became too civilized, and those damn punches hurt."

After playing the antagonist role, Hector got his wish, and the fight was signed.

Six months before the Camacho–Leonard showdown, Junior debuted on his father's card. Forging ahead at 61-3-1, Hector Sr. fought and beat Heath Todd, while Junior beat Lou Martinez in his professional debut. "That was me sixteen years ago," exclaimed the proud father. "Except, I didn't get cut."

On March 1, 1997, Hector faced Leonard. It was the second time Hector warranted a major payday by pulling a fighter out of retirement. (In 1989, he had lured Mancini out in a similar manner.) The back-story was riveting enough. When a young Hector was emerging as a great fighter, Leonard supported him unequivocally. Instead of making it about himself, Leonard came out and said, "This kid can be better than me." Despite his ego, Leonard never mistreated or maligned Hector; in fact, he advised a young and brazen Hector on how to handle himself in a brutal industry. Even in difficult fights, Leonard never publicly criticized him. So when Hector came out and targeted him, the ploy agitated Leonard.

But at the same time, Leonard understood Hector—and his own personal struggle—in ways that other fighters could not. "[P]eople tell you how good you are, how special you are, how great you look, and it becomes seductive," said Leonard. "It becomes a distraction. And especially if you're not doing what you normally do. With Camacho I saw a likeness of me because he was so entertaining and flamboyant and he could get wild like I did. . . . We also used to have those conversations in the [1980s] like I am going to knock you out if we fought and stuff like that," Leonard added.

Going into the fight, Camacho and Leonard weighed under the 160-pound limit. At the weigh-in, broadcast live on ESPN, Hector followed Leonard on the scale, and left everyone with a lasting image by stripping completely naked. Separate backstories converged: Hector fired trainer Pepe Correa in the middle of training camp for a lack of trust (and rehired Jesse Reid) and forced Leonard, who was being treated for a calf injury that almost caused him to postpone the fight, to take a steroid test. Hector's accusation that Leonard was taking steroids was a ludicrous claim that Leonard's adviser, J. D. Brown, downplayed by saying, "[Ray's] taking tacos. He wants to get fat like Camacho."

Initially, the 2-1 odds favored Hector, but those moved to 6-5 man-to-man by fight time. Hector earned $2 million to Leonard's $4 million purse. Leonard had suffered only two blemishes, which were losses to Terry Norris and Roberto Duran, in thirty-nine bouts. The most telling stat, however, was that Leonard had not fought since his knockout loss to Terry Norris six years earlier. Comparatively, Hector was 19-0-1 in his previous twenty bouts. Leonard, at forty, was six years older than Hector and possessed a record of 36-2-1 with twenty-five knockouts.

Hector's ruthless nature reflected how ugly he could be when he felt offended. In the lead-up to the fight, he turned away a Leonard handshake by briskly stating, "I'm going to fuck you up motherfucker." When they eventually got into the ring, Leonard looked at Hector with only one thought in the back of his mind: *I have to break this guy down.*

"That first round was key," said Leonard, "to get a feel and see what he had. He threw and I was thinking, 'That shit hurt.' He hurt me with a jab. And I just knew, I said to myself, 'Ray you can't postpone this right now. People wouldn't accept that.' That's when I knew I shouldn't have been in there."

Before 10,324 fans at the Atlantic City Convention Center, Leonard showed few signs of wear and tear over the first two rounds. As the fight progressed, Hector gained confidence. In the third round, he landed a short, punishing left hook that a vulnerable Leonard would have never let touch him in his prime. In the fourth, Hector opened a cut over Leonard's right eye.

"I was going to feel him out and get a sense for his pace and tempo and what have you," Leonard recalled. "I was going to break him down. I was going to go to the body and slow him down, but that night was Camacho's night, right after the opening bell. Even when guys like Duran hit me, I knew it would take more than that, but when Camacho hit me, I was rocked and I was like, 'Ok, I shouldn't be in here.' I pulled my calf muscle, but I don't even want to use [the injury] as an excuse."

Unable to fend off a right and two uppercuts early in the fifth round, Leonard went down—and looked old doing it. Not long after, referee Joe Cortez stepped in at 1:08 of the round to stop the abuse as Hector battered Leonard. The great champion had nothing left to give; Hector took his will. The damaging fight sent Leonard into permanent retirement.

Years later, Leonard accepted the defeat: "He beat me fair and square. I will take that to the bank."

The fight marked Hector's last hurrah, but not his last payday, as he persuaded thousands to join in his clinch-fest later that year with Oscar De La Hoya. Insatiable in his desire to become the best fighter in the world, De La Hoya viewed Camacho as a necessary stepping-stone to vault himself onto that prestigious pedestal. Looking down on the rest of the boxing world with elite fighters such as Roy Jones Jr., Pernell Whitaker, Felix Trinidad, Ricardo Lopez, and Evander Holyfield, De La Hoya would garner enough votes to be voted *KO Magazine*'s Fighter of the Year that December.

His first order of business, however, was to send Hector into retirement. De La Hoya could have learned a lot from how Hector coped with his own identity crisis. As the young fighter increased in popularity and stature, he still had to deal with a large contingent who were not convinced that this Mexican American was built in the same mold as the Chavezes and Olivareses of the boxing world.

"De La Hoya had to win over Mexican American fans who thought he was too Americanized," said boxing analyst Larry Merchant. "Maybe because they believed that De La Hoya was the anti-Chavez, who was the quintessential Latin fighter. But by sticking to the business at hand, and other factors, he was able to win them over."

In the same vein, Hector had proven that he was just as Puerto Rican as any of his predecessors, but now he had to prove that he was still worthy of being in the ring with this fierce champion.

On September 13, 1997, De La Hoya defended his WBC welterweight title against Hector at the Thomas & Mack Center in Las Vegas. Promoted by Top Rank, De La Hoya, who was 25-0, was making the fourth defense of his title and had few concerns that Hector, now trained by Pat Burns, was a significant threat. Leading up to the fight, De La Hoya joked, "Camacho would be a nice tune-up." When they got in the ring, Hector, draped in a black cape, peered behind an ominous black visor; De La Hoya, looking focused and loose, stared straight ahead.

In the first round, De La Hoya stunned Hector with a big left hook and sent him backward with an uppercut. Turning to the body in round three, De La Hoya heeded trainer Emanuel Steward's advice to "pick up the pace" and raked Hector with a left uppercut and right hand to define the fifth. As in his bout with Chavez, Hector took excessive punishment, fought back, but had to retreat during any significant combination. De La Hoya chased him in the sixth and then sent him to the canvas in the ninth. It marked the first time Hector had been knocked down since 1988, highlighting his durability. De La Hoya battered Hector with fierce combinations, then coasted to a unanimous decision. Chalk up another $3 million dollar payday for Hector, as the final leg of his triple crown was complete.

The physicality of his body had taken a more rounded shape and his boyish good looks had succumbed to the vices and visceral beatings. All the things Hector had done to young fighters on the way in, they were doing to him on the way out. That cycle of punishment was hard to accept for those who loved him.

"I was focused on my career at the time," said Junior. "I remember worrying about my dad more against De La Hoya. He trained hard and whipped himself into shape. But De La Hoya was the face of boxing, a young lion, a young bull. There was a lot of commotion and I couldn't focus. For the first time, my dad wasn't getting all the attention."

After the fight, De La Hoya said, "Chavez couldn't knock Camacho out or drop him; and Felix Trinidad couldn't knock him out or drop him. At least I dropped him."

In the face of De La Hoya's attacks, Hector, candid and honest, said, "When a guy is going off on you like that, the only thing to do is to run or hold. And I couldn't run." With the exception of a good performance against Leonard, that statement encapsulated Hector's identity. Jousting amicably off a spit curl side bet Oscar and Hector had made prior to the fight lightened the mood after the fight. One perk for fight fans was that Hector could still create a stir, as fashionable as always with his leather attire and matching helmet. Unable to undergird his fashion style with any fighting substance proved anticlimactic in the ring, and the irony was not lost on Hector that a disciplined De La Hoya was developing into the fighter that he could never be.

To go down only once against Chavez, De La Hoya, and Trinidad was a feat in itself. Hector's face and body language in those bouts may have suggested otherwise. Two approaches stayed consistent in those three fights: Stay alert and stay away. Truth is, Hector never backed down from any of them.

In January 1998, Hector's wife got a restraining order against him, for an alleged assault. As the relationship deteriorated, Hector looked elsewhere for comfort.

During a work event, a pretty blonde from Detroit named Shelly Salemassi, who worked for Long Beach Mortgage, was invited to a private boxing match at the Caesars Windsor casino in Canada. Her host showed her around the casino and then introduced her to Hector, who was making a special appearance at the casino, even though he was not supposed to have made the trip because he had been charged with a felony and was not supposed to leave the country. But evading the law was nothing new for him.

Unaware of who Hector was and not interested in finding out, Salemassi continued to get drinks and enjoy the evening. Later that night, after the fight, Hector "accidentally" bumped into her.

"Excuse me, I think you bumped into me," Hector said.

"No, I think you bumped into me," she replied.

"I was amazed by how surprising Hector was on that first encounter," Salemassi recalled. "He was shy and cute. Boyish, I would say. Even humble. He had this remarkable smile, and fabulous charisma. We talked for twenty minutes or so till my friends found us and said they were ready to leave."

In an attempt to prolong the evening, Hector asked, "Want to come upstairs and have a grilled cheese sandwich with me?" Salemassi politely declined, but gave him her phone number.

A few days passed by with no phone call. Not holding out hope, Salemassi devoted her time to her work and family. Then she received a call from Hector, who was at the Windsor police station. Not knowing what to expect, Salemassi listened intently: "He said, 'I went to jail for you. Your host got mad and called the cops.'"

Salemassi reluctantly went to pick him up. Still unaware of Hector's stature, Salemassi, absorbed in her work, wanted to drop him off, but he had nowhere to go, so he tagged along to her house. Needing a workout, Hector found the closest thing to a ring.

"Ah, Mom, who is that strange man shadow boxing in the yard?" her oldest son asked.

"I shook my head in dismay. I started laughing," Salemassi recalled. "He's just a friend," she replied.

In the meantime, Hector kept sending subtle hints about his status as the Macho Man. She had trouble getting him out of her head after that.

"I don't know if you know this, but I'm a little famous," Hector said.

"Yah? So am I!" Salemassi said with a laugh.

Admittedly, Salemassi started to warm to Hector. She began to embrace the fact that he was absolutely nothing like a pretentious celebrity or, more important, her ex-husband. Weeks after their initial meeting, Salemassi invited him in after a date and they spent the night together. That morning when she went to work, she left him at her house. The phone rang. It was her ex-husband. Hector answered.

"Where's Shelly?" he asked.

"I don't know. She's not here," said Hector, who quickly hung up.

He called back. "Listen, what if I came over and asked that question in person?"

"Then, my brother, it's Macho Time!" Hector hung up again.

Despite being angry that Hector was answering her phone, Salemassi, now smitten, moved on and the relationship became intense and loving. Periodically seeing Salemassi at intervals in his life, Hector grew closer to her. She witnessed his drug escapades, which often included traveling to the worst projects of new cities and looking for the drug dealers to get his fix. That behavior frightened her.

The affair intensified. However, once Salemassi pieced together the frequent trips to dangerous neighborhoods and Hector's erratic behavior, she began to comprehend the extent of his drug addiction. His cocaine use disrupted their quiet getaway weekends. But Hector was accustomed to handling chaos and adversity, and adept at masking his drug problem. Guilt about leaving his wife occasionally left Hector detached and depressed, but he did not dwell openly on his feelings. Regarding their developing relationship, Hector and Salemassi gave each other ultimatums. Hector told Salemassi that nothing would ever come between him and his mother, Maria, and Salemassi warned Hector never to abuse her.

After ignoring several red flags, Salemassi fell in love with Macho. Hard. They continued to see each other frequently over the next decade, their encounters becoming more intense each time.

Nevertheless, Hector maintained a fast-paced lifestyle that, by all accounts, he was not emotionally equipped to handle. By internalizing his own issues, he believed he could push through any problems. He was the Macho Man. But each public spat or DUI charge extracted something valuable from him. Those who loved him and viewed him as a rock in their lives watched him crumble with regret.

Salemassi overlooked Hector's flaws and thrived off his energy. Hector held Salemassi close and pronounced his love to her. Intimate at times and combative at others, Salemassi and Hector engaged in an ongoing give-and-take, but toward the end Hector always came back to her. During her last visit to Puerto Rico, Hector confessed, "The only thing missing is you." Often the fantasy that Salemassi and Hector were managing quickly morphed into a reality that neither one could sustain.

Hector refused to retire and fought for the next twelve years—his last fight a unanimous-decision loss to Saul Duran on May 14, 2010. He finished his Hall of Fame career with three legitimate world titles (130, 135, and 140) and a record of 79-6-3 with thirty-eight knockouts. Wondrous at 130 pounds, Camacho proved to still be very good at 135 and 140 in a career that spanned thirty years. He placed himself among the pantheon of great Puerto Rican fighters and earned a place in the conversation as one of the most explosive 130-pounders of all time, despite his brief tenure there.

Sadly, as good as he was, Camacho was never able to recapture the ring genius that he exhibited in his first fifteen to twenty fights, when boxing experts were awed by his movement, speed, and attacking style. He continued to flirt with greatness against Jose Luis Ramirez in 1985, but after that fight he never again reached the zenith of the sport.

Hector grew up with nothing in a neighborhood where he saw friends die or get hooked on drugs at any early age, and yet he won three world titles. From the beginning, the outsized expectations were nearly impossible to live up to. Every great boxing analyst sung his praises, and even Sugar Ray Leonard fawned over him. Even the old timers lauded Hector. His future was paved in gold. Those who loved "The Macho Man" prayed that he would stay clean. Those who looked at him as their meal ticket also made a pact with the boxing gods to not touch this perfectly crafted pugilist. But it did not take long for Hector to fall off boxing's beaten path. The oversized expectations and pressure to sustain his greatness did not knock him out. The drugs did. Inactivity, poor training habits, and continued strife with managers and promoters all diluted Hector's legacy. There was no reason why in 1992, twelve years into his career, Hector represented nothing more than a nagging moth to Chavez's vicious attack.

All fighters know how great they can be. If he had kept himself in shape, Hector could have easily changed the narrative from "Chavez to Inflict Pain on Macho Man" to "Camacho Hasn't Lost Much" or "Speed Stymies Chavez." The evidence proved that Chavez struggled with pure boxers, but Hector made it easy for him. He did the same for Trinidad. And made it even easier for De La Hoya.

During an unforgettable period in his life, Hector divorced his wife; was shot at three times in a carjacking in San Juan, Puerto Rico; faced child and domestic abuse allegations; and was arrested for burglary and possession in Mississippi in a computer store. In many ways, Hector had become a caricature of the person that others hoped he would not turn into at that stage in his life, heading into his fifties. He would make a comeback on various shows, including *Mira Quién Baila* and *El Gordo y La Flaca*, on which, in 2012, he was hired to deliver a regular news segment, and he would pose for *Playgirl*. But no matter where or what his celebrity status brought him, Hector could never kick his drug habit.

"You can't tell him nothing: Hector is Hector," said his sister Racquel. "He would take [the advice], but then he would be like, 'Yeah, yeah, yeah . . . leave me alone.'"

Descending into a personal abyss, Hector still maintained relationships, but Jerry Villarreal Sr. had moved away, Tim Cinnante started a family and closed Hi-Tide, his club; and Hector's new posse of friends were heavily involved in drugs. "He would call me at three a.m. . . . to hang out, and I stopped answering his calls," said Cinnante, a hint of resignation in his voice.

★ ★ ★

One of his things about Hector Camacho that people will never forget was his loyalty. He clung to his roots.

During his childhood, Hector's friend, Eddie Pratts, wanted him to understand how much he was valued, and that he had the ability to transcend Spanish Harlem. "I told him, 'Hector, you need to relax. You're somebody special. There is something about you. You'll be somebody someday,'" said Pratts. "'You know that don't you?'"

Hector, startled, stayed silent.

"He looked at me with this look like, *How do you know?* But he was our shining star."

In 1983, Hector, a newly crowned champion, parked his black Eldorado—that had "Hector Camacho" inscribed on the side with little boxing gloves—at the dead end near Our Lady Queen of Angels church. People were in awe.

"Because of him, people in Spanish Harlem suddenly wanted to be fighters," said Pratts. "He inspired all of us."

On a Friday evening in February 1984, Hector showed up at a high school game between Allen Park and Dearborn Heights Crestwood. Then eighteen, Jerry Villarreal Jr., who doubled as a high school senior and Hector's occasional cornerman, heard Hector screaming for him from the sidelines. "For one moment, I knew what it felt like to be Macho," said Villarreal Jr., who ran for two touchdowns in the memorable game. "I will never forget that."

Always in the midst of a "Macho Time" chant with friends who religiously went to every Macho fight, Richie "Rich" Galvan tried to keep Camacho's spirit alive from the beginning. "He looked out for a lot of people when he got famous," said Galvan. "Not many people knew about that. When he was famous, he never changed. Money didn't change him. He would say 'Hi' to everybody. People looked at him and thought, *If he can do it, so can I.* It didn't have to be boxing, it could have been anything."

When it came to his people in Spanish Harlem, Hector stood for something more than just a world champion. "If you didn't have a pair of shoes, he would buy you a pair," Maida recalled. "He was good like that."

So many people wanted to see Hector Camacho—the entertainer, the father, the loyal friend, and son—return to glory, to find himself again. Junior told him, "Change your life around, Pops." To which he received the staple rejoinder: "Everything's good. I'm the Macho Man."

Others waited patiently to see the evolution. "I saw a glimpse of what he could have been," said Junior's aunt Maritza. "He started losing weight again. He started taking care of himself. He was wearing jeans and a blazer on TV. It was like a new point in his life. I saw a glimpse of a person who was growing into that next phase. [But] I always felt we would get a call of an accident or an overdose because of his lifestyle. . . . He had two sides. He was so funny and he would have you rolling on the floor. And the other side, his weakness, was his issue with anger management. Nobody ever taught him how to control his anger. As much as he started to change, sometimes you get pulled into your old self."

Even when he became famous, Hector's spirit and energy still resonated on every corner of Spanish Harlem. "This is where my heart stays," he once said about his connection to his neighborhood. His people felt that love. As one fan from Spanish Harlem put it, "When Hector fought, we all won."

"No matter how much money he had, his heart was always in East Harlem," Cinnante stressed. "He's from East Harlem, born and bred. He never forgot who he was. He helped a lot of kids in the street. He knew a lot of those junkie kids in the street. He would call me up at my bar and say, 'Julio is coming over. Give him some money.' And I would give him $50. He always remembered these kids in the streets. You could take Macho out of the streets, but never take the street out of Macho."

Some fighters turned to drugs because they could not fill the hole that boxing left, and drugs provided that thrill again. Others were introduced to drugs because their stature and lifestyle allowed them to afford such vices. But Hector was different: he grew up with drugs. They were not just part of a hellish phase but a way of life, ingrained in the environment in which he was raised.

"Because he had so much confidence and he carried it so well, there was never any cause for concern," said Sugar Ray Leonard. "He had that sense like 'I can control this.'"

Those who loved him knew as much, but they struggled to challenge him because they knew he was so skilled at deflection. *You just couldn't talk to him about that,* they would say. During the final years of his life, Hector was not ready to die, but he was not sure how to live.

Back Where It All Started **21**

helly Salemassi stayed in Hector's life, but she read the signs. Deep down, she saw a man desperate to get better and to evolve into the man she thought he could be, but there were too many setbacks, one right after another.

"I remember when I found out about his drug habit, but he hid it so well," said Salemassi. "He used to promise me, 'I'll get better. I will.' Then, in New Jersey, he went to drug rehab for a day, hit a girl who worked there with a tray, and got kicked out."

No one was able to explain to Hector that his lifestyle was unacceptable. Trying to manage the most difficult time in his life, he was drifting away from reality, a lost soul replacing the thrill of boxing with drugs.

"He really tried to be a good father," said Salemassi, "but he didn't know how to. He thought he was a good father, but he struggled with understanding what went into being one. But he didn't exactly have good role models growing up, either."

On December 2, 2004, a drunk Hector fell through the ceiling of the ZDI Computer Center in Gulfport, Mississippi. He was climbing through the ceiling space that separated the store from his apartment trying to retrieve his personal computer. Once inside, he stole seven laptops and nearly $6,000 in cash, causing $13,000 in damages. In 2005, Hector hit bottom when officials apprehended him at the Imperial Palace Hotel and Casino in Biloxi, Mississippi, found him in possession of ecstasy, and charged him with commercial burglary and felony possession. Facing years in prison, he had nowhere to turn and no way to spin the story. He was denied bail on the burglary and possession charges, and he signed over his Black Crossfire to pay his lawyer.

After landing in jail in May 2007, Camacho was sentenced to the maximum seven years for the burglary charge. Harrison County Circuit Judge Steve Simpson suspended six years of the sentence and gave Hector a year of house arrest in Puerto Rico as long as authorities agreed to monitor him. The January 2005 drug charge was not dismissed. When he was released on October 7, Salemassi met him in Biloxi, and a refreshed Hector promised to change his ways.

More than a year later, Hector returned to the ring to face and beat Perry Ballard in Houston, Texas, on July 18, 2008. Meanwhile, Junior was busy trying to make his own comeback as he fluctuated between strong and poor performances.

Yet time away had not changed much, as Hector's cocaine use continued. Small moments kept Salemassi hopeful that he would change. While on probation in Florida, he started attending probation classes and traffic school. Salemassi picked him up one day, smiling uncontrollably at the thought that Hector was headed in the right direction.

"You're doing good, Mach," she beamed.

"I'm so happy!" he told her. "I realized what was missing the whole time. My whole life, I always did drugs because I didn't know what was missing. I finally realized that I wanted to go back to school. That was what was missing."

Then, he started to cry.

But soon, Hector was back on cocaine again, shifting aimlessly through life, unable to figure out how to escape drugs or to find a suitable outlet. Small opportunities popped up, and he continued to write in a journal and keep his memories alive with Salemassi late at night, but his past glory was far behind and the future appeared bleak.

His celebrity status still attracted people to him. In one instance, Chicago Bulls basketball star Dennis Rodman came up to him and Jerry Villarreal Jr. and asked to borrow Hector's famous "Macho" chain; at another sports event, professional wrestler Randy "Macho Man" Savage sought Hector out and said, "You are the real Macho Man." Hector soaked it up. He still knew how to thrive in a crowd, but he no longer had any idea how to be himself when not on drugs. His entire existence revolved around the score, leaving him depressed, anxious, and confused.

Living in a dingy apartment in Tampa, Florida, in February 2010, Hector was preparing for what would be his last professional fight, a decision loss to Saul Duran in Kissimmee, Florida, on May 14. Horrified by the state of his apartment, which was crawling with cockroaches, Salemassi pleaded with him to change. His brother, Felix, and his wife, Betsy, attempted to intervene, but it didn't work.

"I am who I am," Hector responded.

For the first time, Salemassi did not feel comfortable, or safe, around him.

Rebounding with the stint with *El Gordo y La Flaca* and moving back to Puerto Rico, Hector started to reinvent himself. The show must go on, and it did. But Hector, an addict, could not stop using. He was shot at in February 2011 while trying to buy cocaine. He tried his best to minimize the incident. "I'm safe here. Everybody loves me here. They must not have known who I am, or they wouldn't have tried to shoot me," Hector said.

On the evening of November 20, 2012, shots again rang out near Hector in Puerto Rico. Then fifty, Hector was in Bayamon, a city in the metropolitan area of San Juan, sitting in the passenger side of a late-model Mustang with his friend, forty-nine-year-old Adrian Mojica Moreno. Mojica was shot three times and was killed instantly. Hector was shot in the face, with the bullet entering through his jaw, ripping up three to four main arteries, and lodging in his right shoulder. In the process, the bullet bounced off a bone, fractured two of his vertebrae, and severely disrupted the blood flow to his brain. The assailants fled in an SUV (or a gray vehicle, depending on reports), and then survived a shoot-out with police. Hector, unconscious, was rushed to Centro Medico, the main trauma center in San Juan. The media and family members descended upon the hospital. Rió Piedras Medical Center Director Ernesto Torres confirmed to the press later evening that Hector was in critical condition.

On life support, the former champion worsened and stopped breathing at one point. A day after the shooting, Hector was in a coma fighting for his life. Torres noted that Hector showed "irregular and intermittent brain activity," but there was little hope. Sordid details confirmed the sad reality that the ambush was drug related. Authorities found nine bags of cocaine in Mojica's pockets at the site of the shooting and another in the car.

Two days after the shooting, doctors pronounced Hector clinically brain dead as Torres released the statement: "We have done all that we can do." Junior flew in to be with the family and, despite his objections, Maria made the final decision to remove her son from life support.

"When the doctor called me in to talk to me, I saw that my dad's heart rate went up from 73 to 85," said Junior. "I thought he was doing good, but the doctor said that he was on a machine, and all the doctor wanted to do was talk to me about what to do with my dad's organs. That pissed me off. I couldn't take it anymore."

Once Junior sat down with Maria to discuss the prospects of what to do with Macho, the stress became overwhelming. "She screamed at me, 'Are you going to take care of him?' And I just didn't see it like that."

Junior did not push back against her decision, and soon Maria told the media, "My son is not alive. My son is only alive for the people that love him." Junior countered that his father was a "fighter," and "would fight until the end," but the decision was final.

On Saturday, November 24, 2012, Hector Camacho was declared dead and officially taken off life support. Thousands mourned his death.

There was no way to spin Hector's death. Drugs and violence had reduced him to a pale version of himself. Still, despite his very public flaws and missteps, he had been a larger-than-life figure who had never turned on his people in Spanish Harlem, and those people never stopped loving him for the loyalty he displayed. If his death left a gaping hole, the ensuing days would create more pain and sorrow.

Salemassi was forced to face reality when she got a call from her sister. "Did you hear, Shell?" her sister asked.

"What the hell are you talking about?" said Salemassi.

"Macho's been shot in the head."

Junior, too, had dreaded that nightmarish moment when the phone would ring. Deep down, he knew it was coming. Then he got the call he dreaded for so long. In mere seconds, his world was turned upside down. His wife answered the phone. "I [saw] her face and said, 'My father, right?' She said, 'Baby, he's been shot, [and he] ain't gonna make it.' I was shocked, but yet I wasn't."

Psychologically, the bullets pierced Junior in ways he had never imagined were possible. Death, or the threat of his father's death, was always present in his life. But never did he think it would arrive as brutally as it did.

"Junior went into a deep depression," said his aunt, Maritza. "It was a shock to all of us, but it hurt Junior the most because he is very spiritual."

Talking about Hector years later, Maida could not let go of the image of the funny and caring man she knew. She could not hold back the tears. "I miss him so much," she said. "Every time I look at my son, I see his father."

When Kisha heard the news, she was far removed from the life she had shared with Hector. Jolted by the realization that a man she had spent so much valuable time with was gone, she had to explain to her family that she needed time to mourn, alone. "When I found out he was shot, I thought he would make it," said Kisha. "I felt like I lost a family member. He was a part of my life for a long time. To me he was Hector, not the Macho Man."

The show, of course, went on, even after Hector's passing. In San Juan, Puerto Rico, on Tuesday, November 27, a scene erupted during a viewing held inside a San Juan gymnasium. Still vying to be identified as Hector's true love, his ex-girlfriends brawled. Claiming to be Macho's last "real" girlfriend before being killed, Cynthia Castillo created a stir when she bent over to kiss Hector in his casket and then join the area designated for family members. Ex-girlfriend Gloria Fernandez along with Hector's sisters, Esther and Estrella, took umbrage and attacked Castillo. The fight spilled over, and people quickly intervened to break it up. No longer was Hector the spectacle; the girls had taken the lead.

No one could forget about Macho, especially now, as his muddled love life seeped into the few moments of class people were expected to show for him. He knew how *not* to be the Macho Man, but never understood how or when to switch from the Macho Man back to Hector, a man who surprisingly was both humble and respectful. The Macho show sadly continued.

What bothered Shelly was the thought that women who, at best, were on the periphery of Hector's life had inserted themselves into the picture. She was the one who loved Hector unconditionally, never leaving his side. To soothe the pain, Shelly told herself, "Some people will never in their life feel love like that."

She encapsulated the chaos in Puerto Rico when she said, "People assumed Macho would have enjoyed it, but I know better. Hector would have been so embarrassed."

Media outlets caught the melee on tape and posted the fight. Junior, however, downplayed the incident at the funeral, and felt relief once he left it and got back into the limo. "I was numb to my dad," said Junior. "I couldn't believe it. I looked to the sky and said, 'God, thank you. Wow, Dad, you made it. Wow, Pops you made it.'"

But Junior dreaded what was to come if they decided to bury his father in New York. What concerned him was the explosion of emotions that would only build in intensity after what happened in Puerto Rico. "I went through hell in Puerto Rico," Junior recalled. "You come out of one problem and expect another."

Media outlets lamented that the shooter "surprised" Hector and Mojica, but few were shocked by his death. Unwilling to ask for or accept help, Hector had maintained a transient lifestyle addled by a drug-induced haze that devalued himself and his family.

By all accounts, Hector put himself in enough dangerous situations that death seemed inevitable. Junior just wanted his father to comfortably move into a stage in his life where he could feel whole again. Moments of bliss were followed by hollow periods of self-delusion and sorrow. As much as Hector tried to distance himself from the label of "Rikers Boy," he could never bring himself to accept a normal lifestyle devoid of criminality. Oh, he raged against the stereotype: "I am a good father." But Hector never truly understood what qualities made up being a "good father." That distinction did not make him a "bad father" but merely a confused one. As for being a good friend or lover, Hector did not think twice about putting his loved ones and closest friends in peril to get a fix.

"You're with me, Mama," he once told Shelly, while laughing. "Nothing is going to happen. I am the 'Macho Man,' and they love me here."

Despite his occasional reckless nature with friends and lovers, his relationship with Maria did not change. She understood every little nuance about her son. Macho could fool some people, but when staying with Maria in her home in Bayamon before his death, something felt off.

"He sensed it," said Maria. "He was in the house a lot. It was like he sensed it. It was like he knew something was wrong. I was like, 'Macho, what is wrong?' He said, 'Nothing Mami, I love you.'"

In the early morning hours on December 1, 2012, friends and fans filed into St. Cecilia's Roman Catholic Church in East Harlem on East 106th Street, a church registered on the National Register of Historic Places, for a public mass. A horse-drawn carriage delivered Hector's coffin to the church. Hundreds waited outside behind a barrier with newspapers and magazines emblazoned with Hector's image. His casket, draped in the Puerto Rican flag, was carried into the church. Hundreds of mourners attended the service.

Frank Skelly, a priest at the church when Hector attended elementary school, spoke gently of the fallen boxer: "He could make us laugh and feel sad. He could lift us up, and he could break our hearts. He was one of a kind, and stood out from the crowd. At the same time, he was one of us."

Former champion Iran Barkley calmly summed up what everyone was thinking when he said, "Macho was Harlem."

No revenge episodes or brawls took place at this service. Hector Luis Camacho Matias was back home.

A horde of fans, friends, and passersby surrounded the church to prepare for the funeral cortege to the cemetery. As family and friends exited the church, a "Macho Time" chant began and thousands cheered when they lifted the coffin into the hearse. After the service, it was clear that the outpouring of love and respect perfectly symbolized what "Little Man," "The Harlem Heckler," or "Macho" meant to the area that spanned from north of the Upper East Side and East 96th Street to East 142nd Street east of 5th Avenue.

Emotional, Maria pumped her fists and said, "Thank you, Nueva York! I love you guys!" After the debacle in San Juan, everyone needed to properly say goodbye to a man who had become an idol to so many people.

The funeral cortege continued until reaching St. Raymond Cemetery in the Bronx. Panicked and grief-stricken, Maria screamed uncontrollably for her son and tried to get back to his rose-strewn casket. She collapsed and was taken to Jacobi Hospital to be treated for a panic attack, but not before shouts of "Mi estrella, mi estrella" (My star, my star) could be heard during the tumult.

Junior all but missed saying goodbye to his father at the cemetery because he was stuck in the office trying to figure out how to pay for the funeral. When all seemed lost, a silver lining emerged through the clouds. As family and friends bickered in the church about who would cover the funeral bill, an old friend stepped up: Pee Wee Rucker, who vowed never to leave Hector's side, because he knew his friend had never left his.

Memories can only sustain those who loved Hector for so long, but remnants of a life remain. Sometimes images and memories would randomly surface for Junior. He would imagine the intimate moments they had spent together, driving in the car. Or he would remember getting a glimpse of his father's newest costume based on one of the creative sketches that Hector made in his downtime. Junior recalled feeling the fabric of his father's costume between his fingers. His fingertips touched the sequins; his mind began to wander. In his memory, his father was sleeping, and Junior draped the fabric over himself for a second, but thought twice about it. There were certain things his father considered sacred. Junior didn't know if he would be upset, but he didn't want to test it. *Maybe this could be mine one day,* he thought to himself. He dreamed of being his father.

Then Junior would return to the present, the softness of the momentary flashback gone.

Six years after his father's death, Junior returned to the Bayamon, Puerto Rico, neighborhood where his father was shot. Resentful about the inaction of officials to close the case, Junior tried to stay composed.

"They had a lead at first and they thought it was two brothers," said Junior. "But the one got shot and killed, and the other was let go because he didn't fit the description of the killer. Now they say it's three guys. Fifteen shots were fired, and no one saw anything?"

Junior spoke about getting closure for his family and the people of Puerto Rico. He kept replaying the scene in his head. *Fifteen shots, a lot of people were around.* But nothing soothed him. He looked straight ahead.

"Nothing will make him come back," he said.

"[I remember] the love I received from the Puerto Rican people," Junior recalled from the Bayamon visit. "They started beeping at me while I was jogging. They loved him; he was never to be forgotten."

Junior's memories of his father's life intermittently washed over him during interviews. Going through his father's belongings, Junior found his journals. He carefully looked over each word, pored over the random thoughts. What did it all mean? Whatever it meant, sifting through the words proved cathartic—and drew him closer to his father.

"I found a lot of things about me. He loved me!" said Junior. "He always had me in his plans. I discovered that I was just like my father when it came to having a journal. The way he would plan things reminds me of how I do it now."

Sometimes Hector's love came in different forms, but Junior received it with open arms all the same. From the beginning, Junior saw his father as his "superhero" who, despite his flaws, stayed simple and humble while existing in a world where everybody wanted a piece of the Macho Man.

"When I got to Bayamon, I felt so empty," said Junior. "My father loved seeing his mother [Maria] so much. We would just be out in front of the house laughing for two hours. That was when he was the happiest."

The two fighters loved to jog, and Hector was notorious for dominating the early morning runs. Even after a long night of partying, he would always get up and do his roadwork. But times had changed, and Junior regularly bested his legendary father. During one run, father and son were headed to Maria's house and they knew that the time would come for someone to forge ahead, and the other to reluctantly accept defeat.

"I used to leave him in the dust," said Junior. "I remember one time he caught up to me and passed me. He started talking shit to me."

Still the same old Macho Man, roaring ahead in a fury, refusing to look back—or slow down—with Junior trailing behind, smiling. That was *his* dad.

★ ★ ★

In 2019, Junior walked through Spanish Harlem, pointing out all of the spots that reflected his father's youth. "He was a bully, a fucking bully," said Junior. "They would say, 'Uh-oh, there goes Macho.' But he was in survival mode. He had to have that mindset." The corners called out to a young Hector back then, but he kept going, moving toward his dream. Comfortable in his own skin, Junior, humble, smiling, shook hands and looked for conversation, content to be home among *his* people.

Some claim that Junior is trying too hard to *be* his father and not himself, but in a real way he embodies the type of balanced life that his father eschewed. More important, Junior understands that the experiences that he had with his father—the long drives just to talk, the forced fights in his childhood, the early, crazy lifestyle—all left an imprint on him, and it did not matter if it was negative or positive.

Some sons may have loathed some of the things Macho did to Junior, but for Junior, loathing was never an option. Instead, Junior embraced every vestige of love that his father gave him. Understanding that he, Junior, had no control over his father's decisions from the beginning made it easier on him, and he was never oblivious to the crippling effect drugs had on his father.

"Me knowing how his life was and how he lived his life, I expected something like this to happen to him," said Junior. "I'm coping with it. It's not easy. It's life." Macho never would have accepted that mindset; instead, he would have numbed himself to his internal struggle. "I loved him. I respected him. I didn't understand him, but he was my idol," said Junior.

Junior then turned a corner in Spanish Harlem, on a street named Machito Square, never looking back.

Afterword

Pops was explosive. You had to be careful around him. He was a street thug. Rob. Steal. He was mean. He wasn't no punk. You had to fuck with him to see that side. Mostly, he was a lovable guy. When he first started out as a professional, he was aggressive. Mix that with speed and martial arts and it was a good mix. His balance and reflexes came from martial arts. He never stood straight up. He was an attacker and would knock you out. He always kept the right distance—the angles—and his boxing IQ was off the charts. Then, throughout the years, I saw that style change. But, even then, he was still strong. One time we were sparring in Puerto Rico and feeling great. I knew him well in the ring. I was quicker, but he had a good jab. I would get the best of him, then I would lay off. The next day came and he started with the tricks. I knew it was coming. I had to be careful. He threw an uppercut and I ran right into it. He loved that uppercut. He swept it under like a hook. I felt it.

Before he hit me with that uppercut, his friend was making fun of him from ringside, saying how I was getting the best of him. I told him, "No, pops, no more sparring." He called me a fucking pussy and told me to get in the ring. But I didn't want to disrespect him. I loved him so much. Even if I got the best of him, he was still my father. I knew my limits.

During the early days, my father would go to the club, and after the club he would run back home from the Bronx. Dancing at the club for him was a workout. He danced all over the place. He grooved and trained with salsa music—Ruben Blades, Willie Colon, Hector Lavoe (a friend). He would stop in the middle of the street and start dancing. He loved to have fun. He was always family oriented.

But he also had this mentality that said, "I started with nothing. I came from nothing. And I'm OK if I lose it all." I loved it. He was who he was. He wasn't going to change. As I got older, I got used to his ways. He was a man of his word. He was up-front. No lying. No bullshit. He would say "fuck you" to your face. He was my idol. He took pride in being from the streets. He had a tough way about him.

But there was a soft side too. People loved him. He was a born entertainer. He started in Spanish Harlem and ended up at the White House. He was living the life at a young age. People in his inner circle were solid. People like Ismael Leandry took care of him. He grabbed the spotlight, but at home he was like a regular person, a big kid. With everything he had, he was still humble. You wouldn't believe how humble he was. Besides the fame, the money and everything, he was just a good man.

But the chip on his shoulder. That was real. He knew how to get under your skin. He meant what he said. He would talk and back it up. That was the street in him. He had that "it" factor. After a while, it was more commercial. You understood it was more of the business side. When Macho did it, it was natural. When Floyd Mayweather tried to do it, it didn't seem genuine. He knew what boxing needed. He said, "I'm going to be me," and when the lights came on, it was "Macho Time." When the lights went off, he would stop the show. If someone spoke to him, he would talk to them and ask them questions about themselves. I saw that. I also saw the crazy side. A bum would ask him for money, and he would start arguing with him, "I gave you money last week." They kept arguing. "I better not see you in the street." Just crazy stuff. I would be like, "What are you doing, Pops? Come on." Shit like that.

In the ring, he wasn't your average slick fighter. He had a street mentality. He would always create angles. It was like art. The way he blocked punches—jab, jab, hold. Inside, he put his right glove hand on your neck to push you where he wanted you to go. And he always knew where he was in the ring. His power was his speed. At 130 and 135 pounds, his power was to be respected. He generated good power from his uppercuts. He would explode up when he threw the uppercut. When he started abusing his body and a fight came up, he knew how to flip a switch and buckle down. But his habits changed before the bout with Ray Mancini. There was more of an "I don't give a shit" kind of feel. Then, toward the end of his career, he just wanted to hang out. At that stage, I wanted to know what he wanted out of life. His taste in women and life; he just didn't care anymore. I would visit him and he had nothing going for him.

When I started fighting as an amateur, I didn't tell him. We were living in Orlando because my mother wanted a fresh start for me. My mom encouraged me to box. She was on me: "Do something," she said. But New York was who I was. "You can't go home," she told me. "You need to do something. Try boxing." When my dad found out, I was sixteen at the time. He called me: "So I hear you are boxing?" There was a crack in his voice. I knew he was upset and surprised because he had to hear about me going to the Olympic Trials through word of mouth. "You can fight?" he asked me. When I first moved to Orlando, I missed him. I couldn't tell anyone who my father was. I was finding myself. My dream was to be known for me. When I was growing up in Spanish Harlem, I had a lot of resentment. I was always wondering, "What the fuck am I doing in the projects?" Then, when I got settled in Orlando, I would see him in the news. He let me down a little bit. He let me down.

When I turned professional, he was in a different place and it was hard to rely on him to be there for me—and support me—because of his lifestyle. But he wasn't a distraction. He didn't have to try to grab the attention. He got the attention. I just stayed humble. He believed in that jab, too. Run and jab, run and jab. It would drive me crazy. He beat it into my head. We would run a lot together in Clewiston and in Puerto Rico. Even the week of one of his fights, we would do roadwork. He always wanted work. And he would always stay in shape, always moving or shadowboxing in the house.

At the start of every one of his training camps, he would say, "Get me three sparring partners." He would start turning it up as the fight got closer. That's when he would get in shape and fuck guys up. When he picked it up, he got very serious and quiet. His attitude would change and he would get grouchy. He always had this aura about him, and he always got up to do roadwork no matter what he was doing the night before.

At the end of his life, I started seeing that he started going through highs and lows. There were times he wouldn't go outside. People called and he wanted to be left alone. He secluded himself. You couldn't talk to him about his problems. If he didn't want to cooperate, he would shut down. One time I had all my friends over for my birthday. I told them all that my father was going to be there. It started at 7 p.m. When the party ended, he was still not there. I was so disappointed. Then at 2 a.m. I heard loud music. I heard someone yell my name. I looked down and there was my dad dressed in a ninja suit with nunchucks, dancing. Other times, when I was younger, I would be sleeping alone at my mother's house, and I would wake up in the morning and he was right next to me. Turns out, he climbed through the window at 3 a.m. after a night of partying. Or I would hear commotion, and my mother would peek her head in and whisper, "Your father's here." It was big. He would give me a hug and a kiss, then he would sit on the couch and make everyone laugh so hard. He had such good energy and spirit. He brought such joy to people whenever he entered a room. It was a gift.

When I was growing up in the Camacho household, Maria, my grandmother, was the dominant voice; but my father was the center of attention with his jokes. He would steal food right off your plate. Grandma would cook her ass off. I remember very clearly one night when I looked over and there was a look of contentment on my father's face. A feeling of success, that he had made it. No money issues. No worrying about tomorrow. He came up with nothing in Spanish Harlem and lived his dreams. That was my father.

Hector Camacho Jr.
New York City
August 2020

Sources

Interviews

Tony Baltazar (October 2018)
Iran Barkley (April 2018)
Al Bernstein (March 2019)
Rafael Bracero (December 2018)
Eddie Pratts Jr. (August 2019)
Mark Breland (February 2019)
Louie Burke (February 2019)
Hector Camacho Jr. (October 2018)
Maria Camacho (April 2019)
Racquel Camacho (February 2019)
Tim Cinnante (March 2019)
Kisha Colon (June 2019)
Steve Farhood (January 2018)
Austin Fenner (May 2018)
Manuel "Pito" Fragosa (March 2019)
Richie Galvan (July 2019)
Jimmy Glenn (February 2019)
Wilfredo Gomez (October 2018)
Tom Hanrahan (Fall 2020)
Greg Haugen (January 2019)
Peter Kahn (March 2019)
Ismael Leandry (January 2019)
Robert Lee (October 2018)
Sugar Ray Leonard (March 2019)
James Levien (March 2019)
Julio Lopez (December 2018)
Ray Mancini (May 2018)
Michael Marley (November 2019)
Maritza Mendez (November 2018)
Larry Merchant (June 2019)

John Montes (October 2018)
Jimmy Montoya (December 2018)
Myra "Maida" Olivio (December 2018)
Yolanda Ortiz (October 2018)
Vinny Pazienza (March 2019)
Felix Pagan Pintor (December 2018)
Alex Ramos (February 2019)
Dennis Rappaport (August 2019)
Ignacio Rivera (February 2019)
Freddie Roach (March 2019)
Tim Ryan (January 2019)
Shelly Salemassi (November/December 2019)
Jose Sanchez (August 2019)
Martin Velez (July 2019)
Jerry Villarreal Jr. (April 2018)
Jerry Villarreal Sr. (April 2018)
Harold Weston (December 2018)
Pernell Whitaker (May 2019)

Articles
Ackerman, Joan. "Now Here's a Macho, Macho, Macho Man." *Sports Illustrated*, August 1, 1983.
Associated Press. "Camacho Captures NABF Feather Title." December 12, 1981.
Baden, Larry. "Mancini Believes He Won, His Future Is Uncertain." *Reno Gazette-Journal*, March 7, 1989.
Berger, Phil. "The Two Sides of Camacho." *New York Times*, June 13, 1986.
———. "Camacho Gains Split Decision." *New York Times*, June 14, 1986.
———. "NOTEBOOK; WBA Sets Deadline for Tyson–Holyfield." *New York Times*, October 11, 1989.
CBS News. "Drugs Found Where Boxer 'Macho' Camacho Was Shot." November 21, 2012.
Democrat and Chronicle. "Macho Man Envisions Easy Fight with Mancini." December 13, 1988.
Diaz, Jesus. "Nobody's Badder than the Macho Man." *Inside Sports,* February 1986.

El Nuevo Día. "Amigo de Macho Camacho tenía drogas en su bolsillo."
November 21, 2012.

Farhood, Steve. "Ray Mancini Will Be an Easy Fight." *KO Magazine,*
May 1983.

Fort Myers News-Press. "Holmes, Dokes Will Defend Titles May 20 in
Las Vegas." April 1, 1983.

Garriga, Ray. "Camacho Winds Up Meticulous Training Program
Saturday." UPI.com, August 5, 1983.

Hartford Courant. "Camacho Wins By a Hair." April 4, 1983.

Hattiesburg American. "Macho Trades Barbs with Rival Boom Boom."
December 20, 1988.

Herbert, Lloyd. "Camacho Wins as Crowd Boos." *Arizona Republic,*
April 4, 1983.

Hoffer, Richard. "Maybe Camacho Is a Kid at Heart, but He's
Growing—and Unbeaten." *Los Angeles Times,* August 10, 1985.

Katz, Michael. "Camacho Defeats Sato in 4th." *New York Times,*
August 29, 1982.

———. "Camacho a Unanimous Victor." *New York Times,* October 31,
1982, A4.

———. "Holmes-Frazier Not for Title." *St. Louis-Post Dispatch,* July
10, 1983.

———. "The Macho World of Hector Camacho." *New York Times,*
January 18, 1985.

Labelle, Fran. "Camacho Hoping for the Best as Spotlight Again
Beckons." *Sun Sentinel,* June 25, 1988.

Lombardi, John. "The Barrio Boxer." *New York Daily News,* July 17,
1983.

Los Angeles Times. "$25,000 Fine, Counseling for Haugen." March 13,
1991.

Marantz, Steve. "Macho Man Rising to the Top." *Boston Globe,*
October 23, 1983.

———. "Camacho Thinking Positively." *Boston Globe,* January 20,
1985.

Matthews, Wallace. "An Alive Camacho Has a Threat for King."
Newsday, January 22, 1986.

———. "Macho Man Says He's a King Man." *Newsday,* March 21, 1986.

———. "Camacho, Rosario Set for Showdown." *Newsday,* June 13,
1986.

————. "Lightweights Left Holding Bag." *Newsday*, September 28, 1986.

————. "Boxing Special Inside: Cooney Bout Tale of Three Cities." *Newsday*, February 27, 1987.

————. "Obsession Mancini's Desire Is to Embarrass Camacho." *Newsday*, March 6, 1989.

————. "Boxing Notes: Camacho Says He May Be Hanging Up His (Driving) Gloves." *Los Angeles Times,* August 13, 1989.

New York Times. "Camacho Winner on Knockout in 5th." November 19, 1983.

————. "Haugen Drug Test Reported Positive." March 2, 1991.

O'Day, Joe. "Camacho shows Loy a Pep Show." *New York Daily News*, July 12, 1982.

Putnam, Pat. "Close Call for the Macho Man." *Sports Illustrated*, June 22, 1986.

Raffo, Dave. "Hector 'Macho" Camacho Got His Wish Thursday when Promoter. . . . " UPI.com, May 9, 1985.

————. "Losing Rounds Issue Could Demolish IBF." United Press International, June 18, 1988.

————. "Boxing Notebook." United Press International, June 24, 1988.

Reno-Gazette Journal. "Crowd Unhappy with Unanimous Decision for 'Macho' Camacho." April 4, 1983.

Ronald Reagan Presidential Library. "President Reagan's Photo Ops. in the Oval Office on September 19–22, 1983." YouTube video. www.youtube.com/watch?v=LX5H5_g7Dqoat, 13:30.

Ryan, Jeff. "An Outrageous Look at Hector 'Macho' Camacho: Too Street Smart to Be America's Sweetheart?" *KO Magazine*, May 1983.

————. "Nobody Understands Me." *KO Magazine*, November 1986.

San Antonio Express-News. "Camacho on Life Support as Family Weighs Options." November 23, 2012.

Saraceno, Jon. "Hector Camacho Pursued Life with Reckless Abandon." *USA Today,* November 22, 2012.

Schmitz, Brian. "Camacho Struggles in Comeback Bid." *Orlando Sentinel*, June 27, 1988.

Schuyler, Ed, Jr. "Hector Long on Confidence." *Associated Press*, November 3, 1982.

Seltzer, Robert. "Rosario Stops Bramble—Camacho Retains Title." *Philadelphia Inquirer*, September 27, 1986.

Smith, Elmer. "Camacho Returns with Fights to Win: Rumors to Dispel." *Philadelphia Daily News*, January 17, 1985.

———. "Camacho Hoping for Legendary Performance." *Philadelphia Daily News*, September 25, 1986.

Smith, Jack. "Mighty Mites' Mettle Faces Final GG Test." *New York Daily News*, March 6, 1978.

Torres, Jose. "Former Champ Takes a Look at Spanish Machismo and What It Meant to Roberto Duran." *Ring Magazine*, May 1981.

United Press International. "Former Boxing Champion Hector Macho Camacho Was Arrested On. . . . " February 3, 1988.

UPI.com. "For Freddie Roach, the Price of Respect Against Undefeated. . . . " December 19, 1985.

———. "Champion Hector Camacho and Challenger Edwin Rosario Are. . . . " June 10, 1986.

Verigan, Bill. "Seales Wins Unanimous, Dull Verdict." *New York Daily News*, April 1, 1982.

Weber, Bruce. "Hector Camacho, 50, Boxer Who Lived Dangerously, Dies." *New York Times*, November 24, 2012.

Winderman, Ira. "Rosario, Boza-Edwards: They Only Speak Softly." *Sun Sentinel*, September 21, 1986.

———. "A Mellow Macho Man." *Sun Sentinel*, September 23, 1986.

Macho Time is set in 10-point Sabon, which was designed by the German-born typographer and designer Jan Tschichold (1902–1974) in the period 1964–1967. It was released jointly by the Linotype, Monotype, and Stempel type foundries in 1967. Copyeditor for this project was Shannon LeMay-Finn. The book was designed by Brad Norr Design, Minneapolis, Minnesota, and typeset by New Best-set Typesetters Ltd. Printed and manufactured by Maple Press on acid-free paper.